Praise for *Keys to Bonhoeffer's Haus*

"This is a terrific book, offering a personal and deeply moving reflection on the life and legacy of Dietrich Bonhoeffer. Having served as a tour guide in Bonhoeffer's family home in Berlin, Laura M. Fabrycky moves easily between the past and present, illuminating Bonhoeffer's all-too-brief life while offering important insights into the relevancy of that life for the world in which we live today."

—Jonathan Addleton, former US Ambassador, author of
**   *Dust of Kandahar* and *Some Far and Distant Place***

"To enter into Bonhoeffer's *Haus,* with Laura Fabrycky as an able and articulate guide, is to fire the moral imagination and to kindle important civic questions. Importantly, Fabrycky rescues Bonhoeffer from hagiography, and her own *hausfrau*-life insists that faithfulness is often modest in the making, accumulated by small gestures in the course of our ordinary days. For these politically turbulent times, Fabrycky's work is probing and urgent, rousing us to inventory our civic responsibilities—and care."

—Jen Pollock Michel, Author of *Surprised by Paradox* and
**   *Keeping Place***

"Through engaging storytelling and clear writing, *Keys to Bonhoeffer's Haus* helps you feel as though you are actually touring Bonhoeffer's home with Laura M. Fabrycky—and with Dietrich himself. As you view Bonhoeffer's home, this book will impact how you view your own home as well, and will press you to ask, 'What does it mean to live faithfully as a Christian today?' I learned a great deal reading this book; you will too."

—Dr. J.R. Briggs, author, speaker, and founder of
**   Kairos Partnerships**

"Laura M. Fabrycky offers a beautifully written and thoughtful reflection on her own journey with Bonhoeffer, considering the people, places, and experiences that shaped him, and how his life and thought might provide us with guidance in our own troubled times. With a measured and honest look at the complexities of Bonhoeffer's life, and an openness about her own questions and discoveries, she shares the keys that unlock more of Bonhoeffer's story, and the wisdom he can bring to the pursuit of faithfulness in a challenging and changing world."

—**Rev. Dr. Jacob Belder, priest and theologian, Diocese of York, England**

"A wonderful read in the style of an '*auf den Spuren von*' ('on the trail of'), this book on Bonhoeffer and his *Haus* is a timely reminder of how embodied and emplaced we all are. As Fabrycky writes, people matter to places, and in her we find a guide not just to Bonhoeffer but to the bigger, existential questions that she herself brought to his house as an American living in Berlin and working as a volunteer guide on the property. Through her attentive gaze, we are able to consider how the Bonhoeffer-Haus came to represent identities, dispositions, and habits, and how we might hone these, alongside Fabrycky, in our own civic housekeeping."

—**Dr. Kate Harrison Brennan, CEO, Anglican Deaconess Ministries, Sydney, Australia**

"Laura M. Fabrycky has written a wonderfully rich book, inviting us into the world of Bonhoeffer's life and the life of his world. With rare grace she understands the distinctive complexity of politics, history, and theology as she weaves them together, reflecting on the moral meaning of his life for our time and place. In *Keys to Bonhoeffer's Haus* we feel that we are in the good company of a trusted friend, someone who asks hard questions of herself and the world, but who on every page honestly longs for more of what is real and true and right, awakening all of us who long with her."

—**Steven Garber, author of *Visions of Vocation: Common Grace for the Common Good*, and professor of marketplace theology, Regent College, Vancouver, BC**

"Laura Fabrycky artfully weaves together travelogue, memoir, cultural commentary, and deep spiritual insight in *Keys to Bonhoeffer's Haus*. This is the work of a masterful tour guide: her expertise as a storyteller at the Bonhoeffer-Haus in Berlin spills over into an illuminating tour of the inner worlds of soul and conscience. In our complex world, where faith, politics, and real human relationships seem to get painfully knotted and tangled, Fabrycky offers the story of her treading in Bonhoeffer's footsteps and, in doing so, leads us on a path to wisdom too."

—**Bronwyn Lea, author of *Beyond Awkward Side Hugs***

"Fabrycky's book is part memoir, part devotional, part history, and part sermon. She writes honestly about Bonhoeffer and her own journey to understand him with clean, descriptive prose, pulling us into the lessons his life has for each of us—if we will choose to listen. This is unlike any Bonhoeffer book I have ever read, and it may now be my favorite."

—**Rev. Steve Bezner, PhD, Senior Pastor of Houston Northwest Church, and adjunct Professor of Theology at Truett Seminary**

"Dietrich Bonhoeffer is one of the most relevant saints for Western Christians in the twenty-first century, and Laura Fabrycky's *Keys to Bonhoeffer's Haus* is a striking meditation on Bonhoeffer and the space he inhabited. Fabrycky deftly weaves memories of Bonhoeffer and his home into a timely narrative about faithfully embodying Christ in a place. We would do well to pay close attention not only to her rendering of Bonhoeffer, but also to her method of carefully exegeting the place she inhabits and the histories to which it gave shape."

—**C. Christopher Smith, founding editor of** *The Englewood Review of Books,* **and author of** *How the Body of Christ Talks: Recovering the Practice of Conversation in the Church*

KEYS TO BONHOEFFER'S HAUS

KEYS TO BONHOEFFER'S HAUS

EXPLORING THE WORLD AND WISDOM OF

DIETRICH BONHOEFFER

LAURA M. FABRYCKY

Fortress Press

Minneapolis

KEYS TO BONHOEFFER'S HAUS
Exploring the World and Wisdom of Dietrich Bonhoeffer

Cover image: Nastasic/istock; Happy_vector/istock
Cover design: Lindsey Owens

Print ISBN: 978-1-5064-5591-4
eBook ISBN: 978-1-5064-5592-1

For all free people, wherever they may live:
Lasst' sie nach Berlin kommen.

Table of Contents

Acknowledgments

Thank you to my family—above all to my husband, David, and our children. Together, we visited the Bonhoeffer-Haus, and then you each patiently endured "Mommy Bonhoeffering" long after. David, your unflagging support, enthusiasm, and faith in me and this story helped me get through my doubts, fears, and serious bouts of dithering. Your companionship in life is one of God's greatest gifts to me, and I love you. Miriam Leslie Fabrycky, Hannah Corbly Fabrycky, and Adam John Fabrycky—you three incredible people lived as Berliners for a season, learned the city's language, and are better Americans and world citizens for it. You make me proud and hopeful. I love you too.

Thank you to my parents, Babs and Jack Merzig, for your love and encouragement, and my parents-in-law, Janet and Alan Fabrycky, for the same. Thank you to my sister Leslie Merzig Deroo, brother-in-law Andrew Deroo, and nieces Talia and Naima for being in the midst, making lasagna, doing dishes, and sharp-eyed reading.

I am deeply indebted to the many who belong to and love the Bonhoeffer-Haus, and those who carry its keys. Special thanks to Rev. ret. Gottfried Brezger (chairman of the board), who read my draft carefully and graciously and contributed critically to it, and to Rev. Martin Dubberke (executive director during my time there), who welcomed me and my family to the Haus so many times. My sincere thanks to the other members of the volunteer group: Martina Dethloff, Ralf Herold, Rev. ret. Michael Kennert, Rev. ret. Kurt Kriebohm, Rev. ret. Dr. Ulrich Luig, Philip Miti, and Ingrid Portmann. Thank you for your open-hearted hospitality to me. I hope more visitors come to the Haus and learn from you as I did.

Thank you to dear friends in Berlin and elsewhere: Emunah Rankin, viriditas forever; early cheerleaders Bill and Laurel Martin (Schreib dein Buch!); Bobbi Jo Brooks, who makes beautiful stuff happen; C. Christopher Smith, to whom I owe a great deal; Jen Pollock Michel, whose wisdom and friendship have been vital and cross-pollinating; my real-life and Voxer pals Julie Nazimek Harner, Maggie Johns, Jody Fernando, Bronwyn Lea, Ashley Hales, Catherine McNeil, and Laura Penney; and also Emily Bliss for reading a painfully early draft. To Shireen David, and Clayton and Megan Anderson. To Shannon and Matt McNeil, and especially to Oliver, who graced Berlin and our home there with his presence and now rests with Waverly in the Lord's arms. To Mareike and Clemens Bethge, and your sweet girls, for your open hearts and minds. To Leah Striker for friendship, beauty, and adventure. To Jonathan Eastvold for the early education. Because our lives have been knit with them, thank you to Steve and Meg Garber, Todd and Judi Deatherage, Abby Deatherage, Karen Marsh, Dr. Heinrich and Conny Audebert, Stephanie and Adam Parken as well as Everett (keep taking good notes!), James, and Lillian, and Tillman Minow. To Michael and Andrea Le Roy, and Ashley and Mary Woodiwiss for teaching me. To Eric Young and Noah and Joe Toly, who were such valuable interlocutors. To Leslie Egge, Jan Aiello, and erstwhile Berliner transplant Heather Morton; to Becky Dye for presence and encouragement. Thank you to all who read early versions of this book.

ACKNOWLEDGMENTS

To our beloved church community of Mosaik Berlin, thank you for your welcome and embrace, and special thanks to Neville and Sue Jones, Benjamin and Brigitte, and Christopher and Stephanie. Special thanks as well to Dr. Victoria Barnett, Rev. Ulrike Trautwein, Dr. Gideon Strauss, Rev. Dr. Richard Mouw, Dr. Bryan McGraw, and other thoughtful leaders with generous minds and hearts.

To all those who visited the Haus and to whom I gave tours in 2017, 2018, and 2019, thank you for listening, asking questions, sharing expertise, and engaging the story with me.

To my editor, Emily Brower, who took the risk and patiently shepherded and strengthened the story. To Layne Johnson, Madeleine Vasaly, Allyce Amidon, Emily Benz, Mallory Hayes, and all who labored on the story's behalf. To Marty Kaz and Don Jacobsen, who offered wisdom. To my MQM readers, who represent family, friends, and acquaintances who have kindly read all along the way, thank you.

I still owe great debts of thanks and love to so many more, and no less despite going unnamed. Moreover, while I have tried to wring out errors and received much help in doing so, I am responsible for those that remain. I welcome feedback and correction.

"Most people have forgotten nowadays what a house can mean, though some of us have come to realize it as never before. It is a kingdom of its own in the midst of the world, a stronghold amid life's storms and stresses, a refuge, even a sanctuary."

Dietrich Bonhoeffer, *Letters and Papers from Prison*

Brief Chronology of Dietrich Bonhoeffer's Life

February 4, 1906	Born in Breslau, Germany (now Wrocław, Poland)
1912	Moves to Berlin with his family
1914	Start of World War I
1918	Brothers Karl-Friedrich and Walter go to war; Walter dies
1923	Abitur exam; begins theology studies at university in Tübingen
April–June 1924	Travels to Rome, Tripoli, and elsewhere with brother Klaus
	Returns to Berlin, enrolls at university
1927	Completes first dissertation, *Sanctorum Communio*
1928	Works in Barcelona as assistant pastor to German expatriate church
1929–1930	Completes second dissertation, *Act and Being*
1930–1931	Academic year spent at Union Theological Seminary, New York, as a Sloan Fellow; travels widely

November 15, 1931	Ordained at St. Matthäus-Kirche in Mitte, Berlin
1931	Begins lecturing at the university in Berlin (now Humboldt University) performing ecumenical and chaplaincy work; teaches confirmation class at the Zionskirche in Berlin (through 1932)
1932	Connects with Niemöller and others who formed the backbone of the Confessing Church
January 30, 1933	Hitler named chancellor of Germany
February 1, 1933	Bonhoeffer's "The Younger Generation's Altered View of the Concept of the Führer" radio address; its broadcast was cut short
February 27, 1933	Reichstag fire
March 23, 1933	Enabling Act passed in Reichstag, granting Hitler emergency powers
April 1933	Jewish businesses boycotted; laws passed targeting Jewish Germans, restricting them and those considered non-Aryan from professions
October 1933	Bonhoeffer leaves for London, begins pastoring two churches there
August 1934	Attends ecumenical conference in Fanø, Denmark; Hitler becomes Führer und Reichskanzler when President Hindenburg dies
1935	Bonhoeffer returns to Germany to establish Confessing Church seminary in Pomerania, meets Eberhard Bethge

1937	Niemöller arrested; Bonhoeffer publishes *Nachfolge* (*The Cost of Discipleship*); seminary closed and collective pastorates work begins
1938	Bonhoeffer publishes *Life Together*
June 2–July 7, 1939	Second journey to the United States
1940	Collective pastorates work ends by Gestapo order; Bonhoeffer begins work with *Abwehr*
1941	Operation 7
1943	Engaged to Maria von Wedemeyer; arrested in the Bonhoeffer-Haus April 5; prisoner at Tegel military prison
July 20, 1944	Stauffenberg plot fails; incriminating files found in an Abwehr bunker (Zossen, Germany); Bonhoeffer is moved from Tegel to Gestapo prison on Prinz-Albrecht-Strasse
1945	Bonhoeffer moved successively to Buchenwald concentration camp, Regensburg, Schönberg, and Flossenbürg concentration camp
April 9, 1945	Put to death at Flossenbürg
April 23, 1945	US Army liberates Flossenbürg concentration camp
July 27, 1945	Bonhoeffer's parents learn of his death on BBC radio, hearing his memorial service broadcast from London

The front door of the Bonhoeffer-Haus, Marienburger Allee 43, Berlin (Unless otherwise listed, all photos: David Fabrycky)

Chapter 1

VISITING THE HOUSE, HOLDING A KEY

It took seventeen minutes, door to door, to pedal from my house to Dietrich's—ten to exchange pleasantries with the Rev. Martin Dubberke, executive director of the Bonhoeffer-Haus, and then sign for a key to the front door. We shook hands and said goodbye, and I unlocked my bike, which I'd lashed to the streetlamp out front, to return home. As I pedaled along the long stretch of road that runs parallel to the A115 highway, I marveled at what this small single object meant. This key symbolized my longing to learn Dietrich Bonhoeffer's story and to put his life in conversation with mine. It also represented an exchange of trust and a new responsibility.

• • •

Becoming a guide at the Bonhoeffer-Haus was not something I sought out when our family first moved to Berlin in the summer of 2016 for my husband's work at the US embassy. Nor had we gone out of our way to find Bonhoeffer in Berlin. But in the early weeks after we arrived, we kept running into evidence of him. After all, it was once *his* Berlin, as it was now also ours for the next three-year season of our lives.

We five first landed in an apartment hotel just off the Robert-Koch-Platz in Mitte, the central downtown neighborhood of Berlin. The hotel was a mile north of the Brandenburg Gate on Pariser

Platz, the symbolic center of this creative, energetic, and historically scarred city. During our first month, the kids and I enjoyed slower starts to our days while my husband, David, set out to work early in the long, bright light of the northern European summer mornings. The rest of us were free to knock about town, gathering the day's groceries and getting our bearings on the buses, trams, and trains of Berlin's public transportation system. The kids were aged ten, eight, and nearly two at the time, and the older two already had deeply formed capacities for patience and long-suffering from years of international moves and cross-cultural living, which they now drew from as I haltingly tried to communicate with people and figure out how we were going to do each day. As all US Foreign Service families do, we live by a motto akin to that of the Marine Corps: *Semper Gumby.* Always flexible.

In the early days of a new posting, the most elemental tasks offer orientation in the foggy bewilderment of calling a new place home. I began writing regular email updates home to friends and family, narrating our days and some of the inner workings of my soul. The growing written record helped me to see that we were, in fact, still alive and kicking, even on the days that felt overwhelming and alien. The most ordinary places can be intimidating in their otherness, and at times I grew frustrated with myself for not knowing "how one does things here" when I wanted not to be an outsider.

Our apartment was close to Berlin's Humboldt University, and the budget grocery store nearby was usually full of students buying grab-and-go items such as the appropriately named Studentenfutter (what we call trail mix, but literally "student feed"). The kids and I drew constant attention in the store as a monstrous, disruptive aberration from the normal clientele. Once, while a university student ahead of me purchased a tidy bottle of beer, a pack of cigarettes, and a premade sandwich, I dumped a day's worth of groceries for a family of five onto the conveyer belt. When I got to the front of the line, the cashier scanned and piled my groceries faster than I could bag them up, as is common practice in Germany for customers to do themselves. Items fell off the small counter and onto the floor, raspberries rolling under our feet. The cashier said something to me—likely asking me if I wanted my receipt—but I did not recognize a single word he uttered. None of it sounded like the simple, slowly articulated German phrases I had practiced in my online language tutorials. With a tired toddler strapped to my back, our two elementary-aged daughters trying to be helpful and fully attuned to how much I was struggling, and a line of customers watching us sullenly, my mind went blank. I said, in halting, poorly pronounced German, "Again please? I'm sorry, I speak only a little German." Then I smiled broadly, hoping to garner a little sympathy, as I felt a raspberry squish under my sneakers. But this only compounded my agony. Smiling at strangers is an American communication trait, but in Germany, it translates as dim-wittedness, which was fairly enough how I felt.

It's a humbling experience to be poor in the social and cultural skills and dominant language of a new place. In public places such as banks, post offices, grocery stores, and government bureaucracies, there are a thousand little rules that one only learns by breaking them, standing out like a sore thumb, and getting schooled in front of others. Buying a single banana in a culture and language not your own can feel like a herculean effort because it is. Yet along that exquisite ridge of learning, with its dizzying heights and jagged valleys of lived experience, one eventually gains competencies and a growing measure of confidence.

Our legs strengthened in those early, carless months too. The kids and I trekked to various places in the city, often hopping a tram on Invalidenstrasse to Berlin's glass-and-steel Hauptbahnhof, the main train station. We also spent a lot of time walking between our apartment and the US embassy, about a mile each way, for various check-in appointments with embassy offices or to have lunch with Daddy. To make our way there, we walked south along Luisenstrasse and crossed the Spree, the main river that snakes through Berlin. The walk goes right through the Charité hospital campus, Berlin's chief medical facility, its large white building standing high above most in the neighborhood. As the late-setting summer sun cast its luminous eye across the city, our sixth-floor apartment had a terrific view as the Charité glowed pink. In those languid evening hours, I found myself gazing at the rose-bathed hospital, the night's advance extinguishing the light show. I was grateful for the building's orienting height.

One weekend afternoon, I went out for a walk by myself, wandering down a side street lined with short brick buildings topped with sharply garbled roofs within the Charité campus. Various signs posted out front indicated that these were academic offices. The little campus neighborhood was sandwiched between our apartment and a canal of the Spree River, and beyond the canal lay the Hauptbahnhof. Walking in the maze of these brick buildings, I spotted a street sign that read Bonhoefferweg, or Bonhoeffer Way. I assumed—knowing only one Bonhoeffer by name—that the sign referred to Dietrich Bonhoeffer, the German theologian and pastor who was put to death by the Nazis at the age of thirty-nine for his role in a conspiracy against Hitler and the National Socialist regime. Only later did I learn I had been walking near the former office of Dr. Karl Bonhoeffer, Dietrich's father, a prominent and widely respected public figure as the director of psychiatry and neurology at the Charité hospital. It was Karl's work that brought the Bonhoeffer family to

Berlin in 1912, when Dietrich was six years old, from Breslau (now Wrocław, Poland), where Dietrich was born. While the legacy of his sixth child has eclipsed him in terms of global recognition, Dr. Bonhoeffer is still a significant figure in German history, even showing up in common parlance in Berlin. One idiomatic expression Berliners still use to say that someone has "gone crazy" is that he or she has "gone off to Boni's ranch," or been "taken to Bonhoeffer's farm," referring to Dr. Karl Bonhoeffer's psychiatric work.

On one of my husband's head-clearing runs in that first month in the city, he ventured east from our apartment through Mitte, running past the Berlin Wall Memorial and Documentation Center on Bernauer Strasse, an infamous stretch where the Cold War–era wall cut through the neighborhood like a knife into living flesh. He spotted a spire in the distance and decided to make that his turnaround point. Finding the door to the stately brown-brick parish church unlocked, he ducked inside to investigate.

David returned from his run with a brochure from the church, which he handed to me as he unlaced his sneakers. "I found a church related to Dietrich Bonhoeffer," he said, pausing to breathe. "They even have a statue outside dedicated to him and a large plaque for him on the outside of the building." I opened the pamphlet and recognized Dietrich in a photo surrounded by a group of adolescent boys on the bank of a lake, which jogged my memory from earlier reading I had done about him. Oh yes, of course—the Zionskirche! The Zion Church was the parish where Bonhoeffer had taught a confirmation class to a group of rowdy boys and won their hearts and minds.

At last, we moved into our permanent residence, a house on the edge of the Grunewald, the sprawling forest dotted with lakes on the city's western edge. Five days later, our children started school and the process of breaking ground with new friends, which reaped quick rewards. On the first day of school, a German girl in my third grader's class approached her and, with an unexpected Scottish accent, said in English, "Shall we be friends?"

Later that autumn, we invited this girl to come play at our house, and her mother, Mareike, and I chatted as the kids raced up the stairs, squealing with fun. I invited Mareike to stay and talk, and I brewed some coffee for us. Thanking her for her daughter's kindness, I offered her some banana bread I had made that morning, a baked good she found peculiar but tasty. "Very much an American thing, isn't it?" Mareike said, also with a surprising Scottish lilt.

We broke our own ground, asking questions that mapped our life stories. Her childhood had been infinitely more interesting—and historic—than mine. She told me about growing up in Communist-era East Berlin, how she rarely ate bananas in her childhood, and how her parents kept coffee in stock in inventive ways. At one point she said, quietly—almost as if she still had to be careful, or did so simply from habit—"The hardest part, really, was not being able to really trust anyone. I don't think that's something anyone recovers from easily." Both she and her husband had lived in Scotland for many years, hence the distinctive accent of their English.

Her family name, Bethge, was familiar to me. It was close to that of an American political theorist whom I had studied, corresponded with while in college, and knew personally in my postcollege years working in a Washington, DC think tank. Even though those heady days are long gone, I still count the late Dr. Jean Bethke Elshtain among my personal and intellectual heroes. *Bethge, Bethke.* I asked whether she was familiar with that name, and whether the *-ge* and *-ke* spellings were interchangeable. "Is it possible she's a distant relation to you?" I wondered aloud.

"No, I don't think so. I'm not aware of that spelling in our family," she replied. But then she pointed up to a thick, blue paperback on the bookshelf behind me, one with Dietrich Bonhoeffer's face peering out from the top of the spine. "I see, though, that you have a book about Dietrich Bonhoeffer right there. Perhaps you are thinking of Eberhard Bethge? He was Dietrich Bonhoeffer's good friend."

"Oh yes, of course! I should have recognized that name," I exclaimed.

She took a sip of coffee and said with complete modesty, "Eberhard was my great-uncle."

Many German guidebooks use a formulation along the lines of "auf den Spuren von" a person or place—that you are "on someone's trail" or finding the traces of something historic. In Dietrich's case, we did not have to go looking far and wide. We had moved into his city and found traces of him still very present.

• • •

On an October day in 2016, I closed my laptop and groaned. The news from home was becoming more difficult to digest with each passing week. The rancor and contempt of the 2016 US presidential election campaign season had clawed into my private world and personal relationships, especially on social media platforms. What had once been a lifeline of connection during our previous overseas assignments now pulsed with acrimony. Suddenly, "friends" and "followers" on social media platforms started acting like contemptuous talking heads on TV rather than as embodied friends and neighbors of one another. Some of those called friends were becoming strangers to us. Every day, it grew harder to watch from afar.

Through my laptop screen, the America I thought I knew was growing more unsettled just as we were trying to settle in Germany. We had unpacked the many boxes containing our household effects, figuring out where to store the coffee mugs and the board games, deciding which drawers should hold the socks and how to organize the books. But the place we called home—the land we represented in this foreign place—looked increasingly strange, even alienating, to us. Something seemed to have snapped in our hyperpolarized and tribal politics that could not easily be put back together; we could feel that even from such a distance. Cords of civic affection were fraying. I felt something fraying within me too, a sense of homelessness and helplessness threatening to swallow me up. I wanted to fight and flee all at once.

A distracting thought that seemed to come out of nowhere interrupted my fear that seemed to come out of nowhere. It was a merciful redirection, however: *Where did Dietrich Bonhoeffer live again? Here in Berlin, but where? Is there a museum there? If so, that might be interesting to visit.* Before we had moved to Berlin, I read a biography about Bonhoeffer, who joined a circle of conspirators in one of the most serious assassination and coup attempts against Hitler and the Nazi government—an attempt that failed. The idea of visiting a place related to him felt like a curious reprieve from the groans of home.

Reopening the laptop, I searched online for places related to Bonhoeffer and saw a small dot on the map, labeled *Bonhoeffer-Haus*, not far from the dot that represented our house on the map. Navigating through to the affiliated website, I saw it was possible to make an appointment to visit. Well, that was easy! I dashed off an email requesting an English-language tour.

A few days later, I received a reply from the director of the Bonhoeffer-Haus, offering an appointment time that I knew wouldn't work; I asked for another option, double-checking that our children could come. He assured me that children were "always welcome at the Bonhoeffer-Haus." We finally settled on a date and time that worked for him and for our family: a morning tour for Saturday, November 12, 2016—the Saturday after the US elections. I felt satisfied knowing we had an expedition like this one on the calendar. We knew it was going to be a very busy week; I needed to finish settling our house in anticipation of a houseguest's arrival and to prepare for a big event at our house later in the week. We also paid close attention to the election news from home, and my husband, like most career foreign service officers around the world, also had additional responsibilities at work for election night. But I felt that carving out some intentional exploration of our new city, and learning more about this significant figure in history, would do us all good. Accomplishing that small task with such little effort helped beat back some of my gloom.

After dropping my son off at preschool that Tuesday morning, Election Day in the United States, I hopped off the bus at a stop earlier than my usual transfer point so I could step foot in the historic St. Anne's Church in Dahlem. During the Nazi era, Rev. Martin Niemöller was the pastor here and an early and significant leader in the Confessing Church—the church movement that opposed the Nazi-affiliated Deutsche Christen, or German Christians. Niemöller was arrested in 1937 and imprisoned in various concentration camps as Hitler's so-called "personal prisoner." His story was well known to the world during those years, and *Time* magazine even put him on its cover in 1940.

A decorated commander of a U-boat during World War I, Niemöller originally supported Hitler, believing that many National Socialist aims coincided with Christian ones—a position Dietrich Bonhoeffer repudiated early in Hitler's rule.[1] Unlike Bonhoeffer,

Niemöller was attracted to the strong nationalist message of the party. But he changed his mind about Hitler and, in close coordination with Bonhoeffer and others, helped lead the segment of the church that opposed Nazi enthusiasm and influence within its sanctuaries, efforts that drew the personal ire of the Führer, Adolf Hitler. Not long after being liberated by Allied forces, Niemöller toured the United States to talk about the Confessing Church and encourage American Christians to donate money for war-ravaged Germany.

Niemöller is now much less known to Americans by name than he was during and immediately after World War II, but many are still familiar with a poem attributed to him:

First they came for the socialists, and I did not speak out—
    Because I was not a socialist.
Then they came for the trade unionists, and I did not speak out—
    Because I was not a trade unionist.
Then they came for the Jews, and I did not speak out—
    Because I was not a Jew.
Then they came for me—and there was no one left to speak for me.[2]

I wanted to come to his church to pray.

After I got off the bus, I walked along Königin-Luise-Straße—Queen Louise Street—until I reached the church gate. I stepped inside the grounds, passed through the cemetery that surrounds it, and approached the main door of this small, historic building, with its simple wooden steeple and stratified stone exterior, the church property dating to the medieval period. Traversing an inlaid mosaic cross on the threshold, I discovered the door was locked. So, standing on that cross, I faced out to look over the cemetery and gardens of St. Anne's and asked God to help my country find our way. I asked for mercy for all the civic stress fractures that seemed to be developing into hard breaks. I prayed for God's will to be done, a prayer that sounded inert and helpless, but I lifted it with open hands.

When Saturday morning dawned at the end of that week, we were exhausted, but our impending excursion to the Bonhoeffer-Haus infused me with energy. Our family of five piled into our newly arrived car to make our way there, at times straddling our vehicle's tires up on the curb in a futile attempt to reduce the footprint of our large vehicle on the slim cobbled roads near the Bonhoeffer-Haus. Lined on one side with parked cars, Marienburger Allee is basically a one-lane road; to pass each other, drivers make delicate adjustments, steering up onto curbs and sidewalks. Beautiful upper-middle-class homes line it, many ringed with waist-high walls, hedges, and picket fences.

The Bonhoeffer-Haus—Marienburger Allee no. 43—stands on a stovepipe extension off the main road bearing the same name. There are only two houses on this small street, a pair of architec-tural twins, both built by the Bonhoeffer family. As we walked up to No. 43, we spotted a large white tile with blue lettering affixed to the house's wall by the front door—a common demarcation of a rec-ognized memorial place. From the door emerged a jovial man, with eyes as large and round as the glasses that framed them, who waved to us and welcomed us in. Holding the door open wide, he asked us to make our way into a conference room on the left, where some other English-speaking visitors were already seated.

I've tried to excavate the memory of that moment, but I do not remember crossing the threshold into the Bonhoeffer-Haus that first time. The moment was suffused with the quotidian efforts of parenting: shepherding our littlest along, hoping we were all being polite and engaging in culturally appropriate ways, and batting away worries that having the kids along on the tour might not have been the wisest idea. But I do remember that my everyday parenting anxieties melted away as I sensed we had just walked into a home—not a museum, a historical theme park, or even a shrine for a deceased hero. The place gave off the homey cues of a residence with the old-bones creak of the floorboards, the warm and pleasant odor of wooden beams and books, and an enveloping and settling feeling of calm and order. This Bonhoeffer-Haus was a home—the door opened for us. Stepping inside, we tourists and gathered strangers transformed into welcomed guests.

Passing through a small entryway, I spotted a large and slightly sun-faded poster of Dietrich Bonhoeffer on our left and a golden pine staircase on our right. Another poster listing dates and events, all in German, hung in the entryway above a small white wardrobe. We passed through glass-paneled doors on the left, where the other guests sat around a large conference table.

The conference room's white walls were adorned with large panels full of black-and-white photographic collages. Nine panels in all hung between tall windows draped with floor-to-ceiling gray curtains pulled back to let in the dappled light. They looked like pages pulled from an old family scrapbook. A haunting image of the destroyed interior of a synagogue is the first image one sees upon entering the room. It depicts Kristallnacht, or Night of the Broken Glass (November 9–10, 1938), the violent Nazi pogrom unleashed against Jewish citizens and places of worship and businesses across Germany. On the same scrapbook-like panel is a photograph of a roadside crucifix—a large traditional statue of the crucified Jesus—sheltered under a little wooden roof right next to a sign that reads *Juden sind hier nicht erwünscht* (Jews not wanted here).[3]

We took our seats at the conference table, and I pulled out crayons and paper for our young son. The guide for the tour, Martin, introduced himself as the executive director of the Haus, and then he asked us why we had come, inviting conversation. Each visitor spoke, passing the question like a collection basket at church. When my turn came, I said, diplomatically, as if casually tossing in a coin, "We're here to learn something about this remarkable man and"—I stopped, searching for the right words, trying to stay casual—"to find inspiration about living faithfully in turbulent times." My answer masked the dull ache within me, which now came roaring back as I thought back over the past week.

It had been a grueling and disorienting one. We had welcomed a guest into our home, our first after unpacking the boxes and hanging the pictures, and we then hosted a large gathering at our house a few days later. We had stayed up into the early morning hours watching the US election results come in, and so were underslept. But deeper than all that, we felt as though the ground beneath our feet had shifted, a map we thought we knew now erased. As I feared, the election had proven to be neither a salve to civic wounds nor a valve to release political indignation and anger. Oddly, the winners were defensive and whiny; the losers shocked and morose. Those caught between the strong political poles found the compass in their hands spinning frantically from all the magnetic interference. Moreover, the pride I often felt about America's democratic practices was, in that moment, in tatters. Our civic habits of the heart seemed weak, and from afar it seemed the formal liturgies of our political life lacked the capacity to revive them. I ached with homesickness for a world that I had taken for granted and that, perhaps, had never really existed as

I had imagined it. Foreign service officers (and their accompanying family members) are no strangers to political transitions, and they work and live within the context of whomever the American people elect. Explaining America and our democratic processes is part of our diplomatic bread and butter. But as our ambassador at the time regularly noted to German audiences before and after the election, it was proving increasingly difficult to explain what the heck was going on back home in American politics.

So, when Martin asked us all why we had come, I knew that the questions I carried with me into the Bonhoeffer-Haus were bigger, more existential, than just curiosity about this one inspiring man. I wanted maps that could help us navigate our way back home, and I wanted words of reassurance.

Next, Martin talked about Bonhoeffer's life, telling stories that redirected my attention away from my inner ache and toward the place where we all now sat. "Dietrich Bonhoeffer did not grow up in this house," Martin began. Designed for the family and built in 1935, along with the adjacent property next door, the house was intended to be a place of retirement for Dr. Bonhoeffer and his wife, Paula von Hase Bonhoeffer, so they could enjoy their later years in the company of their large family. Dr. Bonhoeffer's mother, Julie Tafel Bonhoeffer, also had a suite of rooms and lived out her remaining days in the house, passing away there in 1936. Karl and Paula also reserved a room for their only unmarried adult son, Dietrich, up on the top floor with dormer windows looking out on the backyard next door. There, Ursula Bonhoeffer Schleicher, one of Dietrich's older sisters, lived with her husband, Rüdiger, and their children, including their daughter, Renate, who eventually married Eberhard Bethge, Dietrich's best friend.

Dr. Karl Bonhoeffer continued to see patients from time to time in his retirement, and the large conference room in which we now sat had originally been two rooms: a waiting room and his office. Behind Martin was another set of glass-paneled doors leading out to a small Wintergarten, an enclosed porch where the family could take in sunlight in the dark winter days. Motioning to the large windows, Martin asked us to imagine a dense forest outside, for the Bonhoeffers' houses were part of a new development in this section of the Grunewald. Tucked away at the end of this stovepipe road, with a forest beyond, the house, along with its sister-house next door, was "a perfect setting for conspiring," Martin said—an indication of just how little retiring the Bonhoeffers actually enjoyed there.

Our guide walked us through key moments of the Bonhoeffers' lives, referring to the nine panels of collected photographs: Dietrich's happy childhood with his parents and among his brothers and sisters in Breslau and then Berlin, the beginnings of World War I, the loss of his brother Walter in the war and how his death shattered Paula and affected the entire family, the many places of Dietrich's education and formation, and the growing power of National Socialism. When Martin came to that central panel, with the synagogue, the crucifix, and the sign, he drew our focused attention out from the Bonhoeffer family and toward bigger realities, institutions, themes, and patterns of thought in Germany at that time. The family witnessed how rapidly National Socialism worked its way into nearly every aspect of life in Germany, and the church in Germany was not simply a passive victim to this entanglement. Martin said, plainly, that the church failed its neighbors and fellow citizens during the Nazi era, and these juxtaposed photographs depicted that failure: "The story is told that when the church embraced the message that Jews were not welcome—when Jews were told they were not welcome in the household of God—Jesus himself also left the church." He wanted us to see how the church's failures were moral, to be sure, but also inextricably theological. In the end, a significant segment of the church embraced the ideology of National Socialism and allowed its theological treasures to be raided and exploited for politically expedient ends. Many believed that the movement's successes proved that it was God's will.

Martin finished his summary while standing in front of the panel showing Dietrich in the Tegel military prison, recounting his last days before he was put to death on April 9, 1945, at the Flossenbürg concentration camp. He then invited us to follow him up the two flights of stairs to Dietrich's bedroom, where the Gestapo took him into custody on April 5, 1943. Solemnly, we filed out of the conference room, back toward the front door, and then ascended that pine staircase, the wooden banister on the wall smooth and sturdy as we climbed.

At the top landing of the stairs, the door on the right opens to Dietrich's room. The room is spare. A thin rag rug lies on the floor next to a single twin-sized bed. Trim wooden shelves built by Dietrich and his friend Eberhard ring the room, holding books Dietrich owned and periodicals to which he contributed. Although his actual books and journals were donated to a research library long ago, those now at the Bonhoeffer-Haus are identical.[4] Across from the door is the set of windows that overlooks the neighboring house with a clear view of its backyard. His original desk is positioned beneath the windows with a teal-colored desk lamp. "When Bonhoeffer was in this room," Martin remarked, breaking the group's hushed silence, "the air was often blue with smoke," for Dietrich was a heavy cigarette smoker. Martin pointed out a small cigarette burn on the bluish-green velvet desk blotter, the singe long gone but a hole remaining.

Dietrich's clavichord sits immediately to the right of the room's entrance, and Martin opened the case to show how quiet the instrument is: "Dietrich could play without disturbing others in the house." As a boy, Dietrich demonstrated serious musical talent early on and was especially gifted on the piano. His family wondered whether he might grow up to pursue a career in music; his announcement as a young teenager that he wanted to study theology struck them as curious, even misguided. But he never stopped playing music, and his knowledge and skill in music were closely tied to his theological insights and Christian practices—the clavichord stands as a reminder of this. Just to the left of the instrument is a small alcove with a wardrobe, and a sink and mirror, hidden away by a curtain that stretches across the alcove.

Unlike walking into the house, walking into that room did feel magical, but very quickly the imaginative spell dissipated. The room of this hero looked so normal. Here, a giant slept, yet the room is so small and spare, completely human-sized. The desk is human-sized too; the burn mark is evidence of human habits and even a touch of carelessness. Everything in the room points to Dietrich Bonhoeffer's humanity, putting his insights, courage, and self-sacrificing decisions in even sharper relief.

After some time with the group in that bedroom, we descended the stairs, dropped a donation into the metal canister bolted to the entryway wall, and thanked Martin for his hospitality before heading back to our vehicle.

As my husband and I buckled everyone up for the short drive home, the kids started lobbing questions: "Whose house was that again? Why did we go there? Do we have snacks?" I tried to explain in simple language, especially for our two-year-old, who Bonhoeffer was, how he and his family and many of his friends tried to stop "the bad guys," the Nazis who had come to power in Germany. Simply introducing the word *Nazi* to their lives was meaty stuff for a young

17

family on a Saturday morning. We rumbled back down the narrow cobblestone road toward home.

The roads grew wider and the cobblestones gave way to pavement, and we fell quiet as the rumbling and jostling of the road quieted too. Staring out the window as trees and houses flashed by, I sighed aloud, "That was amazing." Yet I still felt the exhaustion, inner aches, and questions that I carried with me to Bonhoeffer's house. On our way back to ours, we motored past the Grunewald S-Bahn station, with its gingerbread-house styling coupled with a morbid memorial of its own, Gleis 17 (Platform 17).[5] From this station, Nazis transported thousands of Jewish Berliners to concentration camps in their attempt to make Berlin judenfrei, Jew free. At last I said, "I didn't get my questions answered in the way I wanted to." My husband nodded silently.

Oddly, despite not having gotten what I hoped for, I felt a new hope stirring in me alongside the ache. Hearing Martin tell Dietrich Bonhoeffer's story in that house fired my imagination about our home. Even though not a single aspect of my life resembled Bonhoeffer's, the Bonhoeffer-Haus bore witness as a place to human experiences I knew in my daily life. Wordlessly, the Haus disclosed realities, conveyed memories of things I didn't realize I needed to remember. The house had its own tacit form of communication about the silent truths of human life. I sensed that the spinning compass inside me had regained its orientation, my longing for a lost home eclipsed by a feeling of renewed hope alongside the sensation of exile. I wanted to experience more of the silent witness of that home and hear its stories again. I wanted others to experience it too.

Luckily, we received a lot of visitors in Berlin, which gave me a good excuse to return to the Bonhoeffer-Haus. As we considered possible itineraries to explore the city with our guests, I often suggested the Bonhoeffer-Haus: "It's not really on the normal tourist trail." Each time I came with visitors to the Haus, I learned something new about Dietrich Bonhoeffer and his context, seeing some part of his story from a new angle. Each time, I saw how the people who gathered at the Haus influenced how the story was told, bringing their questions in ways that shaped the tours. The different volunteer guides usually asked us visitors why we had come, inviting our participation and dialogue. More often than not, visitors talked about their deep admiration for Bonhoeffer, citing his inspiration in their lives. Some admitted they had questions, puzzles of their own that they hoped to untangle with help from Bonhoeffer's life. In this, I was not so unique after all.

Our visitors influenced our experiences at the Haus too. Prior to their visit to Berlin, dear friends of ours had researched Aktion T4, the Nazi plan to euthanize the "incurably sick"—those with psychiatric disorders and intellectual disabilities who fell outside the Nazis' ever-narrowing definition of valuable human life. With cooperation from the medical establishment, tens to hundreds of thousands of victims were culled from nursing homes and medical care facilities, suffered coerced medical experimentation, and were then systematically murdered, their lives used to test and refine killing methods, especially gassing, that were unleashed on Jews and others at even greater scale later on. Our friends had a personal angle to their interest: both of their children had been diagnosed with a genetic syndrome that, if they had been born in that time and place, surely would have marked them for death. The haunting questions of their life framed how they saw the Nazi era, their minds on fire as they imagined what they would have done if they had lived then and there. So, in addition to taking up my suggestion that we visit the Bonhoeffer-Haus, together we also made a solemn visit to the

T4 Memorial, a relatively new translucent blue-glass wall located on the southern boundary of the Tiergarten, Berlin's central park. The T4 plan derived its name from the address of the building in which it was hatched: Tiergartenstrasse No. 4. Then and now, places themselves bear witness to the horrors of the era; addresses on maps mark the ideas.[6]

The volunteer guides at the Bonhoeffer-Haus issued their own witness, narrating Bonhoeffer's life through the lens of their own questions. One guide—Rev. Gottfried Brezger—conducted his tour much like a theology professor in a seminar class, inviting conversation with guests as he might with cherished students. Pouring cups of tea and offering biscuits, Gottfried asked visitors about their own lives and questions they had about Bonhoeffer, and then he gently steered the conversation to rather lofty theological concepts such as Christology—the study of the person, nature, and work of Jesus Christ. The Jewish identity of Jesus was a key debate in the Nazi era and one that Bonhoeffer labored over in his thoughts, writings, and actions. The Deutsche Christen—literally, the German Christians, those who closely identified with the Nazis—recast the "Jew from Nazareth" into an incarnation of Aryan myth, the physical embodiment of Nazi views of success, strength, and national victory. Gottfried helped us to see that what Christians believed about Jesus mattered to how they treated—and mistreated—others, especially Jews.

Gottfried also drew our attention to the slow work of historical and moral reckoning after the twelve years of Nazi rule. As he put it in one morning's visit, "It took a whole generation before we as a nation even began asking questions about what happened." To hear him say "we" was startling enough; he was identifying himself as a German with the sin-sick story of the Nazis and the shame and responsibility of his people. But it was truly a shock to learn how long it took before the moral reckoning began. After World War II, Berlin was rubble—smoldering and traumatized. Rebuilding the city took substantial physical work, but it didn't even begin to address the sheer effort of surveying the charred landscape of moral and spiritual ruin, the widespread human wreckage of hearts, minds, bodies, and souls. For a long time, Germans avoided this story; nearly everyone still alive was implicated in the ruin. As an American, I had never contemplated what had come after the war, how facts had to be collected, sifted, and evaluated, and how stories had to be rescued before they fell into the great silence of forgetfulness.

On another visit, a German visitor on an English-language tour added some of his own observations on that postwar sifting and sorting, specifically the beguiling nature of words in how one tells the story of the Nazi era and the Holocaust. The mammoth work of "making sense"—the German word is Aufarbeitung, which can mean working through, coming to terms with the past, or reappraising or renovating something—mattered even for words themselves. Pointing to the image of the destroyed synagogue on the conference room wall, this visitor said that even the commonly used term for the November 1938 pogrom against Jewish places of worship and work is not without political controversy. Kristallnacht, whose literal meaning is Crystal Night, is a euphemism, a term that masks the seething hatred and violence unleashed in that destructive series of events that ended in the Holocaust. In other words, the wreckage of the Nazi system, the moral ruin, was still being sorted, even if war rubble had been cleared away long ago. The past is always present here in Germany, and it is both personal and public.[7]

Listening to German visitors and guides during these early visits helped me to see my American interpretive lenses, which focused narrowly on certain elements of World War II history with a dramatic Hollywood gloss to it all. As an American, I found the war's drama captivating, but the story I had learned at the Haus revealed an intoxicating naïveté about war and moral injury. "We" Americans had been "the good guys," and our victory signaled the worthiness of our cause. For the generation of Americans who made great sacrifices in that era, that narrative is not untrue, and the honors we confer on them are rightly earned.

But hearing the witness of other Germans and experiencing the silent witness of the Bonhoeffer-Haus, gravely complicated my neat moral narrative about that history. Perhaps I had given some thought to the moral complications of life under Nazism, mesmerizing in its goose-stepping spectacle, but clearly not enough to the day-to-day non-drama, the million minute decisions that everyday Germans made, consciously and unconsciously, long before the Allied forces advanced against the Nazis in Europe. These decisions shackled them to Hitler's mad vision, moment by moment, and just as efficiently severed the connective tissue of their civic life together. The Nazi idol failed to deliver on his many promises of restored greatness, leaving only a vast field of moral ruin, gasping complicity, and the incomprehensible numbers of murdered humans. The end of the war was the beginning of the long work of moral reckoning, the hard, responsible work of staying free.

But ignorance and silence—telltale hallmarks of civic irresponsibility—are the shadows into which both victors and vanquished can easily retreat. After the war, those who had once been full-throated Nazis were reinstalled into their places in polite German society in rather astonishing numbers. A report released in October 2016 by a commission of German historians and lawyers found that 77 percent of the senior officials in the post–World War II

West German justice ministry had been Nazi Party members, a success made possible by "the fascist old-boys network" protecting its own from punishment.[8]

But the less powerful found ways to avoid their responsibilities too. Anyone could claim that, in their hearts, they practiced "inner resistance," even if they fully complied with Nazi orders. It was a matter of personal survival! Others claimed to have worked from within the system, trying to reduce the effects of the collective madness. It was easy to claim that the goose-stepping obedience had been coerced, to spin the widespread complicity into more appealing shades of gray: No one was a true believer, *really*. Ordinary private citizens shouldn't be held accountable for the rumored atrocities they didn't know about and weren't directly responsible for. One person couldn't make any real difference when the wave of National Socialism crashed upon them all. In all that moral fog, professed ignorance and withdrawal were safe refuges from responsibility. After those terrifying years, it was easier to pretend everything could just go back to normal.

But in the 1960s and 1970s, the children of that generation began to turn to their parents and grandparents to ask what they knew, and what they had done with what they knew. In 1979, the American television series *Holocaust* was broadcast into West German homes. The now familiar and still horrific images from that time—the monstrous heaps of starved and naked bodies; the piles of pulled teeth harvested for gold and the eyeglasses and shoes wrenched from all sizes of human feet; all the careful, calculated organization of torture, murder, and human cruelty—interrupted the practiced, polite silence with searing questions. The moral reckoning—the Aufarbeitung process—began and continues to this day. Whether we acknowledge it or not, the past is still present.

• • •

On my fourth visit to the house, in May 2017, I introduced myself to the guide after her talk, just before she took the group upstairs to Dietrich's bedroom. My visiting friend and I had been a late addition to her group, so I thanked her for including us with such short notice. This guide told us she worked as a teacher at the Walter-Rathenau-Gymnasium, Dietrich Bonhoeffer's old high school, which had been named the Grunewald-Gymnasium when he was a student there. One day, she had noticed a plaque on the school wall, listing names of its students who had died as a result of their resistance to National Socialism, including Bonhoeffer. As a teacher, she saw how friendships forged in school, where neighbors become classmates and classmates become friends, helped them trust one another when trust became rare. These friendships mattered to a nation. She volunteered at the house because of her personal connection to another significant place of Bonhoeffer's life, a place where her life intersects with his. Her unique perspective cast his life in a new light.

After I thanked her, she replied, "Well, I understand from Martin that you come quite regularly to the Haus, so you must be learning a lot!"

I said, not entirely in jest, "Yes, I come so often to the Bonhoeffer-Haus, I think I should volunteer as a guide myself!"

To my astonishment, she said, "Yes, you should!"

With that, I felt like a closed door I had been standing in front of, had shyly cracked open, letting light illuminate my hope. I wanted to be sure it didn't close before I slipped through. Yes, I wanted to come in, into the Haus and more into the story. I wanted this place to matter to the places of my life, to better attend to our story in Berlin and to our home in America with all its fraying bonds of civic affection and decaying trust. I wanted this place and its stories to matter to my neighbors near and far and, above all, to give us hope.

When I got home from that visit, I immediately emailed Martin to ask whether it was really possible, whether I too could volunteer as a guide at the Bonhoeffer-Haus, an opportunity I never imagined when we first made that visit. Now that the door was cracked open, I knew I wanted in.

I wanted "in" with all the meanings that tiny word holds. The house was a place in which I could think more about the tasks of being human, for it was where a very human Bonhoeffer lived—not only the Bonhoeffer of theologians, at times abstracted into ideas, and not only the heroic Bonhoeffer, gauzy, romantic, and two-dimensional. Here, I could imagine the man who rose early to read and meditate on the Bible, who ate oysters and played piano, who was captivated and instructed by art in so many forms, who sang boisterously and conversed brilliantly, who enjoyed all kinds of sports, who wrestled internally with himself, and who wrote fervent, fearful, and sometimes funny letters to friends and loved ones that still pierce hearts with their insight, vulnerability, and strength.

As much as I enjoy playing in the abstract sandbox of the intellect, I wanted to learn the concrete language of the Bonhoeffer-Haus. This home carried a vocabulary, grammar, and syntax that resonated with my Hausfrau-shaped life. Yes, I could read books and watch films about Bonhoeffer, but living as we did in Berlin, just minutes from this place, I wanted to let the house shape the way I thought. I wanted this place—full of the ordinary objects of life—to fertilize my moral imagination, the secret realm where metaphors, images, and ideas disclose possibilities for what is good, true, and right. The house witnesses to all these things, the place offering metaphors from which to embrace agency and responsibility and rekindle hope.

To my surprise, Martin quickly replied by email: "The idea of you joining the team is wonderful. It's not a problem that you don't speak German, because we have so many English-speaking visitors. Please come to our next volunteers' meeting where we can get to know you and you can know us, and we will see what we can offer together in the house."

• • •

"Honestly, Laura, I never heard of Dietrich Bonhoeffer until you mentioned your volunteer work, and only after that did I start to see his name with quotes on social media. So, no, I don't know anything about him, but I like a lot of the quotes I've seen. And, from what you've said, it sounds like he wrestled with what I've also been wrestling with, and about how things are going in our country." My friend's voice streamed into my car through the Bluetooth connection on the voice-messaging platform. "So, are you writing a biography of his life?"

In my reply, I assured her I was not. There are many excellent biographies of Dietrich Bonhoeffer, but as his name and story have become more widely known, they have also become more open to misuse and abuse. Bonhoeffer has become a more malleable figure in our hands, someone we are tempted to fashion for ourselves and to our own ends if we are not attentive to the questions and demands we make on him.[9]

This book serves as a record of my own encounter with Dietrich Bonhoeffer's story as a volunteer guide for two years at the Bonhoeffer-Haus during our three years residing in Berlin. I wrote it to remember what I learned there, to combat forgetfulness of the conversation that happened between his life story as I learned it and explored it with visitors, and mine as I lived it. The narrative of the book moves between his life and mine, for as I learned his story, I found it pushing me back into the realities of my own. The two are inextricable.

This book is also my way of holding the door to the Bonhoeffer-Haus open for you. Here, I've collected my field notes and personal observations from the house, from Berlin, and from other key places in Germany related to Bonhoeffer's story. I also relied heavily on the work of others, especially his friends—historians, theologians, ethicists, and storytellers—to assist my learning. So, whether or not you have the chance to visit the Bonhoeffer-Haus on Marienburger Allee in Berlin-Charlottenburg, I hope my stories assist your imaginative journey there, help you discover the questions you carry, and frame the conversation that might emerge between you and Bonhoeffer. The stowaway questions that clamored within me for attention proved to be the ones I wanted to know and understand better about Bonhoeffer.

Paradoxically, the more I studied Bonhoeffer's life and learned to tell his story with visitors to the Haus, I also came to see more clearly that Bonhoeffer's story is not *my* story. Though I wanted to discover the secrets that allowed him to live with such courage and tenacity, and though I was tempted to discern analogies between his world and mine, I saw that his times are not my times, and the world he lived in is not my world. That is not to say there is no correspondence—far from it. It is more to say that, like Bonhoeffer, we also choose whether to enter more fully into the questions of our time and step into them courageously with hope or to ignore them and try to evade our responsibilities, shrinking back in fear, disconnection, or despair. Above all, I wrote this book as a sign that I have chosen hope and invite you to do so too.

• • •

Having signed for a key from Martin, I slid it onto my keychain. It jangled among all the other keys, the ones for our house and car, my bike lock, our mailbox, and others, each representing different aspects of my life, the places and people I care for, my relationships and responsibilities. Similarly, the collected insights I learned about Bonhoeffer's life through the Haus are keys. None of them are *my* discoveries; none unlock some secret biographical passageway into the mysteries of his life. Many of them correspond to my questions, elements that we have often forgotten in our civic storytelling.

So, this story moves from place to place, from question to question, from life to life, from key to key. Together, these keys represent the Bonhoeffer-Haus's lessons, a place of civic housekeeping, where memories and stories are maintained and passed along to others, and thus the final chapter explores what is necessary to maintain our civic house too.

Just as Martin issued me a key that opened the Haus to me, I offer these keys to you, to explore Bonhoeffer's life and peer into rooms that hold truths that are small but also so personally demanding that we sometimes try to avoid them. When we emphasize the grand, dramatic, and public parts of Bonhoeffer's story, it is easy to miss these humbler aspects, all that enabled him to step as he did onto the stage of history.

Spending time in Bonhoeffer's story and his house prompted me especially to revisit my civic housekeeping habits. In his life, I saw ways of being, relating, thinking, imagining, and participating in the life of the world. The Haus came to represent identities, dispositions, and habits that I recognized in myself but needed to hone. These rusty, perhaps forgotten skills are ones we all can recover and relearn. And each of us doing so may make all the difference to how the story of our own houses unfolds.

Memorial to the Murdered Jews of Europe, also known as the Holocaust Memorial, Berlin

Chapter 2

LEARNING
THE STORY

→ *Key: There's a bigger story than my own.* ←

The email said I should join Gottfried on a tour in late July 2017 to observe him. I carefully noted it in my calendar. My training program as a volunteer guide was underway, and when I had time, I sequestered myself away with books to rehearse details of Bonhoeffer's life, talking out loud in my house to no one to practice the facts.

I attended my first volunteers' meeting on an evening in May 2017. We volunteers gathered around a table in the Wintergarten, the glass-enclosed porch off the conference room. Martin briefly introduced me to the other volunteers in attendance, and I shook hands around the table. We conversed effortlessly in English, and they asked me questions about where our family had lived in the world with the foreign service and about my studies of Bonhoeffer. I likely surprised a few of them when I admitted that I was working hard at learning more about his life.

But as the actual meeting got underway, my heart sank as I realized how linguistically hindered I was. Despite tossing out a few expressions of polite greeting, I could not do any meaningful business in German. One of the volunteers glanced at me as the meeting got underway and asked, in German, whether I understood. Knowing enough to understand what he said, I answered in English to underscore just how hamstrung I was, that I could only pick out a few words here and there in the discussion. Graciously, Martin stopped the meeting and proposed that they proceed in English, which some at the table agreed to. But then one volunteer pleaded for the meeting to be held in German, saying his English was not strong enough.

Inwardly, I cringed as this conversation took place, chagrined at how much my presence disrupted their normal proceedings. I apologized, thanked them, and begged them to continue as they normally would in German. I assured them, and myself, that I could get a summary of the agenda at the end of the meeting. And then I sat, silently, for the next two hours, straining to cobble together fragments of meaning from words I gleaned here and there. Surprisingly, the volunteer who had requested the meeting continue in German periodically whispered English translations to me, a gesture that made me nearly giggle. He spoke far more English than he gave himself credit for, and his gentle hospitality touched me immensely. I already felt like an interloper to the group, and his willingness to interpret for me was the olive branch I needed.

As the evening's light dimmed, the attendees' body language—a few final fountain-pen scribbles into planners and the subsequent packing up—signaled that the meeting was over. Several volunteers then stood and said goodnight and goodbye. As everyone began to leave, I pulled Martin aside. I still had some business to discuss, which I assumed was going to come up in the meeting.

"So, my training. In terms of my being prepared for giving a tour, how does this work? Is there a script I should follow?"

Energetically, with that uniquely German conversational directness, Martin said, "No! There is no script! Although," he added, his eyes turning away in thought, "I do have something that might help you. I think we have one last copy in English."

He disappeared to another room and returned with a bright orange paperback in hand: an English-language catalogue to the exhibition, the collection of the nine panels in the conference room, with hand-lettered printing on the front: *Dietrich Bonhoeffer, Pfarrer* (Pastor), *Berlin-Charlottenburg 9, Marienburger Allee 43.* I thanked him, tucked the book into my purse, and stepped out into the night air.

Driving home, my doubts about having stepped into this little world crept out. *This isn't my world. I don't speak German! What have I done? I don't belong there. How will I ever learn to tell this story?*

Walking into our house, I found my husband reading on the sofa. He looked up, smiling, and said, "So, how was it?"

"Well," I said, slinging my purse down and flopping onto the couch. "I am *not* German, and I do *not* speak German, and I do *not* know if this was the best idea. I think I may be in over my head."

He looked at me knowingly. "You do manage to connect to places in unusual ways, Laura. I'm sure it will be fine."

I retrieved the exhibition catalogue from my purse and began paging through it. Looking at the hand-lettered cover and title page, I read an explanation just below it:

The front-cover shows one of three entries Dietrich Bonhoeffer hastily scribbled with a thick pencil into his copy of Plutarch on April 9, 1945, immediately before he was deported from Schönberg Jail to Flossenbuerg Concentration Camp, where he was murdered the next morning. He left the book on the table—the address at Marienburger Allee was the clue, that was to be found in the later chaos. One of his fellow-prisoners, a son of Friedrich Goerdeler, took the book and handed it to the family later on—the last sign of life of Dietrich Bonhoeffer.

So, the handwriting was Bonhoeffer's, under immense stress. I pulled a pen from my purse as well, and wrote my name and the date on the title page, my own handwritten sign of life to the story in those pages, a small gesture that I would step toward learning, despite my own cultural bewilderment, rather than shrink away in discouragement.

Over the next few weeks, I pored over that catalogue, seeking to make what was in it my own. I knew I had a lot of work to do before I gave a tour to anyone. But every time I opened the catalogue's pages, I felt as if I were peering into a drawer of odds and ends in someone else's house. Everyone has those drawers, full of sauce packets and toothpicks and bottle openers and weird tools. The contents make sense to us, but to anyone else, they are just jumbled miscellany. The catalogue contained explanations to each of the exhibition panels, captions for every photograph, and brief statements of background to some of these elements. Accompanying them were excerpts of primary sources related to each of the panels' themes, snippets of text and letters, and meditations written by members of the Bonhoeffer family, including Eberhard and Renate Bethge, and those close to them. Each section also contained excerpts from some of Dietrich's published works.

Despite its clear organization, I couldn't see the bigger story well and struggled to make sense of it as a whole. I began skipping around the catalogue, like a bored child in a museum quickly and mindlessly glimpsing many paintings on a wall but failing to understand the larger story to which they belonged, the curated meaning from the disparate parts. The problem wasn't the catalogue; it is, in fact, very thoughtfully arranged, spare and serious, saying what it can say and no more. The problem was me. My failure to make sense of it, early on, had more to do with what I thought I knew—and obviously didn't know—about Bonhoeffer as well as about German history and culture, including the Nazi era but well beyond it too. The story I thought I knew now collided with a more intricate and lived reality.

• • •

I began to learn about Bonhoeffer long before we moved to Berlin, but the information was more gleaned than studied. I suspect I saw Bonhoeffer's name mentioned in *Christianity Today*, a magazine to which my parents subscribed when I was a child and which I began to read more earnestly when I was in high school. I doubt I ever heard him quoted in our church's pulpit or at youth group. But I knew of some of his more popular devotional writings about Christian life, such as *The Cost of Discipleship* (1937), which Bonhoeffer published after the Gestapo closed an illegal seminary he headed, or *Life Together* (1938), his meditation on Christian community. Because what I knew of the man himself I had learned from others, their perceptions and opinions shaped that knowledge. At times I heard his name uttered with some suspicion, a wariness about some of his theological beliefs despite his opposition to Hitler and the Nazis. Some of what he wrote made certain folks squirm—phrases such as "religionless Christianity," which sounded *continental* and made him a more complicated figure, someone not easily pegged. My actual knowledge of his life and thought was spotty, derived from hearsay.

Bonhoeffer's name came up more during my undergraduate days at Wheaton College in Illinois, where professors referred to him with respect and intellectual regard. My studies in political science, in which I focused heavily on political theory and theology, gave me exposure to ideas that coincided with Bonhoeffer's life and thought. I learned more about how his Christian commitments shaped his political resistance work in Nazi Germany, a coherence I had never grasped from those devotional writings.

But my earliest teacher in Bonhoeffer's thought was a friend, a fact that, knowing how friends so deeply influenced Bonhoeffer, now seems quite fitting. Jonathan, a classmate of mine, began to study Bonhoeffer for himself, and his growing facility with the man's life, thought, and historical context began to trouble him in personal ways. As fellow majors focusing on political theory, we were both prone to rather immersive thought. We relished the realm of ideas and took long hikes of conversation up what seemed like mountains of truth, savoring the heady clarity of what, for us, was pretty high-altitude thinking. Jonathan was deep in Bonhoeffer, while my mind was in Thomas Hobbes's *Leviathan*, an early modern political treatise on social contract theory in which the English philosopher argues that life is so "nasty, brutish, and short" that to survive it, human beings should surrender all to a strong figurehead. I was trying to figure out why Hobbes quoted so much of the Bible in establishing what I had largely understood as a secular foundation of the social contract.

As Jonathan trekked deeper into Bonhoeffer's thought, he found his own world coming under intense interrogation. Raised in a pious and politically active home in the 1980s and 1990s, Jonathan once identified closely with the Moral Majority, the Republican Party, and certain key organizations and figures on the so-called religious right, such as the Christian Coalition. But now, peering into Bonhoeffer's world, he found the tables of his life being overturned. At times, when we shared what we were learning in our respective studies, he spoke like a man whose world had been set on fire, and he wasn't sure whether or how to put it out. He recognized troubling parallels between the complicit church of Bonhoeffer's time and that of his childhood, a church subservient to politicians and political parties, skilled at offering religious fig leaves to cover naked cravings for power. Jonathan heard in Bonhoeffer's writings indictments that shook the earth under the foundations on which he was raised. The tremors were upending his story.

• • •

My memories of Jonathan's intense interrogation of his own life returned to me often as I studied the exhibition catalogue. I was also reading a Bonhoeffer biography at the time and starting to piece elements of the Bonhoeffer-Haus panels onto a mental board of my own. Each time I sat to study, I immersed myself in the documents associated with each panel of photographs, drawing my gaze back to see how the events of history intersected with Bonhoeffer's life. But a document affiliated with Panel 5—the central panel featuring a desecrated, vandalized synagogue—refused to make sense to me. Clearly the exhibition's organizers thought this primary document important enough to print it in the catalogue, but I could not figure how it related to the theme of Panel 5, which was "The Church and the Jewish Question."

This theme was also the title of a critical essay that Bonhoeffer wrote in April 1933, just weeks after Hitler came to power and not long after the government announced a boycott of Jewish businesses. In it, Bonhoeffer detailed three ways the church could interact with the state. He saw early how the norm-breaking Nazis could exploit the traditional relationship of church and state and argued that the church had responsibilities to the secular state as well as to its victims, which was a significant departure from traditional teaching. First, he argued, the church could "ask the state" whether it is fulfilling its God-given responsibilities of just governance. Second, the church could care for the victims of the state, bandaging their wounds. And third, he argued, the church must not only care for those caught under the state's "wheel" but be willing to fall into the spokes of the wheel, or to drive "a spoke" into the wheel itself. The church might be called upon to be the jamming agent to prevent the wheel of the state from crushing those under its purview.[1]

The arguments from that essay were already somewhat familiar, but this other primary document before me was completely alien. It was a memo with the title "II D3a (9) Nr. 214/42 g. Rs." The date, June 5, 1942; the place, Berlin; the classification, "Top Secret." I scanned the memo and then tried reading it, but it was written in a way that seemed to inhibit rather than assist my comprehension. It began "I. Memo, Regarding: Technical Modifications to be Added to the Operational and Presently Being Prepared Special Vehicles," and it didn't seem to have anything to do with Dietrich Bonhoeffer, the Nazis, or the church. None of these were named in it. It was full of technical jargon. The language felt coded, and it was laced with the passive voice.

I read it over and over, blankly at first, my eyes skimming the surfaces of the words. Then, as when a page in a Magic Eye book suddenly discloses its obscured picture after one has stared cross-eyed at it long enough, the memo's meaning coalesced with nauseating clarity. It concerned vehicles—vans or trucks, I think—that the Nazis designed to kill people—Jewish people, mostly. These mobile units killed through asphyxiation. Nazis loaded Jewish people into them, filled the vehicles with carbon monoxide, and then emptied the dead from the killing machines.

Whoever wrote the memo, however, used language to tap-dance delicately, almost soothingly, around the subject at hand to obscure the heavy murderous footfall of its horrific realities. The vocabulary and syntax worked together to veil facts in ways that allowed the reader to escape moral reckoning. At their best, words and language aid communication and bridge gaps; in service of the truth, words reflect reality and assist meaning. But in this memo, the words and sentences play tricks. These quicksand sentences swallowed more than they said; these ear-ticklers softened the blow that plain and direct speech would easily level on the human conscience. The memo's writer did not use common human terms to describe what these vehicles were intended for or what happened in them. The words made the killing sound mechanized, clean, industrial, reporting that in the span of six months, "97,000 were processed with three vehicles operating." *Processed*, like an insurance claim.

But, of course, large-scale murder of human beings is in no way like processing an insurance claim. It is never clean. The memo addresses certain "problems"—technical problems—that emerged in these "processing" operations. When carbon monoxide is pumped into a sealed van packed with people, these panicked human beings try to escape. Their frantic attempts to get out of the van resulted in, as the memo describes it, "a disadvantageous shift of gravity [in which] the load carried in the operation [tries] to reach the rear door" (44). The memo suggested installing a functioning light bulb in the vehicle so "the cargo" or "the load" wouldn't clamor toward the light beyond the vehicle's locked door. The memo writer made this suggestion as a soothing precaution to keep the panic down. Moreover, because people are bodies—flesh and bone, blood and water—these vehicles held the gruesome marks of the violent crimes perpetrated upon human flesh. Thus, someone had to clean the vans, and the writer offered technical solutions to the burden of this necessary chore, highlighting again the value of a functioning light bulb and some drain modifications, nothing that processing an insurance claim requires.

When my mind finally translated its substance, I saw that the memo was the stuff of the most terrifying nightmares any person could imagine—and also unavoidable historical reality. But it taught me something after I wrestled with it, namely how even language has a morality, or immorality, in whether it discloses or seals off facts and responsible thought, in whether it serves the truth or lies. The memo's avoidant language—its heavy use of the passive voice and of dehumanizing terms such as "load" or "cargo" for people—was a telltale sign of a particular kind of evil, one that the German Jewish political theorist Hannah Arendt aptly described. She called this evil *banal*—a word that can mean boring, unimaginative, tired, trite, doused in tricky language that makes the cruel and barbaric appear routine and neutral.

By reminding the world of evil's banality, Arendt challenged a dominant narrative that the Nazis were blood-thirsty monsters, red hot rather than coolly, mindlessly indifferent. In her reporting on the significant trial for Adolf Eichmann[2]—one of the administrators of the Final Solution, the Nazi plan to slaughter all Jewish people—Arendt saw Eichmann as the pathetic embodiment of the rule-following bureaucrat, incapable of his own thought, desperate for direction from those stronger than him, a person who has surrendered his agency to others. Nazi pabulum and propaganda *were* his thought and speech, and he saw himself as fulfilling his duties but did not believe himself to be morally responsible for his actions.

I tried to imagine the person who wrote the vehicle memo, sitting at a desk to work on a typewriter, drafting and editing the memo, checking the task off a list of things to do for the workday, and then heading home, maybe picking up some ingredients to prepare for dinner that evening. I imagined the memo's recipient, who was expected to carry out the suggested modifications; maybe this person read the memo while sipping coffee, wiping their mouth, laughing with a coworker, and later enjoying a meal with family. And then I imagined the engineers who were assigned these "problems" to figure out these "technical solutions," who consulted with the memo writer. At each step, I shuddered at their collective smallness, their pathetic surrender to the system, their refusal to jam the wheel, their banal cooperation that kept it spinning and crushing.

Few of these people behaved like cackling devils with fire and pitchforks—I suspect none gave off the Hollywood cues that so often accompany the popular Nazi narrative. But it is right to describe their participation as evil, their dull minds and emaciated hearts cold with indifference and moral inertia. Evil of this kind whispers escape from responsibility. The memo writer wasn't *killing* these people. He or she was only writing a memo! The engineers weren't *killing* these people. They were merely solving problems as part of their normal work! Whoever it was that actually shouted and shoved these doomed and terrified human beings into vehicles were simply following orders. They didn't personally *will* these murders. These pathetic creatures were just normal people doing their jobs without any sense of personal responsibility, fed a diet of words that helped them escape reality. They were cargo handlers, load processors. The language of the memo allowed them to slip out of knowing—and out of being responsible for what they knew—into a place where they could avoid any responsible thought.

As a curious artifact of that era, this strange memo issued a clear warning about words and stories. Part of learning to tell Dietrich Bonhoeffer's story to visitors at the house required me to give thought to language itself—not just the story but the way I told it. How I used

41

words, how I crafted sentences, even how I thought mattered to the work of the house. The language I used when talking about Bonhoeffer had to be morally responsible. I had to make sure I was telling the truth and doing so in an active voice. There was a bigger story than my impressions; there was even a bigger story than Bonhoeffer. I had to understand the condition of the time, the prevailing thought, and do so as responsibly as I could.

• • •

"You should read this book. It's really creepy," my husband said to me one night in the fall of 2015, as we lay in bed reading in our northern Virginia home. A year earlier, he had received his assignment for a position at the US embassy in Berlin. Since beginning his studies in the German language and culture, his mind had already been moving there in ways that mine had not yet begun to. I was limping through an online language-tutoring program that the State Department offers spouses and partners. My stated goal in my language studies was to learn how to be polite and not offend others, as if I was a child learning how not to hit another when angry. And indeed, that was not too far from my daily realities, ferrying my older two to their respective elementary schools, and making sure our littlest was fed and napped and read to and played with, and all the other normal household tasks of family life. I tried to schedule my check-ins with my tutor during our son's nap times. And while I had learned to rattle off the German pronunciations of its twenty-seven-letter alphabet—including its double-s, the Eszett (ß), that looks to English speakers like a funny-looking capital B—Berlin felt far off from my American day-to-day life.

But I knew reading would help bring it closer, so when my husband finished with it, I picked up the ominous book from his nightstand, Erik Larson's *In the Garden of Beasts*, and started in. I expected to find the narrative gripping, but I wasn't prepared to find points of personal familiarity with it, especially aspects of diplomatic life. In it, Larson tells the story of William E. Dodd and his family upon his appointment as the US ambassador to Germany during the rise of Hitler. The story includes the family angle: their transition to a new place, Dodd's dreams and career ambitions, their work of setting up a home, and their efforts to try to make sense of their new surroundings. These were things I knew, but they were set in the oddly alien realm of the early Nazi era. Of course, the Dodd family's experience in the old US Foreign Service was very different than ours is today. But I could easily relate to the upheavals they experienced in an international move and what it feels like to press one's face up against the glass of another culture's window, trying to find a way in, trying to make sense of it all. These experiences we knew well.

To tell that story as well as he does, Larson pays as close attention to facts as he does to language, especially the violence Nazis did with and to words. He introduces the Dresden-based philologist Victor Klemperer, who, as a university professor, kept careful daily documentation of what happened to common language under the Nazis, the terms that were coined or corroded, words that gained new, almost inverted meaning, noting how once negative connotations became positive. The word *fanatical*, for instance, usually connoting unhinged enthusiasm, became a laudatory term during the Nazi era to denote intense personal loyalty to Hitler and the regime.

Klemperer was also Jewish, so his astute observations as an expert philologist gained a poignant clarity from his experience of living under Nazi persecution. The diary he kept catalogued rapid social changes such as when he and his fellow academics, civil servants, and professionals started facing ever-tightening limits to their freedoms. Despite being a university professor, he was denied access to libraries, dismissed from his position at the Technical University of Dresden, and forced to work in a munitions factory. He figured his "mixed marriage" to an "Aryan" woman protected him during those years. Having survived, Klemperer's diary served as his source material from which he could draw to show how everyday discourse suffered under Nazi tyranny and how powerfully language shaped life itself. Klemperer saw how words functioned like shields against reality in people's minds, even as they, paradoxically, could not help but reveal kernels of truth.

From his diaries, he distilled his book *Lingua Tertii Imperii*—or *The Language of the Third Reich*. Klemperer admitted that early on in the regime, he much preferred to avoid paying attention to the language of the Third Reich, repressed his instinct for observation, and kept busy with his professional work, which at the time was a study of eighteenth-century French literature. But as the Nazis rolled out new bans and persecutions, he finally felt forced to pay attention, and the diary took on greater importance. Later, thinking back to those days, he recalled a vignette in a storybook from his youth in which a man and his son watch a circus-performer walk across a tightrope. The boy asks his father what the bar in the performer's hands is for, and the father says that it's "holding him steady," and the boy cries out, "What if he lets go of it?" The father replies that the man is holding the bar steady too, the bar and the man working together. Klemperer saw his diary-keeping as his balancing pole on the narrowing tightrope of his life.[3]

In the historical downstream, Klemperer's work proves critical. He depicts a world making less and less sense, a world in which people were letting go of balancing bars everywhere and in which words themselves were suffering, denuded of their meaning, forced into chimerical sentences that had dramatic moral consequences. One of Klemperer's most searing observations from that time is that *language often does our thinking for us.* We take in words and phrases like air, mindlessly, and this ambient language forms our thoughts without ever stimulating our minds to interrogate them. We so often do not stop to ask whether they are true.

The most powerful effect of Nazism upon German life, Klemperer believed, did not come through the grandiose speeches and torchlit rallies, nor from the posters, fliers, or other overt forms of propaganda. Rather, the party spread its ideas in the beguilingly commonplace ways that Nazi terms became everyday terms. Nazi ideas "permeated the flesh and blood of the people through single words, idioms and sentence structures which were imposed on them in a million repetitions and taken on board mechanically and unconsciously," Klemperer wrote.[4] This language burrowed deep into society, forming emotions and thoughts. Klemperer compared these minuscule adjustments in language to the subtle buildup of arsenic in a body. One is hardly aware of its deadly work when it's introduced in small doses, and that is its unique power.

Besides delivering a steady stream of corroded language, the Nazis also deployed certain storytelling techniques that were "copied from American cinema and thrillers."[5] The Nazis mimicked these cinematic techniques in "a deliberate effort to generate a kind of daily suspense," a way to keep people tuned in but also off-kilter, increasingly dependent on the central figure of the Führer to shape reality. Adolf Hitler could be quite charismatic, behaving with a frenzy of his own. He knew how to whip up a crowd and stoke the fires of fear that were critical to his rule. Hitler's frenzied demeanor was odd, Klemperer observed, for it undermined his desire to "convey omnipotence." The truth peeked out in these performances. Klemperer wondered,

"Do you talk with such blind rage" if you claim to be inaugurating an unshakeable thousand-year-long kingdom that guaranteed the final destruction of one's enemies?[6] Of course not. But, Klemperer argued, as debased as the language was, it still contained vestiges of truth: far from being the strong leader he claimed to be, Hitler was a pathologically narcissistic man, insecure and fragile to his core.[7]

• • •

I planned to observe Gottfried from a chair in the corner for my first time at the Bonhoeffer-Haus as a volunteer, in July 2017. When the large tour group arrived, the two of us met them at the door, but rather than inviting them inside, Gottfried asked them to join him in returning to the street so he could point out a few features of the house from the outside. I headed outdoors with the group. Out front on the street, Gottfried pointed to Bonhoeffer's bedroom windows up on the top floor—the third floor as Americans count, or the second floor by European standards. He then pointed to the house next door, No. 42, also built by the Bonhoeffers, where Dietrich's older sister Ursula lived with her husband, Rüdiger Schleicher, and their children.

Once we were inside the house, Gottfried moved through the exhibition's panels, pointing to certain pictures, skipping others. Having been a visitor on several of his tours already, I saw that he did not follow a formula but tried to begin a conversation. With the eyes of a newbie volunteer, I saw how agile he was with Bonhoeffer's story, engaging this group in different ways than he had with others. He wove the narrative with key themes, changing angles and emphases from tour to tour, finding the footing that resonated with those in the room.

Midtour, the doorbell rang. Briefly pausing in his lecture, Gottfried motioned for me to see who it was. I hustled out of the room to the front door. It was not uncommon for people to drop by the house without an appointment in hopes of stepping inside, and on this day a group was gathered at the gate, so I went out to speak with them.

"Please," one of them said, "we have come all the way from Korea. Can we see the house?" They were seminarians and professors traveling on a Reformation-focused tour, like so many in 2017, the five hundredth anniversary of the Protestant Reformation, when Martin Luther so famously published his *Ninety-Five Theses* in Wittenberg. I told them I needed to check with the guide inside about what we should do. "There's another big group here, you see, and I'm a new volunteer. I'm not sure of the rules." (And if there's anything one should know in Germany, it is the rules!) Then I apologized to them, like a new cashier ringing the bell for managerial help. I assured them I'd be right back, leaving them standing awkwardly at the gate.

Back inside, I saw that Gottfried had finished speaking with the large group in the conference room, and they had broken into two smaller groups to take turns going up to Bonhoeffer's bedroom. I pulled him aside to ask him what I should do.

"I'm going to take this next group upstairs, and you're going to give that one a tour," he replied directly and calmly, pointing out the front window to the group standing forlornly outside. Then he headed to the stairs to rejoin his tour.

I gulped inwardly, wondering whether I was actually ready to tell Dietrich Bonhoeffer's story, especially to a group that might be very well versed in his life. Over the past two months, I had studied the catalogue and read several biographies, but immediately the facts started swirling incoherently. I wasn't expecting to have to say anything to anyone that day; my job was to observe. I wasn't sure I had enough words—the simple facts such as names, dates, laws, key phrases—or even the story itself, the connective tissue on the bones of the facts, to fashion a worthy account. But seeing the group waiting outside, and receiving Gottfried's direction, I resolved to make my unexpected start as best I could. I did not feel ready, but I decided to be ready to be responsible for the story, to say what I could truthfully. So I stepped back out and more properly introduced myself.

We spoke together in English, and the group's leader expressed their surprise (and confusion!) that an American was going to give them a tour.

"Well, yes," I said, smiling as confidently as I could. "As I said, I'm new. *Quite* new. This is, in fact, my very first tour, and so let me again welcome you to the Bonhoeffer-Haus."

The leader asked me to pause for a moment. "We'll need to translate today," and then he turned to repeat in Korean what I said to the group in English. Of course, I understood that need, and I was relieved by it. The lag time for translation after each sentence or two would buy me time to think and prepare. Gottfried's agility in Bonhoeffer's story had been formed by years of study and dialogue with visitors. My own private studies now felt flimsy, barely up to snuff for dialogue. I felt the need to tell a story that far outpaced what I had yet learned.

So I did what even the worst students are capable of: raw imitation. I imitated Gottfried, nearly word for word, mimicking even his hand motions, pointing up to Bonhoeffer's bedroom window, then over to the No. 42 house. And after each sentence, one of the leaders offered translation in Korean. When I'd exhausted all I could remember of what Gottfried had said out in front of the house, I asked the group to follow me inside, and we made our way into the conference room to work through the exhibit's panels.

We rounded our way through one half of the room, and thus about half of the panels of photographs, when Gottfried returned and sat down. Our roles were reversed; now he observed me. None of this was part of the plan, I groaned inwardly, and my confidence dimmed as I began to monitor myself. *Am I getting the facts right? Did I pair the correct name with that face in the photo? Ugh, who is that again?!* Some of the names completely escaped me. I tripped over parts of the story as I spoke and tried to smooth over my inadequacies with exuberance. Gottfried listened and watched, then volunteered to take them up to the bedroom when I finished with the last panel in a clumsy attempt to finish the story of his life. After the group left the conference room with Gottfried, I stood alone, exhaling deeply. The group finally departed the Haus, and Gottfried returned to the conference room.

"You have an engaging way of speaking," he said, kindly.

"Well, I'm an American, aren't I?" I replied, all smiles and probably too glibly.

Gottfried did not laugh. "You did a good job," he repeated sincerely, and so I thanked him this time without any guile.

His words meant a lot, but I didn't think I deserved it. I could feel just how little I knew, and I did not want to do another tour feeling so unequipped. All in all, it worked out fine. They were a merciful group, and our shared language barriers afforded me the luxury of staying a few sentences ahead of running out of things to say.

When I got home, I took out a green pen and sat down with the catalogue again, like a student checking the textbook after a big exam. That first unexpected tour in the Bonhoeffer-Haus had primed me to pay a different kind of attention to the catalogue; I carefully looked at the photos where my mind had drawn a blank. I wrote notes by them, labeling locations, names, key dates, all the things I had failed to recall on my feet. The story was so big and complicated and so tied to such big themes and moments in history that were, to be sure, foreign to me.

The only way to master the details of Bonhoeffer's life was to become a student of them, submitting to the story as responsibly as I could. I knew I would still make mistakes, as students do, and I would have to say that I didn't know things. I could not wing it, but I had to start somewhere. My faithfulness in study or my failure to tell the truth mattered to those who came, who were depending on me to do both. What I said there—the language I used, the quality of my private preparations—mattered to those waiting outside at the gate.

• • •

What I learned about Bonhoeffer mattered not just for my role as tour guide but for my life as well. I was driven personally into his narrative and wanted him to matter to me. But as I studied his life, developing more awe for him as a human being, I saw that, at times, I wanted him to do something for me that he could not do. I approached him imaginatively, the way a young child might with an imaginary friend. Imaginary friends are wonderful, but they don't really exist in all the stubborn ways actual people do. They can be unfailingly loyal to those who conjured them. They are never alien or peculiar; no translation is ever necessary. They do not confront, rebuke, annoy, or refuse. An imaginary friend is perfectly instrumental, and completely unreal.

In a true friendship between real people, there is give and take, acceptance and growth, always with the possibility of criticism, disappointment, or rupture, as well as repair. If I wanted to make friendly inroads with Dietrich Bonhoeffer and his story, I had to confront some of my own gaps in knowledge about him. I had to relinquish impressions and practice facts. Even more, I had to acknowledge that my American mind might not be able to effortlessly understand his German one, or German history and culture. Above all, I needed to resist the temptation to make him *mine*, to narrate his life as a mere reflection of my own opinions and tribal belongings.

Eberhard Bethge warned about this temptation, not only as it related to Bonhoeffer but for anyone deemed a hero of Christian faith, as Bonhoeffer so often is. Bethge wrote that there is "great harm caused when Christians are preoccupied with measuring the record of achievements and with worries about the proper Christian identity. The latter might even tempt us to reinterpret our own martyrs."[8] Bonhoeffer had to become a human being in my mind, a more fully fleshed stranger known from the distance of hard, cold facts, situated in a loving family, a living faith, and a culture with real differences from my own, before I could possibly make sense of his life in the light of mine.

My instinct to want Bonhoeffer to mean something to my life wasn't altogether bad, but I still needed to gain clarity on the questions that drew me to him. I also needed to bring my expectations of him into the light of scrutiny. Learning his story required that I also came to see how it was not mine, how he could not answer my questions for me. It is not fair to him to ask "What Would Bonhoeffer Do?" not only because he cannot answer it—he is deceased—but also because, and I cannot stress this point enough, it is not *his* responsibility to do so. We can take counsel from the wisdom of his life, but it is our responsibility to act wisely in our own lives.

Assuredly, Dietrich Bonhoeffer *is* a hero of the Christian faith, but the Bonhoeffer-Haus reminds us quietly that he faced the same kinds of human constraints and limitations that we each face. Mere affiliation with Bonhoeffer as "the good guy" does a grave disservice to his legacy; it doesn't take his witness seriously enough, and it relegates it to a realm that none of us actually inhabit. I am grateful that those who prepared the catalogue materials for the Bonhoeffer-Haus anticipated some of these thorny interpretive temptations around Bonhoeffer's life, writing in an introductory essay:

> We hope that visitors will not place Dietrich Bonhoeffer on a pedestal of holiness. When you visit this house, honor him, but also relate to the claims he and his theology make upon us today. The exhibition seeks to point back to a way of being faithful which also confronts us with an urgent, present question: What does it mean today to live faithfully as Christians?

• • •

Months after my first tour as a guide, I was back at the Haus for another volunteer meeting. At the table was a new volunteer, Phil, who had recently finished an advanced degree studying Bonhoeffer, focusing on theologies of disability. Speaking in British-accented English at first, he easily switched into German, speaking with considerable facility. His ability to speak German drew him immediately into the life of the volunteers more deeply than I had experienced, a dynamic I completely understood. Looking back at me, the group deliberated again about whether to conduct the meeting in English, but again they settled on German. With his characteristically kind smile, Phil turned to me and said he was happy to translate what was happening in the meeting for me, which I still needed and which he was fully equipped to provide.

A few weeks later, he asked me whether he could sit in on one of my tours to observe, and of course, I agreed wholeheartedly. I told him that on my next scheduled tour, I'd be guiding a small group of visitors who were pretty familiar with Dietrich's life, so I didn't expect to lead it as I normally would. Phil's addition to the group ratcheted the expertise level up even higher, and, realizing this, I decided to take on some new risks with this group.

Unlike on other tours, during which I typically stood, circling the room and pointing to photographs on the panels, that morning I sat at the conference table with the visitors.

"I'd like to do this tour a little differently than I usually do today. I often ask for Bonhoeffer scholars or students of his to identify themselves to me," I said, with my dreaded glibness sneaking out, "just so I know where they are and to watch their faces to see if I'm getting some detail wrong. Knowing that the caliber of minds in this room is pretty high, I thought we might have a conversation and learn from each other. I'd like to try out some thoughts on you and welcome you to do the same." They agreed to the plan.

I brought up three points with them, each of which I had learned from my widening reading of Bonhoeffer's life, evidence that my studies of faces and dates were beginning to take shape into a story. Each point pulled the lens back away from the singular facts of Bonhoeffer's life to discern patterns, tendencies, and possibilities. (They proved to be early prototypes of some keys I include in this book.)

First, I spoke about how important family was to and for Bonhoeffer and how his family shaped some of his lifelong habits. His parents taught him to speak with economy, clarity, and courage, and he relied on them for much of his life, even as an adult, when he returned home to the Bonhoeffer-Haus from time to time. "When we talk about a significant public figure in history, we do not often think about and credit those close to that figure in helping them be who they are. How we narrate those lives often reveals more about us than it does about the figure in history. Perhaps we imagine ourselves as singular and independent heroes rather than as interdependent human beings who need relationships and families to be who we are," I suggested.

Next, I posed the possibility that Bonhoeffer had been shaped by much older cultural norms and ideas that gave him a deep well of authority from which to draw when faced with the loud and false claims of the Nazis. A short discussion in one of the earliest biographies about his life had prompted me to wonder about citizenship. I told the group, "The free imperial cities of the Holy Roman Empire—many of which maintained this independent streak even when incorporated as German cities—developed an idea of a citizen that was subject to no one but the king. Was it possible that Dietrich drew on this idea of citizenship, that it shaped his sense of responsibility? And it causes me to wonder what stories we are telling about our citizenship and the authority and responsibilities that come with it."

Finally, we talked about how Bonhoeffer's life was characterized by boundary crossings, all of which allowed him to better see his own world. From his first international trip with his brother Klaus to Rome, after his first year in university, to his expatriate years in Barcelona, New York, and London, Bonhoeffer grew as he encountered new people and places, and yet, he also found his love for his particular German place and his particular people sharpened and clarified by them.

Together, around the conference room in the Bonhoeffer-Haus, we discussed these ideas. In a wonderful role reversal, I asked questions and scribbled a few notes, jotting down suggested readings that these guests raised and some new angles of thought to consider. Phil sat quietly through the whole thing, taking it all in and smiling. This time, drawing on my knowledge of political theory, I felt like a translator, or at least more of a true volunteer guide.

I invited the group to join me, and we climbed the stairs to stand in Bonhoeffer's bedroom and look out of his window. Standing there, I felt more at home in the Bonhoeffer-Haus and in the story of Bonhoeffer's life. I had learned to tell his story, beginning with imitation and months of studying, practicing, making mistakes. At last, I felt I could tell a true story about him—a story that invariably reflected my own search for meaning and purpose but also necessitated that I pay attention to facts and to a much bigger picture than just my own perceptions of them. This was my first key to the Bonhoeffer-Haus.

• • •

The stories all changed when the Nazis were defeated and the war was over. Those who had once cheered at rallies for Hitler began to tell different accounts about what they thought, said, and did during those twelve years of fear and increasing levels of murder. Very few wanted to talk about any of it; there were no words, and many preferred to pretend there was no real story to tell, or that if there was, they had no role in it. These were the new moral hiding places, created through tired old ways to shield the conscience from truth, banal ways of keeping reality from breaking in on one's preferred surreality. Suddenly, their stories all changed—but, rest assured, the truth never did. There is a bigger story than our own.

On the stairs of the Michaelskirche, or St. Michaels, in Schwäbisch Hall;
the *Rathaus* in the background

Chapter 3

SOURCES OF IDENTITY

*→ Key: We are who we are because
we belong to people and places. ←*

I would love to know," the woman said to me, somewhat privately, "if you could say anything about his habits, how he lived his life." This American visitor had come to the Haus with a larger tour group, and she pulled me aside on the doorstep of Bonhoeffer's bedroom as the others milled about the room, taking pictures. She spoke quietly and directly and wanted me to answer *her*, to know more of what made him *him*, the private everydayness of his life, his interior self. His bedroom with his books, clavichord, and cigarette-hole desk blotter is a natural place to wonder such an intimate question.

I didn't have a very satisfying answer for her that day, even standing on that third-floor landing so close to a space that held his life and is still furnished with the objects that were so important to him. Here, on the doorstep of the room in which he slept, read, wrote, smoked, made music, and wrestled with his thoughts, we guests are offered a tantalizing sensation of intimacy that leaves us hungry to know more. We want to peer in more deeply, to glimpse how Bonhoeffer lived with such purpose, clarity, and courage—character qualities that can feel so elusive to us. And from our place in history, we can only stand on the doorstep of his life, hoping that whatever inspiration we feel here lingers with us, even on us, after we have left this place.

My time at the Bonhoeffer-Haus taught me, though, to pull back my mental spotlight that I had trained so singularly on Bonhoeffer's life. In the Haus I learned to tell his story with a wider view across the stage, to see him as someone who belonged to many people and places, a belonging that was significant to his identity.

Seeing him this way helps us see his inheritance—not money or real estate but the ancient stories, habits, and traditions that shaped him and informed the way he lived. Like Bonhoeffer, we too are shaped powerfully by belonging to others, or by the painful experience of not belonging. Asking to whom and where we belong are some of life's most critical questions.

• • •

The rooms of Marienburger Allee 43 give us a natural setting in which to meet three very important people in Dietrich Bonhoeffer's life, who lived at the Bonhoeffer-Haus, like he did. These are his parents, Karl and Paula Bonhoeffer, and his grandmother, Julie Tafel Bonhoeffer, who lived with the family from 1925, when she moved to Berlin, until 1936, when she passed away in the Bonhoeffer-Haus.

Dietrich's childhood was, by and large, a happy, privileged, sheltered, and culturally rich one, and his first community was his family. The sixth of eight children, he came into a small universe already full of people and activity when he was born on February 4, 1906, arriving ten minutes before his twin sister, Sabine. Dietrich entered the world accompanied, not alone.

The family moved from Breslau, Germany, where he was born and where his father was working as a professor of psychiatry, to

Berlin in 1912.[1] They eventually settled into a house on Wangen-heimstrasse in the stately Grunewald neighborhood, No. 14, a home large enough for the family and the staff they employed to keep life running smoothly. That staff included a governess, a nurse for the little ones, two maids, a cook, and a chauffeur from time to time.[2] Then as now, the house is situated in a neighborhood full of highly educated professionals and the relatively well-to-do. Large homes line narrow cobblestone streets, and huge sycamore trees shade the thoughtfully designed boulevards that frame the neighborhood.

In Bonhoeffer's childhood, many prominent intellectuals and political leaders lived in the Grunewald neighborhood, and the children of these families became playmates, classmates, and friends of the Bonhoeffer children. In time, some became spouses, joining the family through marriage. One of their neighbors, the historian Hans Delbrück, hosted regular evening discussions at his house with other leading figures in Berlin.[3] It was a lively and comfortable world of intellectual, cultural, and political engagement.

Karl and Paula fit right in. As chief of psychiatry at the Charité hospital, Dr. Bonhoeffer occupied a position of significant public influence, not just in Berlin but in all of Germany. He enjoyed a reputation as a careful, modest, prudent man of science and professional integrity. In his work and life, his frame of reference was strictly empirical; he did not dabble in the field of psychoanalysis. His expertise in psychiatry was psychosis, having researched "degenerative psychosis" following his postdoctoral studies among "mentally disturbed prisoners."[4] Later on, his professional position and reputation drew him into the spotlight when he was asked to evaluate the mental state of the young Dutch communist Marinus van der Lubbe, whom the Nazis accused of setting fire to the Reichstag, the building housing Germany's parliament, in February 1933. Hitler exploited this infamous event to consolidate his power and curtail the rights of citizens under the pretext of a national emergency. Based on Dr. Bonhoeffer's opinion that the prisoner was mentally fit to stand trial, the trial proceeded, and van der Lubbe was executed.

As a father, Karl was relatively engaged given the demands on his time and norms of his era. He attended family meals and periodically read to and played with his children. Though he'd likely not be described as warm by modern standards, he was sensitive and empathetic and taught his children to respect others. But he maintained a firm sense of control over his own emotions, which sometimes made him seem distant or aloof. He often spoke quietly. He was an authoritative but not domineering parent, and he had high expectations for his children's discipline and upbringing.[5]

As adults, his children remembered their father for his particular care for words and responsible speech, expecting simplicity, precision, and brevity. Noting that his expectations for disciplined speech often intimidated but likely protected them later on, Sabine said:

> His rejections of the hollow phrase may have made us at times tongue-tied and uneasy, but as a result we could not abide any clichés, gossip, platitudes or pomposity when we grew up. . . . Sometimes our papa delighted in making us define concepts, or things, and if we managed to do so clearly without being vague, he was happy.[6]

Dietrich was also shaped by his father's disciplined approach to thought and self-expression as well. One of his students, Winfried Maechler, asked him who had especially influenced him, and he replied, "Above all, my father." Dietrich prized his father's "scientific achievement, judgments free of prejudice, and personal modesty which rejected empty phrases and superlatives."[7]

Although he cared deeply for words and thought, Dr. Bonhoeffer did not share his wife's faith in God. He was a man of science, agnostic about faith, though while he did not personally engage in religion, he respected the faith of others, including his wife's. When Dietrich, at the relatively young age of thirteen, announced to his family that he planned to study theology at university—unlike his older brothers, who trained in the worldlier fields of science and law—his decision marked a departure from his father's world and a turning toward his mother's.

Religion was a significant part of Paula von Hase Bonhoeffer's world. Before becoming the wife of a prominent psychiatrist and mother of their eight children, she already had a fascinating life and lineage. (The inclusion of "von" in a German name can signify ties to aristocracy, but not always.) Her grandfather, Karl August von Hase, was a professor of theology at the University of Jena; her father, Karl Alfred von Hase, was a pastor with experience in the thorny political realm. Karl Alfred von Hase served as a chaplain in the court of Emperor Wilhelm II, which was headquartered in Potsdam, just to the southwest of Berlin, but he was dismissed after a short two-year tenure, likely for criticizing the emperor.[8] He eventually took a position in theology at the university in Breslau. Clara, Paula's mother, was born the Countess Kalckreuth, and the family's home served as a meeting place for local intellectuals and artists. It was there that Paula met the young doctor Karl Bonhoeffer, who was instantly taken with her. For all their differences in temperament and orientations to the world, they were utterly devoted to one another and, in their fifty years of marriage, spent very little time apart from one another.[9]

Their differences were considerable but also remarkably matched in strength. Whereas Karl was the quiet and careful authority figure, Paula Bonhoeffer was the vibrant, energetic engine of the family, wielding her own form of authority. Prior to marriage, she earned a teaching certificate at a time when it was rare for women to do so. Paula held strong opinions about the proper education of children and was critical of German civic formation. She believed German society broke the backs of its citizens twice: first in school, and then again in the military. Ensuring the strong development of her children's spines to withstand the unknown pressures ahead, Paula made the family's home a school for the eight children when they were young. She expected them to behave with discipline and decorum, but they were also given much latitude to roam, discover, and experiment. In their Breslau house, there was a veritable menagerie of animals that the children had collected when playing outside, including "snakes, lizards, squirrels and pigeons."[10] Mrs. Bonhoeffer also instructed them in religion and read to them from an illustrated Bible.

For all the organization and discipline in the house, the home was a bustling, vibrant place, reflecting Paula Bonhoeffer's engaged, extroverted, and imaginative personality. She hosted elaborate parties, with games, boisterous singing, puppet shows, and poetry recitations. Emmi Delbrück, daughter of the neighbor and famous historian, who eventually married Klaus Bonhoeffer, one of Dietrich's older brothers, recalled "Mother Bonhoeffer" singing Beethoven, and Delbrück also recalled that the parties at the Wangenheimstrasse house were "countless; no one was ever bored. Only a snob would be, and that was about the only type of person you wouldn't meet there."[11] Strong backs and strong voices were cultivated in the Wangenheimstrasse house, literally, for all the emotive singing and musical expression. Being there gave Emmi Delbrück "an opportunity to express [her] feeling in a big chorus without being noticed."[12] Paula "was not easy to put off" and had a way of inspiring people to get on with living, believing that "mistakes were more forgivable than boredom."[13] Dietrich was so clearly her son; he resembled her physically more than his father, and he took after her in so many other ways: in his orientation to people, his skill in fostering community and belonging, in music-making and singing, and in his sheer indefatigable activity.

But one day, Paula fell silent, shattered with grief, when the family received word in 1918 that Walter, their second born, had been killed just weeks after shipping to the front in World War I. Despite his and his brothers' youthful—and naïve—nationalistic enthusiasm for the Great War, Dietrich witnessed what war does to a home and a family when his two oldest brothers were conscripted and when the younger of the two did not return. Walter managed to write a letter between his battlefield wounding and his death, which the family received. Paula closed herself away in the house, then left completely, spending weeks in bed at a neighbor's home. Her immense grief made it feel as if the home fire had been snuffed out. It took years before the family believed she was herself again. The military had broken more than just a back, and by the end of Paula's life, in another world-swallowing war, she would lose four more in her family—two sons (Dietrich and his older brother Klaus, Emmi's husband) and two sons-in-law (Rüdiger Schleicher, Ursula's husband, and Hans von Dohnanyi, who married Dietrich's other older sister, Christine, who was called Christel). All of them were part of Germany's Widerstand (resistance).

In their temperaments and perspectives, Dietrich Bonhoeffer's parents represented life's diversity, and together they formed a small community of strong children with equally strong views, disciplined practices, and life skills. From his father's judicious care in thought, word, and deed, and his expectation for precision and brevity, to his mother's courage and conviviality, cultivating a home rich in music and communal bonding, Bonhoeffer experienced family as a community of difference in the midst of belonging. He also witnessed in his parents' marriage the possibility that people who hold robustly different views about religion, and even orientations to the world, can love and respect one another and can stay together and enjoy each other for a lifetime. From them, he learned that his life of manifest privilege was not solely for his own private benefit. They taught him, too, that his life belonged to others and the world.

• • •

In addition to the Bonhoeffer-Haus, I wanted to see more places to which Dietrich Bonhoeffer belonged. For our daughters' fall break from school in 2018, we planned a family trip to the Black Forest region in Germany's southwest, which, in many ways, couldn't be further from Berlin. As a family, no matter where we live with the foreign service, we usually explore places as fully and as deeply as we can. Germany was no exception, but I often steered suggestions for side trips to Bonhoeffer-related spots as we planned our trips.

After a lovely stay in the Black Forest, and with a long drive ahead back across the country to Berlin, we decided to break it up with two of these Bonhoeffer-related stops. The first was Tübingen, the university town where Bonhoeffer spent the first of his university years (1923–1924) and where his father and his brother Karl-Friedrich had also studied. The second was Schwäbisch Hall, a town to which Bonhoeffer traced his ancestry on his father's side. I wanted to step foot, even for a short time, into both cities to get a better view of Bonhoeffer, to picture him in some of his places.

Although we had left the Black Forest, we were still in the half-timbered realm of Swabia, comprising the German state of Baden-Württemberg, in which both Tübingen and Schwäbisch Hall are located, separated by a two-hour car drive. These higgledy-piggledy cities feel rich in history with their narrow alleys of well-maintained houses, conforming well to the Disney-like formula of what many think of as historic Germany.

In Tübingen, we found a place to park the car—not often an easy feat in historic quarters—and then walked into the old section of the city. Flower boxes lined many windows, heavy with red trailing geraniums. The cobblestoned streets featured deep gutters that necessitated small bridges to cross from the street to a house or a building. Some of the half-timbered structures had very small doors—"Perfect for a hobbit, right?" I whispered to my kids. My husband would have had to fold in half to walk inside one.

Needing a bite to eat, we found the single-letter-named X, also known as Das X, a popular little hamburger restaurant on Kornhausstrasse listed in our guidebook. It was packed with lunchtime patrons when we arrived, and the few standing-room tables were all occupied. While my husband went to place our order, I stalked tables; when one finally opened up, the kids scampered up on the bench along the wall while I held the space standing on the other side. A few minutes later, David returned with two small plates of pommes frites (French fries), one piled with mayonnaise and the other with ketchup, and our respective burger orders. Just before tucking into her cheeseburger, our middle child asked me cheerfully, "So, did Dietrich Bonhoeffer eat burgers here?"

It was a fair question. As popular as X's burgers are among students and tourists now, the little eatery did not exist when Bonhoeffer spent his first year at university in Tübingen studying theology. In 1923, his letters home to his parents did mention food, but they showed more concern for the price of it than anything. Germany was in the grip of post–World War I hyperinflation, and Bonhoeffer reported home that each meal cost him one billion marks. His parents were enduring the same economic conditions in Berlin: Dr. Bonhoeffer had cashed out a mature life-insurance policy of one hundred thousand marks and hoped he could purchase some wine and strawberries with it. By the time he got to the store, the money had lost even more of its value, and all he could buy were the strawberries.[14] But my daughter's sweet curiosity was not ill placed, for as much as I was taking in Tübingen, I was also imagining Bonhoeffer here.

Revived, we bused our table and headed out toward the Rathaus, the main city hall, as common a feature in German cities as the souk and mosque are in Middle Eastern ones. These are the places of common life, where people market and worship, where good food is found, where decisions large and small are made, where problems are solved, where disagreements erupt, and where they can also find possible resolution. In the lovely plaza in front of the Rathaus, our son chased tourist-weary pigeons, sending them into flight; they landed high and wisely out of reach on a fountain's statue.

A signpost for a walking tour about National Socialism in Tübingen stands just off the plaza, a stark reminder that so many of these quaint and storybook-looking places were once nightmarishly dark. These places that cultivate forms of civic life have also been places of compromise and complicity. After strolling from the Rathaus through the botanical garden in the old city, we happened upon another of these National Socialism tour signs, this one in front of the university's Neue Aula (the new auditorium). Here we read horrifying stories about university-affiliated culprits, all leading men of learning. Here, in this very place, Nazi academics culled human victims for medical experimentation from among both the living and the dead, dissecting many of the latter in a medical lecture hall on campus.

Stepping into the grand building, we discovered two large marble memorials affixed to the wall, one listing the names of prominent Tübingen students who died as part of the Widerstand, the resistance movement against National Socialism. Among them, we spotted those names so familiar on historic plaques: Dietrich Bonhoeffer, his brother Klaus Bonhoeffer, and their brother-in-law Rüdiger Schleicher. Another memorial plaque features two lines from Bonhoeffer's famous poem "Stations on the Road to Freedom":

Freedom, how long we have sought you through discipline, action, and suffering.

Dying, now we behold your face in the countenance of God.[15]

Tübingen claimed him too; for a time, Bonhoeffer belonged here as well.

Our four-year-old son was outside, playing, laughing, and running along the broad rims of the fountains as our twelve-year-old daughter watched over him. He begged us to come back out and watch him too. The two of them created a little show for us in which he ran one way around one of the fountains and she ran the other, both of them making circles of laughter. He took a flamboyant bow at the end, a toothy grin spreading across his face. Watching him, clapping as he bowed, I couldn't shake my moral disorientation—my children laughing and playing in this distinguished place of learning, with all its charming lanes and flower-boxed houses alongside small signs that reminded us tourists that human medical experimentation happened not far from all this charm, here in this particular building, by these named people. This adorable city once thoroughly embraced hatred, dehumanizing terror, and violence.

Dietrich Bonhoeffer's grandmother, Julie Tafel Bonhoeffer, lived in Tübingen when he was a student there, and she moved from there to Berlin in 1925 to live closer to her son and his family. She was another significant figure in Dietrich's life and the Bonhoeffer-Haus, and I thought about her too as we stretched our legs and clapped for our kids in Tübingen. During Dietrich's two semesters as a student, the conditions for National Socialism's flowering were already crystalizing. In the days of postwar hyperinflation, when the mark had so little value, Germans felt demoralized, shouldering indignities that gave way to resentment. Those resentments took root, metastasized, and prowled for a scapegoat, someone upon whom to fix blame and unload the hard burdens of responsible living in difficult times. It's a pattern as predictable as it is horrific in history: the resentful nurse their wounds, identify enemies to blame them on, and then shun and lead their scapegoat to slaughter. It was nauseating—but not hard—to imagine those medical lecture halls as a kind of pagan temple to the false and deceptive gods of national pride.

During the two-hour drive from Tübingen to Schwäbisch Hall, we assured the kids we'd take another break from driving for Kaffee und Kuchen (coffee and cake), a beloved German midafternoon tradition. At last Schwäbisch Hall came into view. Knowing how significant the Bonhoeffer name was to this city, I was keen to find evidence of it. Parking just outside the city's old wall, we walked along it and came up behind Michaelskirche, St. Michael's, the grand central church with a luxurious staircase that extends from its front edifice like a bridal train, an opulent skirt of stairs. Facing it from the lower end of the plaza sits the city's Rathaus. As if by instinct, the kids began running up and down the stairs, adopting the place as their own by playing in it. We took in the church and its commanding setting, the view from the top of the grand stairs down across the plaza and on beyond to the city's tiled rooftops, and then made our way inside.

As we entered the sanctuary, we were enveloped immediately in a rising swell of a cappella singing, a warm polyphony in the air. Just as quickly, the voices unraveled and collapsed, the director of the choir tapping his baton and shaking his head. A guide welcomed us, whispering that we would have to remain here at the back of the church, since the choral group was preparing for a concert that evening. The nave was aglow with warm light, full of artwork and statuary. Up the aisle near the front of the church, the choir stood in listening silence as the director issued a few words of guidance, and then, raising his arms to draw the choir's attention even deeper and back into song, he brought the music back to life. Harmonies reverberated again off the stone floor and pillars.

As I bent down to urge our youngest to be quieter, I spotted Bonhoeffer's familiar face out of the corner of my eye. It was printed on a simple single-page folded bulletin among other pamphlets and notices on the back of the last pew. I grabbed an English-language version and read: "There are quite a number of statues of members of the family of Dietrich Bonhoeffer in our church of St. Michael. The first ancestor recorded here was Kasper von Bonhoven [sic], a poor goldsmith's assistant who came from Nimwegen and who later became a citizen of Schwäbisch Hall." If this was Caspar von

Bonhoeffer's city—as his name is usually spelled in English-language material—this was also his church, and my heart swelled to see the word "citizen" printed on this small pamphlet.

Months earlier, a short discussion in one of the earliest Bonhoeffer biographies grabbed my attention. The author, Mary Bosanquet, spent a noticeable amount of time describing the free imperial cities of Germany, including Schwäbisch Hall, as part of her own attempt to situate Bonhoeffer in context. She saw these cities as important to understanding him. As someone who studied political theory in college—the political ideas and texts that inform how we think about and practice common life, the assumptions, concepts, and metaphors that shape our moral and political imaginations—I was intrigued by Bosanquet's attention to these free cities, and it sent me hunting. Our Kaffee und Kuchen pit stop in Schwäbisch Hall was one piece in the puzzle of Bonhoeffer's places of belonging.

The Bonhoeffers dated their connection to Schwäbisch Hall to 1513, when a certain Caspar von Bonhoeffer moved there from the Netherlands, and members of the family served in the city's public affairs for almost three centuries. These free cities of the Holy Roman Empire (800–1806) formed the "cradle" of the later German empire (1871–1918) and were a "remarkably stable institution" with a rich history that paralleled that of the German empire. These cities were mostly concerned with themselves, developing their growing trades in resources, and were "unconcerned with the political life of Europe."[16] That meant they avoided the costly conflagrations of the royalty. Those brutal political power struggles, which characterize the bulk of European history, squandered lives and money, often solely for a sovereign's ego and territory. The subjects of a sovereign lived under his whim and will with little recourse to defend against them.

• • •

Before our move to Berlin, we read as much as we could about Germany, especially what was available at our local public library. One book I read in that preparation period was Steven Ozment's *A Mighty Fortress*, a history of the German peoples. Since the dark Nazi era and World War II so eclipse most of what we think of as German history, Ozment's book tries to depict the German experience in history before those catastrophic years. It was an odd reading journey to take, post-Holocaust, to try to hear the stories and refrains that contributed to German identity and culture, an altogether recent idea. Tribes, territory, and war compose the history of the Germanic peoples, as do violent interactions with the so-called civilized peoples of the Roman empire.

One line in Ozment's book stood out to me: "Historical experience has . . . left Germans more fearful of anarchy than of tyranny, inclining them to hedge, if hedge they must, on the side of good order. This they have done in a compelling belief that it is not freedom, once attained, but discipline, carefully maintained, that keeps a people free."[17] Of course, it's easy to see how this old cultural pattern emerged in the years during and immediately after World War I, when the chaos of hyperinflation and brawling street fights between nationalists and communists deepened a popular ache for a strong authority, a bold leader who promised restoration of law and order. That cultural instinct proved yet another means for Hitler to exert his chaotic tyranny and call it order. But the gamble for Nazi promises of good order failed to deliver any true freedoms.

Another political tradition, besides a strong central authority, developed in German history as well. In the medieval period, there were the troublesome principalities—areas governed by princes, whose capricious lusts for power and wealth jeopardized the daily lives of their subjects. But in the late medieval period, when the area was part of the Holy Roman Empire, free imperial cities began to grow, and people belonging to these cities were called citizens, not subjects. Bosanquet writes:

> While the fortunes of the princes and their subjects ebbed and flowed, life within the free cities took its even course, leaving the citizens at liberty to develop those traditions of culture and of civic responsibility which were to have so profound an effect on the character of succeeding generations. It was in the rich soil of these long-established cities that the solid burgher families who have made so large a contribution to the most valuable and enduring elements in Germany's culture, slowly grew to maturity.[18]

The only figure to whom these cities were subject was the Holy Roman Emperor. In the feudal dealings of the medieval period, when the royal, noble, and ecclesiastical classes dictated so much of people's lives, these cities carved out a political counternarrative. I needed to understand what these cities were for myself, to see how they connected to Bonhoeffer's civic inheritance and how his imagined belonging to the city of Schwäbisch Hall mattered to his life. I needed a key to the free imperial cities, and, absent time travel, I turned to books.

I visited Fritz Rörig's *The Medieval Town*,[19] an old classic study (and not a particularly easy read!) of a new kind of power—the city, the town—that developed in the mid- to late medieval period. From Italian city-states that supplied and benefited off the Crusades to northern European towns that established powerful trading networks all across the Baltic region, trade was the ground from which this "new power" grew. Towns were distinct from, organized differently than, and, most significantly, threatened the prevailing feudal ideas and structures of Europe: "The ideal of personal bondage" as practiced in the feudal system "disappeared within the walls of the towns; the innumerable relationships of dependence in the countryside—in short, the feudal ordering of society—were broken and subdued."[20] An identity of citizenship developed—a person's sense of belonging to a place, having agency and membership within it—and economic power based on trade secured that identity. Not all medieval towns became free imperial cities; only three hundred or so could claim that official title, and, as mentioned, those that did were subject only to the emperor himself, not to middling princes or lords. As one of these especially powerful cities, rich from trade and thus endowed with real political power, Schwäbisch Hall grew because of its trade in "white gold": salt.

Those people living outside a city's walls, in what we might call the suburbs today, could belong to the city even if they did not reside in it, and they did so by owning property. These were "citizens of the pale," people who belonged to the life of the town or city even though they lived beyond its walls and under the jurisdiction of a prince or lord. (Interestingly, those found "beyond the pale"—a common idiomatic expression in English meaning crossing a line of acceptable behavior—were those who dwelled beyond the town's legal boundaries and who neither belonged to it nor enjoyed its freedoms and protections.[21]) By owning property, the subject of a prince could claim citizenship in the city and thus establish a measure of protection against the prince's exploitation. One common medieval legal maxim was that "town air brings freedom," a free city being a place where subjects could become citizens.[22]

The Bonhoeffer ancestral line was full of men (and a handful of recognized women) who worked in public service to the free imperial city of Schwäbisch Hall and were shaped by its culture, especially its value on learning, which, alongside trade, was a common feature of these cities. Merchant families prized so-called "secular learning" because trade necessitated worldly knowledge and diplomatic skill; traveling merchants needed to have a facility with languages, customs, and geography as well as some real know-how with accounting books. They had to keep extensive records and be able to develop and maintain relationships with people in places very different from their own. So, in addition to exchanging hard currency and merchandise, they also had to work in currencies of trust.

Educating the next generation of merchants directly benefited the trade businesses and, by extension, the cities, which saw the value of establishing universities.[23] Besides cultivating a general love of knowledge, these universities also supplied a steady stream of trained lawyers.[24] Prizing education and benefiting from it, these towns were the seedbeds of "the great new spiritual movements of Humanism, [the] Renaissance and [the] Reformation," whose values and ideas were also cultivated and cherished in the Bonhoeffer family.[25]

Holding that pamphlet in St. Michael's, my heart leapt to see that one little word *citizen* in the paragraph, a word that signified so much, and the powerful narrative in which a once-poor goldsmith's assistant came to belong as a citizen of a free imperial city. Here, a Bonhoeffer was transformed from subject to citizen; here, town air brought him, and his descendants, a form of freedom. Many of those Bonhoeffers served the city, a lineage of public service that Dietrich was taught to honor as a boy.

The free cities also figure in the Bonhoeffer family's lineage as a point of tension, particularly between the class backgrounds of his parents and the different ideas Germans held about their common life. Besides Karl and Paula's religious differences, their marriage also represented political diversity between their respective family trees. Paula hailed from the nobility; her mother was a countess. But Karl traced his lineage to this city, as a member of its non-noble "middle" class. The family mirrored in small scale some of the political and class tensions within competing power centers in German history.

Significantly, those tensions existed—and, at times, spawned open conflict—among those engaged in German anti-Nazi resistance. Of the many attempts on Hitler's life, the last serious one was executed on July 20, 1944. (Dietrich Bonhoeffer was not central to the action of the plot, but he was aware of the plans and supported it.) Many of the conspirators in this particular plot, a last-ditch effort to communicate to the world that not all Germans were Nazis, hailed from noble lineage and entertained ideas of restoring a monarchy.[26] Others hoped to revive a liberal democracy for Germany. Both streams of political identity repudiated the raw and unchecked authoritarianism of the Nazi fascists. Both streams of political thought motivated their resistance; and, despite the many differences, this group of conspirators worked together in a last attempt to defeat the strong man. But the plot failed, and when Bonhoeffer heard in prison of the failure, he figured his doom was sealed.

In some ways, Bonhoeffer was attracted to the idea of a nobility, but not a nobility of bloodline and privilege; rather, he was attracted to a "new sense of nobility," one that prizes quality and renounces celebrity and lineage, that keeps an "open eye both upwards and downwards," makes friends with and thus belongs to people from all social classes and backgrounds, and joyfully participates in private life while courageously entering public life. In a reflection on the times he wrote at Christmas 1942, before his arrest, Bonhoeffer casts a vision of the culture of this new nobility, which he imagined would involve "a return from the newspaper and the radio to the book, from feverish activity to unhurried leisure, from dispersion to concentration, from sensationalism to reflection, from virtuosity to art, from snobbery to modesty, from extravagance to moderation."[27]

• • •

In an unpublished memoir, Karl Bonhoeffer grieved his lack of success in acquiring property in Schwäbisch Hall. Recalling that medieval legal maxim quoted earlier, Dr. Bonhoeffer described his quest to purchase property as his seeking to apply for "the freedom of the city." One hears his anguish at being cut off from his civic lineage when he wrote, "Although I have not lived any long period in Schwäbisch Hall, the little medieval town still gives me a strong sense that I belong there."[28] Though he was not a citizen of that city, he still lived *as if* he were. He *imagined* himself a citizen of the pale and cherished the city to which he did not legally belong, where he would never live as his ancestors had. Dr. Bonhoeffer passed that civic inheritance to his children, however, in the values he cultivated in them. This too gave Dietrich and the rest that sense of belonging.

But their civic inheritance still had boundaries because Bonhoeffer family culture forbade flaunting their lineage. Bragging about ancestry was considered completely off-limits in the Bonhoeffer household, even as the Nazis demanded proof of everyone's ancestry.[29] But, at a critical point in his life, Dietrich Bonhoeffer broke with this long-honored taboo, a marked aberration from his family culture. The record of this moment was captured by the Schutzstaffel, commonly known as the SS, in its records at the Reich Security Headquarters in Berlin. The Gestapo had grown skittish of Bonhoeffer's influence and banned him from speaking in public. Apparently, during an interrogation in which he attempted to mount a defense against this Nazi injunction, Bonhoeffer referred to his family's long and deep connections to Schwäbisch Hall:

> [My father's] ancestors lived for centuries as highly esteemed craftsmen and councilors of the then Imperial City of Schwäbisch Hall, and even today our pictures hang proudly in the city's main church. . . . In conscious affirmation of this spiritual legacy and moral position of my family, I cannot accept the charge of "activity subverting the people."[30]

Bonhoeffer's statement could hardly be called putting on airs, but when pressed, he invoked his identity, one rooted in people and a place, and did so with the authority as a citizen of that place in the face of the meddlesome power.

Standing in St. Michael's Church that late afternoon, we saw from a distance some of the pictures of these illustrious Bonhoeffers hanging on the walls, these free citizens who belonged to and served Schwäbisch Hall, and even more was written about them in the church's thick history book in the narthex. We stood in the place of Dietrich Bonhoeffer's imagined belonging, the city to which he himself was a kind of spiritual citizen of the pale.

None of the free imperial cities were free of rank injustice. None offered unalloyed goodness to all within their realms. Their systems of citizenry were, like many before and after, predicated on privilege and patriarchy, a certain level of wealth and power, most of which was concentrated in the upper classes. These free cities tolerated, knowingly and unknowingly, all kinds of inequality and injustice, even as they provided a serious check on the instability and fecklessness of the princes.[31] Human rights and notions of citizenship not predicated on male property ownership were still largely alien at that time in history. But the seeds of those ideas were in the ground, waiting to germinate.

Looking at my own place of belonging, the American experiment is predicated on ideas and ideals that have yet to be fully realized in the lives of its citizens. But its ideas are worth tending and preserving, especially to those of us who know that, at its founding, we would have been considered beyond the pale. Those who first belonged to the imagined America were a narrow and select few. I would not have been counted among its citizens.

I was reminded of this sober reality in a visit years ago, when our family made a trek from our home near Washington, DC, to Williamsburg, Virginia, and explored that city's historical park. After stopping in at the milliners' shop and the old-time pharmacy, we gathered with other tourists to listen to a lively debate conducted on a wooden platform. Two actors dressed in period clothing debated as if they were two of America's founding fathers who held very different views about the idea of religious freedom in the fledgling democracy. When the debate came to an end, the actors turned to us, the now quite large listening audience, to vote on which founding father had won the debate.

I was excited to vote, having listened to them and holding a position of my own on the subject. But just as quickly, these actors reminded us of the time—that is, their place in history. To the growing (and vocal) consternation of the crowd, the actors declared they would poll only those who would have been deemed true citizens during that time. Despite their different positions about the new American government, the characters were in marked agreement in defining who was a citizen and who was not.

"First off," one said, straightening his coat and flouncing the lace cravat around his neck, "I would kindly ask all the female members of this crowd to sit down and stay silent. You are not eligible to vote." Ah, of course. My daughters and I reluctantly sat. The actors then further whittled down the citizenry. Only whites! Only those who hold property in Virginia! For a time, my husband stood (and I think he was gloating), believing he would be able to vote. But then the actors specified a man had to own far more land than we did to be considered a true property holder, and with that, my husband—bearer of a mere still-under-mortgage two-thirds of an acre in a northern Virginia suburb—was finally forced to sit. In the end, only two men out of the crowd of hundreds cast a vote.

Much has changed for the good since those days. There has been struggle in America and around the world to ascertain how a city's freedoms (and responsibilities) might belong to more than just a select few. Despite the struggle, I see how the *idea* of citizenship in towns such as Schwäbisch Hall are still valuable. Here and there, new forms of authority were tested and tried, the freedom and responsibility for governance expanded beyond the divine line of kings and their troublesome progeny. Here and there, some non-royal and non-noble people lived free, vested both with agency and responsibility, as unequal as it was for so many others. New ideas upturned long-neglected soil, and new understandings of the human person emerged. While I would not like to turn the clock back, I can honor those efforts and breathe some of that town air for myself. And to honor it best, I can pray and work to keep expanding the freedoms, keep nurturing the sense of responsibility, so that more people can take in that air, unpolluted and free.

Standing in the stone interior of St. Michael's and glimpsing pieces of art commissioned to honor Bonhoeffer's ancestors—the very place he might have held in his mind as he defended himself against charges intended to silence him—I saw how powerfully *this place* had formed him. This church embodied the privilege of belonging to a city as well as the responsibility of belonging. Not insignificantly, when faced with the proud, freedom-crushing, and violent powers of the Nazis, Bonhoeffer invoked his citizenship in this place. He too breathed that free air, even when held in unfree places.

• • •

Julie Tafel Bonhoeffer, Dietrich's grandmother, was one of the most important persons in his life. An avid reader, she embodied the intellectual and civic virtues that were passed along to her grandchildren. Throughout her life, she was "politically alert" and especially active in advancing women's issues.[32] She established a home for older women and vocational training centers for young women.[33] Her model of intellectual and practical engagement was critical for Dietrich as well; she was well practiced in living out her beliefs, and that mattered when the Nazis began pressing their heavy power upon civic life.

Early in their rule, on April 1, 1933, the Nazis announced a boycott of Jewish businesses. It was the first in a long campaign to eradicate Jews from Germany, beginning with persecution, making life for Jewish citizens more and more unbearable so they would leave Germany under the pressure. These policies also normalized long-held prejudices that German society had indulged violently from time to time throughout history. These early measures also trained non-Jewish Germans to grow inured and indifferent to their fellow citizens' suffering.

Even at her advanced age, Mrs. Tafel Bonhoeffer enjoyed shopping at the Kaufhaus des Westens, whose name means "the

Department Store of the West" and which was owned by "a prominent Jewish family of the Grunewald," as Bonhoeffer biographer
Charles Marsh puts it.[34] As it was then, it is still Berlin's central
department store, offering up haute couture on the ground level and
all kinds of wares in the floors above. Usually referred to by its shorthand name, the KaDeWe, it's located on Tauentzienstrasse not far
from Kurfürstendamm, or Ku'Damm, a grand boulevard lined with
shops, grand and common—another place Berliners love enough to
nickname by contracting its name.

To enforce the boycott, the Nazis set up cordons and blockades
in front of Jewish-owned businesses. Crowds gathered to harass and
intimidate those tempted to cross the line. These places of refinement
and fashion—the KaDeWe and other shops along Ku'Damm—became
terrifying settings of tension when the Nazis initiated the boycott:

> Eyewitnesses recalled the division amongst the crowds—
> between those who forced their way into shops despite the
> abuse hurled at them; those who hurried by with an embar-
> rassed glance in the direction of the store or building; and
> those, like the mass of people in front of the Ka De We, who
> stood around the entrance spontaneously giving the Hitler
> salute and chanting anti-Semitic slogans.[35]

The ninety-one-year-old Julie Tafel Bonhoeffer was out shopping in
this frightful spectacle, and, rather than shrink back, she marched
right through "a cordon of SA brownshirts" posted to block entry.[36]
In some accounts of the story, she astonished the young guards by
charging past them, unfazed. According to other versions, she verbally confronted them, asserting that she would shop where she
always shopped, wherever she liked.

Whether she verbally rebuked them or not, this elderly woman was not cowed, even in the face of a phalanx of security forces, intense social pressure, and mob intimidation. She acted and spoke with a courage anchored in an identity and authority deeper than just herself. Both she and Dietrich shared a fascination with Gandhi's methods of nonviolence; Grandmother Bonhoeffer had even encouraged Dietrich to visit Gandhi, although his attempts to do so never came to fruition.[37] She exercised the kind of civil disobedience in this moment that, arguably, at this early stage of Nazi rule, if practiced on a large scale, might have thwarted the grip of National Socialism.[38]

Dietrich Bonhoeffer gave the eulogy at his grandmother's funeral, and his words reveal just how deep an imprint she made on him. He names certain virtues, ones cultivated in the free imperial cities, civic traits that coupled privileges and responsibilities:

> The uncompromising nature of law and justice, the free word of a free man, the obligation to stand by a promise once it is made, clarity and sobriety of speech, uprightness and simplicity in public and private life—on these she set her whole heart. . . . She could not bear to see these aims held in contempt or see the violation of another's rights. Thus her last years were clouded by the great sorrow she endured on account of the fate of the Jews among our people, a fate she bore and suffered in sympathy with them. She was the product of another time, of another spiritual world—and that world goes down with her to the grave.[39]

He expressed gratitude that she preserved these values, which he and others had inherited as their duty. With her passing, the inheritance passed as well—both the rights and the responsibilities. Dietrich knew the people and the places to which he belonged. It was like he carried within him a free imperial city, an imagined place of belonging, a reservoir and rootedness to guide his decisions and actions.

• • •

Imagined belonging shapes the moral imagination, revealing possibilities that may not yet exist. But imagined doesn't mean unreal. It can mean otherworldly or immaterial. Imagined communities can be quite formative, and in them, it's possible to experience belonging and membership in a community, even with a relative stranger. What matters in an imagined community is who belongs—who is included and who is excluded. The Nazis answered that question in a certain way, and they too shaped moral imaginations, hardening latent anti-Semitism and prejudice in policy and law and ensuring that those included in the community shaped by Aryan mythology would fear extending a hand to those excluded from it. All kinds of imagined communities now spring up online. Almost effortlessly, social media allows us to connect with and disconnect from friends and strangers alike. We can reconnect with old acquaintances from long ago or, just as easily, find ourselves engulfed in social media swamps of contempt. In those spaces, in discussion threads and on message boards, it is easy to grow inured and indifferent, to learn to dehumanize those who do not belong to our imagined community. And when dehumanizing trends begin, the effect lands ruthlessly on minorities and the vulnerable.

In the medieval age, as under National Socialism—and worryingly, even now—Jewish people suffered exclusion, discrimination, and recrimination for all kinds of grievances. Mob law and violence against Jews punctuated medieval town life. When the Nazis revived and gave state sanction to prejudiced myths and enacted new, horrifying forms of exclusion in their attempts to secure German identity in those myths, Dietrich Bonhoeffer argued that the church in Germany could not simply stand by as if it didn't matter to them. Christians needed to see how they belonged to Jews and other victims of an increasingly belligerent and bloodthirsty state. Indeed, how Christians responded to these vulnerable populations revealed the actual content and strength of their faith—how they would respond to Jesus the Jew himself, the Christ who journeyed hidden among those excluded from belonging.

While Bonhoeffer invoked the free imperial city to defend his name against Gestapo accusations, it hardly explained why he worked so hard to support the Confessing Church in its opposition to Nazi influence among Christians or why, when he was offered an escape from Germany in June 1939, he returned home after only a few short weeks in the United States. As significant as his family's heritage may have been, that rather obscure connection hardly explained his journey from theological opposition to political struggle. Not unlike that visitor who asked me about Bonhoeffer's daily life and habits, I too wondered what animated Bonhoeffer to the point that he was willing to risk his life to oppose the Nazis. And I wondered, as is natural, whether I would do the same, extending a hand to someone suffering exclusion and persecution.

To answer those questions, I turned to the research of Dr. Kristen Monroe.[40] She has studied moral choice in frightful social settings, such as genocides in various countries, including Nazi Germany. Monroe wondered what determined whether someone would take on personal risks to assist another person, such as a stranger suffering persecution or just needing help. She wanted to know why some just stand by as inert bystanders while others reach out to help. Monroe's research gave me a new angle from which to think about Bonhoeffer.

One determining factor in how people act, Monroe discovered, is how they perceive themselves in relationship to others. Self-perception, she explains—both a person's understanding of their own identity and their sense of belonging to others, even just the simple connection of being a fellow human being—largely determines whether a person feels obligated to help another even if it costs them personally. Even more interesting, a person's identity and belonging also influences their ability to imagine possible courses of action. When they see their moral obligations, their imaginations are fired and able to see possibilities that wouldn't have been apparent without those obligations. As Monroe puts it, "identity constrains choice." When she asked people why they did or did not assist others during reigns of persecution, terror, or genocide, both the uninvolved bystanders and the heroic risk takers alike used the same expression: they said they had "no choice but to" do what they did, even though that meant two very different courses of action. The difference wasn't in their *knowing* the right thing to do. What mattered was how they understood who they were (identity) in relationship to others (belonging). How they imagined their belonging to others is what determined how they behaved.[41]

In these admittedly difficult social and political situations, bystanders saw themselves as isolated individuals (identity), powerless and disconnected. They also imagined themselves as merely one person in the face of larger forces that could not be countered alone.

Bystanders were paralyzed in their perceived isolation, even if they felt tugs at their conscience. Perceiving themselves as alone and weak also kept them from seeing what possibilities were available to them to act differently. Naturally, they saw none.

But those who took personal risks for others felt compelled to do so because they saw themselves as connected to the sufferer, at least in their shared humanity. If the roles were reversed, they figured, they would want someone to help them. Their sense of identity and their imagined belonging to that person constrained their choice: they felt they had *no choice but* to act for the other person. Remarkably, possibilities opened up before them to help—newfound courage, or a clever way of intervening against powerful forces. Their identity and sense of belonging shaped their moral imagination, and, in turn, their moral imagination enabled them to see and act for someone enduring persecution.

• • •

On a warm autumn afternoon, I took a walk in the Grunewald. For centuries, this huge forest on the southwest side of Berlin was preserved for imperial hunting. Now, it is open for us common folks to enjoy, and our family was lucky enough to live on a street that literally backs onto this forest. I walked beneath the trees and took deep breaths of the forested air, crunching leaves beneath my feet. As they cropped up along the paths, I peered into the deep holes dug out by foraging Schweine (wild boars). In our three years here in Berlin, I have glimpsed these shy and sometimes aggressive creatures only a handful of times, but their handiwork is everywhere.

I followed the dirt path that circles the Grunewaldsee, a small and picturesque lake, and took in long looks of the Jagdschloss (Hunting Palace), Berlin's oldest preserved castle, a fairy-tale place perched on its bank. Built in the mid-1500s, it was the hunting lodge of the kaiser, the Prussian emperor, and the surrounding forest and all life within it were his and for his pleasure. The industrious Schweine of today are the descendants of those who were hunted then. In tribute to that traditional pastime, within the cobblestone courtyard of the palace—with its half-timbered café serving Kaffee und Kuchen and an art gallery showcasing works of both Lucas Cranach the Elder and the Younger—stands a life-sized statue of a boar, its eyes and mouth open in wild terror, being taken down by three snarling hounds. In this statue, the hunt lives on.

The building survived Allied war bombing, and its graceful towers and steep red-tiled roofs look like a movie set of yesteryear. A delightful Christmas market happens here every year on the second weekend of Advent, with actors in period clothing conjuring its past. For all its picturesque architecture, however, the whispered legend was confirmed by historians: during the decadent latter days of the German empire, in 1891, Kaiser Wilhelm II's sister hosted huge parties of imperial courtiers that turned orgiastic, and those who attended fought duels over the threat to make public their scandalous behavior there.[42] Despite its graceful setting and elegant, otherworldly appointments, this little palace represents the toxic brew of power, money, and vice. The once-virtuous past is an illusion.

The Jagdschloss's history is a warning, a reminder of the limits of all these broken inheritances, these messy and turbulent lineages. Most national identities—German identity, or my American one—include emotionally compelling but murky, dubious myths. Adolf Hitler exploited these myths, adding some of his own invention to them, and sold them like a carnival barker to an insecure people who were hungry to make the myths true, desperate to restore a lost and shattered identity. The "blood and soil" refrain that Nazis so often invoked captures both the natural and the human element, as if this one mythical people had grown like trees in the national soil and all other life was alien to it, theirs to exploit, even to hunt and kill. Craving this sense of rootedness, an already debased people were even further debased, proving again that idols—including those of cultures and nations—never deliver on their promises. Worse, they leave worshippers even more broken than before they found them. That palatial artifact on the lake cast a warning to my imaginings: nothing in Dietrich Bonhoeffer's ancestry could save him or the nation from its self-destruction. The only way to save Germany from its national myths was to expose and defeat them.

Bonhoeffer knew that too. Privately, in a letter, he wished for a "new nobility"—not one of blood and soil but of quality and conscience, one that prized freedom and responsible action instead of power and privilege, a new generation of people willing to walk, "not [as] lords," but as "instruments in the hands of the Lord of history" along "the very narrow way, often extremely difficult to find, of living every day as if it were our last, and yet living in faith and responsibility as though there were to be a great future."[43] When, in 1939, his friends in New York City offered him an escape from Nazi Germany in the form of an invitation to return to Union Theological Seminary, his identity, his sense of belonging, also constrained his choice. Thus, Bonhoeffer returned to Germany in 1939 to step into the political struggle. Doing so, he fully embraced his identity as a German, with all its guilt and shame, and his sense of belonging to what was left of the church in Germany, to Germany and its people, those who thought they alone belonged and those they had excluded. He stepped toward the possibility that he might suffer, and he proved himself to be a citizen of a much freer place.

Herrnhuter stars during Advent, in Herrnhut, Germany

Chapter 4

THE
WATCHWORDS

→ *Key: When we hold on to the truth, we find the truth holds onto us, even when we are tempted to despair.* ←

The summer of 2018 was a scorcher all across Europe. On a hot day at the beginning of June, I rotated the sprinkler around our Garten (yard); although I had dreams of vesting it with flowers and vegetables, the heat had severely pruned my hopes back to the sparest of goals. I was now just trying to keep our grass and new hedgerow alive.

When we had moved into our permanent residence two years earlier, it was clear that the yard was midproject—or midfailure. The grass was in terrible shape. The embassy's residential handbook, which lay on the kitchen counter upon our arrival, informed us that we were responsible for the care and upkeep of the yard and grass. But we had inherited a mess. The yard was patches of dirt and moss, interspersed with little tufts of green grass and a lot of weeds.

About a week after we moved in, a gardening crew showed up to our place unannounced, scraped off all the green material, and reseeded the exposed earth. When they were packing up to leave, they informed me that I needed to water regularly and keep the kids off of the yard so the new grass could grow. The ground was now brown and covered in delicate seeds, even more homely looking than when we first arrived. My lone task was to ensure that the grass grew. It was hot, tiring, and tedious work.

A waist-high hedge of evergreens ringed part of the yard, and a higher hedge stood between our yard and our German neighbor's. But outside the kitchen window was a large gap in that higher hedge, an opening in the green curtain that crossed the cream-colored cinder-block wall of our neighbor's garage. As if the growing grass wasn't enough of a challenge, the hedge gap was clearly another unfinished project—one that involved our neighbor.

Over the course of those first months, I had many discussions with the neighbor about that wall. Based on her regular briefings, it was clear I was inheriting some of her past consternation with the embassy as well. She informed me that she wanted to paint the wall of her garage that faced our house now that the hedge had been torn out. Since the project site for painting was our yard, she needed to get the work done before the new line of bushes went in. I tried to inform the embassy what my neighbor wanted to have happen and then relayed to my neighbor what the embassy wanted too. Between trying to get our new house organized, accomplishing my daily grocery-store runs on the bus, and continuing to help our kids settle into their new rhythms of school and the bewilderment of a new language and culture, I was barely keeping up with my role as yard project manager and neighbor-diplomat.

When it looked like the weather would cooperate, my neighbor hired a painter. I was happy for her, and I told the embassy we were nearly ready to schedule the gardener. But when her contracted painter showed up one morning and began setting up his workspace in our yard, he made an unfortunate discovery.

That morning, an unannounced meeting was brought to order with a sharp rap on our front door. There, I found my elderly German neighbor standing in her bathrobe, exasperated, with a cartoonishly angry painter. He was throwing up his hands, sighing, his twitching mustache as bushy as the paintbrush in his hand. Apparently, there was an abundance of yellow-jacket nests all along one side of our house, and the wasps were hounding him as he began to work. We had never really been bothered by them—thanks to the delicate grass seeds, we weren't spending any time in the yard, and as a result we hadn't done anything about them. So here I was, the pajama-clad American nitwit who had—in the painter's mind—allowed a whole apartment complex of yellow jackets to take up residence and thwart his work.

Despite her excellent English, my neighbor was so frustrated that she was using a lot more German than she normally did with me. Having spent years training each newly arrived American family in *proper* social norms (as best she could), and having already invested in me rather heavily, and now in a painter, she was struggling to remain calm. I assured her, seasoning my sentences with whatever nice expressions and words I could think of in my very limited German, that I was on her side. "We will get this done," I said, instinctively smiling. "We will figure this out." No smiles were returned, and they both marched off.

By the time winter arrived, we three improbable teammates had brought the many moving parts of the project to a satisfying place of completion. I informed the embassy about the wasps. They contracted a pest-control specialist, who helped to draw down their numbers. The garage wall was finally painted just before the early winter rains began, and at long last, the hedgerow gap was filled with new bushes, all Christmas tree shaped, which I found endearing and perfectly timed for the approaching season. In all respects, the view from my kitchen window considerably improved.

• • •

Come spring, the new hedgerow bushes showed signs of stress. My next-door neighbor urged me to water them better than I had been—which was not at all since they had been planted in the late fall. I wasn't in the habit of watering them with the relatively wet winter, but it was clear they needed it, so I began a watering regimen, but not in sufficient time to keep one of the new bushes alive. Again, I informed the embassy, and a few weeks later, a gardener came to remove it, assuring me that the other bushes would grow to fill in the new gap. He told me I needed to be watering, and I assured him I would.

But in time, some of the other bushes began to show stress too, and across the hedge, my neighbor guessed it was disease. She urged me to prune them, with that abrupt directness that Germans communicate with and we Americans can find so grating and painful. I was starting to feel a little like a bush in the hedge myself. I had already done so much to tend the yard, which was among the lowest of my priorities as we acclimated to our life in unyielding Berlin. I was sick of being a middle manager to an inherited project. And in that very American way, in which we are cloyingly nice to new acquaintances until pushed to a snapping point and then we snarl, after getting that last bit of advice, I marched into our house in passive-aggressive frustration and returned holding a meat cleaver—the only object in our house that I thought could do the job. Making sure she saw me from her kitchen window, which looked out onto our yard, I began to hack out the dead branches in the hedge with my meat cleaver. As I hacked, probably looking somewhat deranged, I hoped it would bring the nagging to an end.

Spring turned to summer, and my meat-cleaver hacking had left some unsightly pockets in the hedge. From time to time, my neighbor suggested that I train some of the living branches, tying them to better fill in the gap. I replied, stone-faced, that it wasn't a high priority of mine. I had long abandoned any hopes of beautifying the yard; it was enough that it was mostly alive. The grass was greening up, and the hedgerow was heading in the right direction, albeit imperfectly.

But the summer of 2018, our final full summer in Berlin, was historically hot, not just in Berlin but throughout Europe. Temperatures spiked in places it normally never did, and all of life wilted under its oppressive hand. Wildfires raged in parts of Scandinavia and in tinder-dry forests outside of Berlin. For a few days, we could smell the smoke when we stepped outside. Everyone discussed the heat, how unusual it was, how it was unlike anything they had experienced in living memory.

Our neighbor wisely avoided the heat and the sun, staying indoors as much as possible. After a few health problems earlier that year, she seemed a bit frailer than when we had first met. We didn't bump into each other as much as we used to, nor did she have the energy in the heat to keep up her training of me, her hopeless American next-door neighbor, to improve my evident gardening gaps. I still tried to get out into the yard most days, heavily watering the hedges and the grass in hopes of keeping them alive.

As I moved the sprinkler around to the next patch of yard, an American neighbor across the street came out to do the same. Many of the yards along our street were scorched, brittle and brown. We waved to each other, ritually lamenting the heat.

"We finally broke down and got an air conditioner," she called, smiling.

"Good for you," I called back, smiling broadly in reply. "I can't stand hunkering down in the dark house with the shutters down, but without an air conditioner, it's what we have to do."

Then my German neighbor came out to check her plants, and I thought I'd get a jump on the conversation to try to steer it away from house and yard tasks and into life. I told her that my daughters were being released from school early again that day—"for Hitzefrei," I said, heat free, a snow day but for the extreme heat. Like most homes in Germany, as in most parts of northern Europe, schools and office buildings are not usually air conditioned. The US embassy is unique in the city for its air-conditioned workspace, and my husband was having great success booking meetings with his German counterparts at his office rather than at the sweltering German Foreign Ministry.

"Ja, Hitzefrei. That's good," she said quietly, nodding and squinting in the bright morning sunlight. "No learning today." I nodded and squinted back, unsure whether she meant me or my kids. But on this, we agreed, and it was a balm. She headed back into her house, bunkered like mine against the unusual heat. It was so small, but I was so gratified to have had a more personal exchange with her.

After rotating the sprinkler, I, too, returned to the dark of the house. Besides my usual chores, I wanted to review Bonhoeffer's second trip to New York in the summer of 1939. His friends there and in the Confessing Church in Germany were worried for him. With the Nazi war machine gearing up (the invasion of Poland and beginning of World War II was only a few months away), he was required to register his place of residence and keep the police informed of his whereabouts; he needed special permission from the authorities to leave Germany. He applied for permission to go to New York, and the recruiting office overseeing his case granted him a year during which he could leave Berlin.

Bonhoeffer was tired. His work for the Confessing Church and the stress of the deteriorating national situation in Germany had left him depleted. Knowing that men his age, born in 1906, would be called to report for military duty, he knew he was caught. His conscience compelled him to make a stand as a conscientious objector, but then equally prevented him from doing so in order not to draw attention to the Confessing Church, already under grave suspicion. Military service meant swearing an oath to Hitler, as so many pastors in the Confessing Church had already done, heading off to their compulsory military service. Bonhoeffer's proposed yearlong sabbatical to New York seemed to him, at least, to offer him some space, if not reprieve, from his dilemmas and doubts.[1]

He set out from Germany on a hot June day, not unlike that day for me, I noted, as I wiped my brow and took another sip of water, sitting right under a ceiling fan spinning at full speed. In a letter to his friend Bethge, Bonhoeffer described the pink evening light as he flew from Germany to England; it was from here, after a long layover visiting his twin sister and her family, that he voyaged across the Atlantic.[2]

But as I read and imagined his life with such neat congruence to my own, I made a discovery, and my imagination turned off and my critical mind engaged. The narrative I had been telling in tours about these critical weeks in Bonhoeffer's life did not match what I was now reading. In fact, I was horrified to see, clearly, that I had forced his story into fanciful imaginings of my own. His story was not for my inspiration alone, and I needed to let go of places where that imagination wanted it to be. My narrative needed pruning and hacking, replanting and watering.

The diseased narrative concerned the Moravian watchwords, or *Die Losungen*. These were, and are, daily Scripture meditations published every year by the Moravian Brethren, a Protestant group that traces its religious heritage to a pre-Reformation movement of pietists who were committed to Scripture, prayer, and evangelism. In the early 1700s, they left Moravia and Bohemia, areas that are part of the Czech Republic today, to escape religious persecution, settling in an area east of Dresden, Germany. They named their town Herrnhut, the Lord's protection. Bonhoeffer and many others used their so-called watchwords—pairs of verses, one from the Old Testament matched with one from the New Testament—as a daily devotional practice, and it was one he commended to others as well.

The watchwords figure prominently in the records of this short and momentous season of his life in part because he referred to them in a diary of that time. Journeying away from Nazi Germany in June 1939, Bonhoeffer's burden of anxiety seemed to grow, not lessen. The further he ventured into the purported safety of America, the less settled he felt. The plan to bring him to safety was well intentioned, and his friends Reinhold Niebuhr and Paul Lehmann were very glad to help him avoid the Nazi military dragnet. But even as he boarded the ship bound for New York's harbor, Bonhoeffer already wondered whether he had made a mistake in leaving Germany.

The tormenting thoughts did not abate when he arrived. He felt more acutely that he had left loved ones behind, the weight of their suffering growing within him, they who remained in the ever-darkening nightmare of Hitler's rule. His ache was the agony of responsibility. He knew his actions mattered. Even the noblest of intentions and the purest of motives—such as the prospect of a university position and a lecture tour in the United States and many opportunities to communicate about the situation in Nazi Germany to the world—could not reframe the truths gnawing in him.

His daily readings in *Die Losungen*, the watchwords, heightened Bonhoeffer's inner ache. In the paradoxical nature of truth, his handhold on the word of God proved to be a comforting anchor of truth in the growing storm of his soul. He found some reprieve as he meditated on the verses, but he found, too, that the word made his inner waves pitch to new peaks. In this season, Bonhoeffer was like the prophet Jonah, but in a German retelling in which the prophet fled his own country and people. The storm was within him as much as it raged in the world, and he began to see that he, too, would have to be thrown overboard, to return and likely be swallowed up. His journey into the safety of New York's harbor was dangerous, and the right course was toward danger—toward the crushing wheel of the state.

I had been telling a story that made this all too dramatic. I thought I had read that there was a single verse that had tipped the balance in his heart, a determining word that pointed him home. As compelling and entertaining a tale it was to tell, I saw now that there was no one watchword, no single fortune-cookie paper that cast magic lamplight on his heroic path. He was still at a crossroads of decision; he was a free man, tormented with free choice.

I went back outside, squinting in the blinding summer sun. I shifted the sprinkler again, pulled a few more weeds from the lawn, and called "Morgen!" to some dog walkers on the sidewalk. Like they had in this yard, weeds had grown up in my story that needed to be identified and pulled. I had to practice the facts of Bonhoeffer's life and keep the story well-watered with regular study and a willingness to be corrected. On this hot day, I returned to my dark house to practice aloud those hot June days when he both clung to the word as a life raft and, at last, let himself fall like Jonah into its churning waves.

In his short summer stay in New York in 1939, Bonhoeffer wrestled with himself, examining his motives for leaving Germany. His thoughts were scattered and his writing more labored than usual.[3] The tasks that usually came so easily to him now seemed to be failing him. Many saw his presence in New York as an answer to prayer, but he felt lost.[4] After arriving on June 12, he made up his mind to return to Germany on June 20, referring to the watchwords in his diary entry when he announced his decision to his friends.[5] He boarded one of the last ships leaving for Germany on July 7.[6]

Even though he believed it had been a mistake, there was still value to the journey. It had refined him, and he wrote in his diary, "I am glad to have been over there, and glad to be on my way home again. . . . Probably this visit will have a great effect on me. . . . Since I have been on the ship my inner ambiguity about the future has ceased."[7] Through it all, Bonhoeffer held on to the truth, and the truth held on to him, even when doubt and disorientation threatened to swallow him up. And that same truth, that same light, would hold on to him as he made his way back to the darkness that was Nazi Germany.

· · ·

Another Advent was upon us, the heat and long days of summer a forgotten memory. Daylight hours were now short, and the lights of the season had gone up again all over town. In front of the Brandenburg Gate, the city placed a huge menorah to honor the Jewish holiday of Hanukkah alongside a large, brightly lit Christmas evergreen. The illumined columns of the gate stood in artful complement to the large electrified candles of the menorah and the tree. The gate at night holds bitter memories, the backdrop to ominous Nazi rallies of marching brownshirts and flaming torches. The menorah's witness before this monument cast a gentle glow of hard-won victory, the juxtaposition still a miracle to many.

Glowing paper stars, some with so many points they nearly resemble sea urchins, hung over doorways, in windows at houses and apartments, and inside the cavernous grand sanctuaries of the city's churches. The cold winter air, cloudy, dreary, and typically wet as winter is on the great European plain, pierced the many layers of clothing and winter gear we donned.

In our final year in Berlin, we made mental lists of the places we still wanted to visit. The clock ticking with its unrelenting, steady pace forced us to prioritize. With Christmas markets opening up all over town and country, we contemplated visiting some of the famous ones outside Berlin, such as those in Dresden, Hamburg, or Nuremberg.

With stalls set up on main squares and outlined in strings of light, each market claims to be the best, the quintessential Weihnachtsmarkt (Christmas market). And having sampled many of Berlin's markets, I cannot disagree, for most markets manage to charm in some unique way. The German Christmas-market scene is an endearing sort of festival of booths, drawing us out of our houses, improbably, into the cold, dark night, where we are warmed with mugs of Glühwein (mulled wine), rolls stuffed with hot bratwurst, and bowls of steaming Grünkohl (stewed kale) in an atmosphere of holiday togetherness.

"Perhaps we should do another trip to Dresden," I said to my husband as we considered possibilities, "especially if we could swing a visit to Herrnhut." As I said it aloud, I knew that what was even more important to me than visiting yet another Weihnachtsmarkt was getting the chance to see Herrnhut, the city where those Moravian refugees, fleeing religious persecution for their Reformed-minded beliefs centuries ago, found safety and finally settled. That community, founded in the eighteenth century, extended an outsized yet still humble influence on the world through the Moravian Brethren's prayer meetings, missionary efforts, and annual publication of *Die Losungen*, the biblical daily texts or watchwords. This daily devotional practice was one that Bonhoeffer cherished and personally recommended to others, especially as a beginning way to listen meditatively to the word of God. With those paper stars casting their distinctive glow all over town, I also saw that the timing couldn't be better for a visit. What we in America know as a Moravian star is a Herrnhuter Stern, a star of Herrnhut, for the eponymous town where it was designed. Getting to Herrnhut felt like an important piece of my mental Bonhoeffer map, for Dietrich belonged in some ways to this town too, through his mother, his nannies, and his scripture reading practices. To be able to see it at Christmastime, festooned with Moravian stars, would make it all the more memorable.

Lying due east of the city of Dresden, Herrnhut is the spiritual center of the Moravian story. The Moravians were pietists, a Christian group emphasizing individual conversion to Jesus and separated from the established Roman Catholic church, one of many pre-Reformation Protestant groups that grew out of the Bohemian Reformation in what we now call the Czech Republic. Later on, under threat from the ruling Roman Catholics during the Counter-Reformation, they fled west from Moravia as refugees and were welcomed by Count Nikolaus Ludwig von Zinzendorf, a German nobleman trained for the royal court in Dresden. Zinzendorf permitted the Moravian refugees to settle on Berthelsdorf, his estate in Saxony. The Moravians called that settlement Herrnhut—the name meaning "the Lord's Protection" or "the Refuge of the Lord"—and Zinzendorf served as a leader in the group.

In 1727, Zinzendorf and these Moravians experienced a revival, a movement of charismatic expression and enthusiasm, speaking in tongues, and holding extensive prayer meetings, and they were inspired with an earnest longing to evangelize. Many Moravians committed to a round-the-clock prayer meeting, a covenant of continuous praying, which lasted over a hundred years. These early Moravians were fearless about missions, going to great pains to journey around the world, carrying the light and living water of God's word.

The Moravians significantly influenced later modern missionaries such as John Wesley, who witnessed their daring faith firsthand. On a transatlantic voyage he took to the American colony of Georgia, Wesley found himself traveling with a group of Moravians. During the crossing, a rough storm battered their ship, and most of the passengers panicked. Wesley feared he and the others were going to die in the storm, but he glimpsed a group of passengers singing, calmly. They were German Moravian Christians.[8]

There were, in fact, twenty-four Moravians aboard the storm-tossed ship *Simmonds*, and they and their bishop, David Nitschmann, were also on their way to Georgia.[9] When the storm finally abated and the inner terror that gripped most passengers quieted, Wesley asked the Moravians whether they had been afraid. They told him they had not been afraid and, more so, they were not afraid to die. Kindly, almost pityingly, they asked Wesley whether *he* had faith in Christ, a question that startled him since he, too, was traveling as a Christian missionary just like them. Later, back home to England, he pursued friendship with a Moravian leader in London by the name of Peter Böhler. After visiting a Moravian worship service "in Nettleton Court on the east side of Aldersgate Street" in 1738, Wesley knew his heart had been changed—"strangely warmed," as he put it—and he felt assured that he *did* trust in Christ and that he was truly saved in a way that he had never experienced before.[10] Wesley made a pilgrimage of his own to the Moravian community at Herrnhut later that same year to see it for himself and to be further equipped in faith.

Like Wesley, Bonhoeffer had links to the Moravians and Herrnhut through his mother, Paula, and his nannies. Paula Bonhoeffer had spent time in her youth at Herrnhut and had been influenced by Moravian Brethren ideas.[11] Since she gave religious instruction to her children when they were little, it's possible she passed along Moravian thought to them as well. The Bonhoeffers also employed in their household two sisters, Maria and Käthe Horn, who worked as nannies to the youngest of the eight children—the twins, Dietrich and Sabine, and the baby of the family, Susanne, were under their charge. Both Maria and Käthe had also studied at Herrnhut and identified as Moravians.

Then as now, the Moravians publish a small devotional book of Scripture verses, and each day's entry contains a verse from the Old Testament—called "the text," or Losung—and one from the New Testament—the instruction text, or Lehrtext. There is also a brief prayer that incorporates the theme of the passages.[12] Selected by lot in the city of Herrnhut, the verses are drawn up three years before publication, so the passages I read during Advent 2018 had been drawn in the year prior to our move to Berlin. I found that thought incredibly comforting.

At some point as a young adult, Bonhoeffer began the devotional practice himself, and he introduced it to many others as a small but meaningful step in making oneself more available to the word of God, to be in the presence of the truth, and to be addressed personally by the truth, as he understood it.[13] Bonhoeffer practiced the devotion, meditating on the Losungen long before he entered particular seasons of difficulty when the practice meant so much to him, like during that second journey to New York or his time of imprisonment later on. Besides the watchwords, he also read deeply and widely in the Scriptures as a whole. And when he faced those particularly trying seasons, having invested his life in the truth, he found the truth holding on to him even as he was plunged into stormy seas of doubt and, at times, despair.

He developed his own hybrid version of this meditative Scripture practice for the illegal Confessing Church seminary on the Baltic coast he led from 1935 to 1937, drawing from other traditions and making them his own. Like Wesley visiting Herrnhut, Bonhoeffer visited some Anglican monastic communities before leaving London (where he pastored two expatriate churches from 1933 to 1935) as well as Presbyterian, Methodist, and Quaker Christian communities. He was struck by the rhythms of life and practices these various traditions observed. As a self-styled abbot of a "new monasticism," as well as a new kind of Reformer in the style of Martin Luther, Bonhoeffer selected what seemed appropriate to him for the spiritual community over which he was asked to preside.[14] Not unlike a gardener experimenting with growing methods, he sampled from the traditions of the Christian communities in England as well as the meditative practices of the Moravians. The form mattered only insofar as it drew from the "only source capable of exploding the whole enchantment and specter [of the Nazis]," a life lived in response to the word, formed in the shape of Christ's Sermon on the Mount.[15]

Like John Wesley, Paula Bonhoeffer, and the Horn sisters, I wanted to visit Herrnhut too. I wanted to set foot in this place that exerted significant influence on Bonhoeffer's life, even from a distance. We booked our trip for the days just before Christmas 2018, the only time our busy holiday calendar would permit. My husband and I were excited about the timing of this visit to the Moravian town, and when the kids looked at us blankly in response, we promised them we would swing through the Dresden Christmas market on our way back home to Berlin.

• • •

When I first read about Bonhoeffer's Scripture reading, long before we moved to Berlin, I signed up to receive *Die Losungen* and the Moravian Daily Texts by email. Looking back, it was naïvely ambitious of me to sign up for both the German and English versions. When I typed my email address into the subscription box, I thought I could practice German as I wrestled out a short translation of the verses and then check my work when the North American English translation came to my inbox later in the day. That translation work never became a habit.

But I read the passages often during our tour in Berlin, looking to see what they said together, what emerged from their joint witness, what light each drew from and on the other. On some of those days—though not every day—the pairs of Scripture cast a distinct fragrance into my experience. They offered a handhold on a truth, and at times, their truth would come roaring back to me later in the day. Other days, they were a simple manna, a far-shore beam of light to steer by. Some days, I didn't look at the verses at all, or I'd glimpse but not wrestle, read but not inwardly digest. And, on others, despite my pouring the water of my attention on the little verse seeds, nothing seemed to grow.

Before Advent began in our final year in Berlin, the idea struck me that it would be good for our family to have more Scripture in our lives—specifically, to read the entire Bible through in one year. I thought it might be nice to begin a reading program and time it to begin on the First Sunday in Advent, like a New Year's resolution but timed with the Christian liturgical calendar. Before I proposed it, I prayed about it, asking God whether it was wise, whether this seed of an idea could actually sprout and take root in our family. I didn't want to just impose my idea on everyone, and I know I am prone to enthusiasm and equally so to petering out on an idea when my enthusiasm inevitably dries up. So I prayed.

Over the weeks of quietly praying, not mentioning a word of the idea to my family, I saw that my concept was still alive, having survived my initial burst of enthusiasm, so I proposed it to the reading members of our family—four out of the five of us. I offered a few possible reading schedules for us to choose from and suggested it might be a nice practice that we could carry with us as we departed Berlin for our next assignment, a comforting continuity even as our dwelling place changed. To my delight, my family agreed.

I suspect that sense of continuity gave Bonhoeffer comfort too, as he returned to his *Losungen* practice during his time of agony over whether he should return to Germany. No matter where he was in the world, whether in New York or Berlin, the word was with him too.

• • •

"Of course, many of these people who were committing these horrible acts against the Jews were still dutifully reading *Die Losungen!*" she declared with a volume markedly uncharacteristic of Germans in daily conversation. She and I were in the conference room of the Bonhoeffer-Haus, and she knew this morbid fact better than most. A pastor and regional bishop (Generalsuperintendentin) of the Berlin diocese in the Evangelische Kirche—the official Protestant Church in Germany—and a board member of the Bonhoeffer-Haus, Rev. Ulrike Trautwein was joining me on a tour. She and I had met privately beforehand to get to know one another and review our plan for the tour. I had been turning my anxieties about the tour like worry-beads in my hand, fearful that I would get the story wrong or take imaginative liberties with it.

I couldn't have had a better partner that day. Rev. Trautwein put me at ease and made many beneficial interjections into my standard discussion points on the tour. After it was over, we spent a few minutes debriefing. It was mid-August 2018, and the heat bore down as the afternoon advanced. I wiped my brow, smearing some makeup off as I did, and we laughed about that together. I felt like we had both just walked off a stage and were now collapsing into the background of the set. We both admitted that a glass of wine sounded appealing after the big performance, but all we had to drink was water. Given the heat of the day, that was definitely for the best.

She had a busy schedule ahead of her, but she took time to talk with me. She also invited me to an opening event at the newly refurbished Martin-Niemöller-Haus in Berlin-Dahlem. As part of her portfolio as regional bishop, Rev. Trautwein oversees memorial efforts. At each service, or tour, or an unveiling of a new memorial, she regularly faces the shame and guilt of human moral failure— especially the failures of those who claim to follow Christ, who claim to cherish and obey his word. Regularly, she wrestles with how much the church still needs to face its complicity in the injustices and sin of history, how much the narrative needs correction and confession, both in history and the present day. It's a mission she carries as she preaches in pulpits throughout her diocese.

Her stark words about Nazi collaborators also reading the *Losungen* slapped me awake. Bonhoeffer was not unique in reading the *Losungen* most days; then and now, it remains a cherished practice by many in Germany and throughout the world, and many read them during the Nazi years despite walking in spiritually deadly paths. The mere ingestion of the watchwords is not a magic pill that guarantees right living.

Knowing the truth and living in truth are intricately related, but they are different things. Bonhoeffer's disciplined reading in Scripture was, of course, a critical part of his life, but he still had to wrestle with what the truth of the Scriptures meant for him and how he lived, the claims it made on his life, and, having heard, he then had to live it out. Moreover, he had to listen for the whole truth, the many voices of witness that, together, make up the Bible. As the German Christians pushed to ignore the entire Old Testament—the Jewish, and thus non-Aryan, Bible, including the Psalms—Bonhoeffer insisted that the whole word of God be allowed to resonate in the lives of those who followed Jesus.[16] Scripture was not only a comfort or refuge. Far from offering an escape from the world, the Scripture Bonhoeffer prayerfully meditated on pushed him more deeply into the murky realities of life in the world. He held on to the truth through these practices and because of them he became ever more engaged in the world and its turmoil.

I remembered the bishop's warning as I ticked off the little boxes on my Scripture reading plan for the year. Uttered in the summer heat of an afternoon, Rev. Trautwein's insight returned to me again later in Advent, months after we had met together. Her wisdom joined that of John the Baptist, whose voice permeates the Advent readings in the common lectionary. The Advent calendars that line grocery store shelves have little doors that open and release a chocolate or a candy. If John the Baptist sold Advent calendars, each door opened might release a warning, a cry to repent, to turn around and go in the right direction. No candy coating.

The *Losungen* are intended to help us keep watch, but we can fail at that watch, even as we dutifully attend to the daily passages. Many read the daily verses back then, just like Bonhoeffer did, yet some still went marching in torchlight, arms raised, under the Hakenkreuz—the twisted cross better known as the swastika.

• • •

It was the evening of the fifth candle, and we were late. We climbed the stairs up to the top floor of a magnificent old building in Berlin's Kreuzberg neighborhood, the warm noise of good cheer tumbling down the staircase, drawing us up. Arriving a bit out of breath after the long climb up to the penthouse suite, we were kissed and welcomed, and we ditched our shoes at the doorstep. Glasses of wine placed in our hands, we joined the human flow toward the tables piled with food: big trays of latkes, bowls of sauces, olives, cooked fennel, zucchini, eggplant, and platters of hummus. On another table was a big box of sugar-covered donuts right next to a homemade menorah, fashioned out of bolts welded to a humble strip of metal. In the bolts stood candles, now blown out. We had missed the menorah lighting, to our chagrin.

Balancing my cup and plate, I joined my husband and one of our hosts just as he asked her about the curious-looking menorah.

"Well, menorahs were often made out of household objects, sometimes from things as simple as potatoes. One wouldn't be questioned for having potatoes in the house." She stopped for a moment, looking around their apartment packed with guests. "Whenever it has been safe to do so, we Jews celebrate Hanukkah, and it's a joy to have you here."

Celebrating with them that night in the city the Nazis once tried to make judenfrei—Jew free—was an honor, albeit an unavoidably sobering one with all of my Bonhoeffer study in mind. The tables were full of family and friends, some Jews, some gentiles like us, and together in the darkness of midwinter we gave thanks for the miracle of light, for courageous endurance, remembering life lights that had been brutally snuffed out but would never be forgotten. The Festival of Lights tends the memory of light when it seems most dark.

These dark days of winter somehow draw us together and toward light. Even after great stretches of darkness, new lights still dawn. Decades after the horrors of the Nazi era and the Holocaust, we marveled with our friend that a large menorah stood in front of the Brandenburg Gate, floodlit. It was a complicated witness but still an important one to make. It was one way to keep watch, to recognize that the last word is a true word.

Before we left for the evening, our host said she wanted to talk about my volunteer work at the Bonhoeffer-Haus. Earlier, I had told her I was writing a book about that experience, and she wanted to hear more. "I'm working on a project of my own too, in that time period," she said. A gifted filmmaker, she was beginning a project on that same dark time in history. I assured her we would find time to talk soon.

Later the next week, we spotted each other across an auditorium where each of our daughters would be performing in their school's winter holiday concert. Even though it was a full hour before the performance was scheduled to begin, the room was already packed, and there were only a few seats left, here and there. Parents were scrambling to find decent places to stand. My friend was standing along the wall close to the front of the large room, and I rushed over to greet her. She urged me stay with her there for the performance and keep her company for the long wait ahead.

"We had such a nice time the other night. Thank you for inviting us," I said, setting my purse down on the ground to begin staking out territory next to her.

"We were glad to have you. Thank you for coming."

As the auditorium continued to fill, we sat cross-legged on the floor, ducking down under the noise to return to the conversation begun at the fifth candle evening. For her own project, she had been researching Mildred Fish-Harnack (1902–1943)—the only American woman Hitler ordered put to death for her resistance efforts[17]—among others. We found ourselves talking about the significance of even very small moral actions, about why some people use their talents to benefit themselves, exploiting times of trouble, rather than working to serve others. She was searching for other stories to tell. "But the fact remains," she said with regret, "that many who made small efforts for the good are just not that well known. As each year passes, their stories are more lost to history and public memory."

The orchestra began to tune its instruments, and the lights dimmed, so we wound down our conversation. Our eyes adjusted to the darkness, spying the few parents who still circled, looking for a last free seat.

• • •

"When the Nazis enacted the Aryan Paragraph in April 1933, requiring that professionals throughout society, including pastors and academics, prove their Aryan lineage to work, Bonhoeffer could no longer stomach working in Germany," I said to a large group of visitors, pointing to the panel with photos of leaders from the Confessing Church and snapshots of the seminary. "So, he left for England and served as a pastor to two expatriate German churches in London. He prepared and delivered sermons and assisted the many German refugees that were already desperate for help. He even received a letter from the well-known Swiss academic theologian and pastor

Karl Barth, begging him to return to Germany, to stay engaged in the church struggle, which Bonhoeffer had already served so valiantly."

I continued: "The Confessing Church was the group of Christians who stood, first, against the Deutsche Christen—the German Christians who embraced Nazism in the church and society. Primarily, the Confessing Church organized to protest church Nazification, not to protest Nazism in society. Few, sadly, even in the Confessing Church, spoke up to oppose the Nazis' persecution of Jews; very few acted to resist it."

The Bekennende Kirche (Confessing Church) comprised a number of groups. The Deutsche Christen, or German Christians, formed in 1932 as an official movement of pro-Nazi Protestants. The National Socialist, or Nazi Party, had strengthened politically in the late 1920s and early 1930s but had yet to gain real power on the national stage. When Hitler came to power in 1933, the Nazis effectively made the church their own instrument, consolidating its governance under a single Reichsbishop (their Nazi puppet) and issuing policies and laws that directly affected church affairs. As these laws began negatively affecting more people within the church—especially those who could not prove their Aryan heritage—early iterations of the Confessing Church formed to assist those suffering as a result of Nazi law. Bonhoeffer was among its earliest leaders, and he believed that the church was in status confessionis—a state of confession, like a witness in a courtroom sworn to tell the truth. This Confessing Church must speak and act according to its confession of faith, a faith that he believed the German Christians had abandoned.

As the church organized into factions, the German Christians increasingly mirrored the Nazis as they consolidated power, enjoying the political support of the state. With the Nazis ratcheting up their pressure on all aspects of society, the Confessing Church had to take on experimental approaches to training its seminarians, adopting strategies and practices that would not have been considered under other circumstances. The five seminaries of the Confessing Church were set up away from places of political power and cultural influence, their remoteness proving to be a key strength: "Protected by their relative obscurity, the new seminaries were able to turn themselves into remarkable power centers of theology."[18] When the Confessing Church approached Bonhoeffer to establish one of these pastoral training centers, it was an opportunity for him to lay the groundwork for "a new kind of monasticism."[19] Bonhoeffer started his seminary in bare-bones fashion in the Baltic coastal town of Zingst, where classes were often held on the dunes. But when the weather turned colder in late 1935, the seminary moved to Finkenwalde, near the town of Stettin (now Szczecin, Poland). Few, if any, of the incoming students knew of Bonhoeffer's plans for this seminary, and they might have been leery of them if the times were not so desperate.

Bonhoeffer decided the community, like any monastic order, would have a rule of life—a rhythm to the day, incorporating prayer, work, and study. The most grating of these new monastic disciplines for the seminarians was the required half-hour-long meditation and silent prayer on a piece of Scripture, held after breakfast and before a session of theological study. The students largely found the exercise so frustrating, so alien to their Christian practices, and increasingly such a source of resentment that the community met to discuss. They debated things like whether one might smoke a pipe during their time of meditation. This meditation exercise was one among many that set the Finkenwalde seminary apart from the other Confessing Church training centers; these robust practices of communal living were simply not the Prussian way of doing things.

The council of the Old Prussian Church, the Confessing Church body that had extended its invitation to Bonhoeffer, questioned his approach too. Even the famous theologian Karl Barth, who was expelled from his teaching post at the University of Bonn for refusing allegiance to Hitler in 1935, expressed his concern over "an indefinable odor of the eros and pathos of the cloister," which he worried Bonhoeffer was fanning as the self-styled abbot of the community.[20] Wilhelm Rott, the inspector of studies at the Finkenwalde seminary for the Confessing Church, shared skepticism of the whole enterprise, but he was won over in time. He wrote that while he had initially been concerned about the possibility of fanaticism at Finkenwalde, he learned there "the practice of meditation on the Bible to my lasting profit."[21]

When asked about the required practice of Scripture meditation at Finkenwalde, Eberhard Bethge replied, "Why do I meditate? Because I am a Christian, and because therefore every day is a day lost for me in which I have not penetrated deeper into the understanding of the word of God in scripture." Bethge described the practice: seminarians meditated on a selection of Scripture, a single passage of ten to fifteen verses, for an entire week. He surmised that a half hour was the *minimum* amount of time that should be given to this practice each day. Bethge said that when he engaged in scripture meditation alone, practicing the discipline within the larger community, he became more aware that others were praying too, not only the brothers at Finkenwalde but the community of the entire church. The silence of the solitary prayer connected him to the company of heaven and earth.[22]

The seminary community held classes for two short years, from 1935 until the Gestapo shuttered its doors in 1937. But even then, the community reorganized, basing at churches in Eastern

Pomerania (today northern Poland) where seminarians were trained in apprentice-like settings at Confessing Churches. The Scripture meditation practices Bonhoeffer inaugurated at Finkenwalde persisted even after the institutions were formally closed.

• • •

Bonhoeffer's last legally published piece of writing was about the Psalms: *Das Gebetbuch der Bibel,* or *The Prayerbook of the Bible.*[23] When it was published, the Reich Board for the Regulation of Literature issued Bonhoeffer a fine for failing to submit the manuscript for review. Eventually, they repealed the fine but then banned him from publishing again.[24] Despite its small size, the book is loaded with spiritual dynamite.

Bonhoeffer believed prayer could be taught and learned and that the book of Psalms was the great schoolhouse of prayer. His commentary opens with the plea, "Lord, Teach Us to Pray!" These are the same words Jesus's disciples said to him and in response to which he taught them the words commonly called the Lord's Prayer. As a Christian, Bonhoeffer placed the figure of Jesus in the center of his meditation on prayer and the Psalms, reminding his readers then that as a Jewish boy, Jesus himself learned to pray in the Psalms, and as a man, dying on a Roman cross, some of his last words came from the Psalter. Because Jesus prayed these prayers, Bonhoeffer wrote, we can pray them too—a radical statement in Nazi Germany, where the compliant Reichskirche sought to "de-Judaize" the Bible.

What Bonhoeffer did not write in this slim book, but is evident from some of his letters, is that praying the Psalms also helped him make sense of and manage his intense emotions as his life grew increasingly complicated.[25] During the last half of the 1930s,

Bonhoeffer was teaching, traveling, meeting with all kinds of people, and maintaining heavy correspondence loads. As the decade turned, he then began his double-agent work in German military intelligence, the Abwehr, as well. By the time he was arrested and taken into custody on April 5, 1943, Bonhoeffer had developed deep habits of leaning on the Scriptures in prayer. When Bonhoeffer joined his heart in prayer, whether when traveling before his arrest or after, when he was in prison, even though he was very alone, he joined the prayers of the scattered Confessing Church community and the company of heaven and earth.

Praying drew him out of himself and equipped him to serve others, even when he was in prison. His prayer practices prevented his "conspiratorial actions from degenerating into self-righteousness," recentering his gaze on the truth, renewing his grip on the word.[26] Prayer kept the heavy weights of his responsibilities from crushing him entirely. It was the great stream in which he could connect his own life with God's, his solitary and peripatetic life with a larger community, and keep a sharp watch on the needs and injustices around him. Prayer offered him solace and simultaneously plunged him more deeply into the needs of the world.

• • •

"Wherever the Psalter is abandoned, an incomparable treasure vanishes from the Christian church. With its recovery will come unsuspected power," I read aloud to my best friend from college as we drove from Minneapolis to Duluth, Minnesota, on our way to her graduation from her doctoral program in May 2016.[27] I had packed Bonhoeffer's book on the Psalms in my luggage, the only book our local public library had on its shelves that Bonhoeffer himself wrote.

As she drove, her fancy robe and doctoral hood hanging in the back seat, I read portions from the book out loud. She listened quietly for a while, noticing how moved I was by the book.

"Why are you so into this material?" she asked.

"You know how I've been reading a lot for Berlin; that's part of it. But it's more than that. I feel like things are shifting in the world that I'm completely helpless to change. These words about prayer are so, well . . . they help me feel less despairing and stuck. Remember when I was so excited about Kathleen Norris, the poet, and her book about writing and acedia—that vicious combination of sloth, pride, and apathy? How she prayed the Psalms to fight acedia? Reading Bonhoeffer's thoughts about the Psalms reminded me of that."

Two and half years later, this same friend left me a message, asking how my writing of this book was going, adding, "You're going to have to remind me how you came to study Bonhoeffer so much! Was it just proximity?"

Proximity helped, but there were patterns in Bonhoeffer's life that I recognized in myself—not his adventurous and breathless pace of life, nor his standing in society or the church, but more so his inner life, his thoughts and moods, aspects of himself that aren't accessible in his theological writing. These elements of his soul are also far more commonly experienced by others. Several popular books have reintroduced the word *acedia* to public parlance, chiefly posed by Kathleen Norris. In her 2008 book, *Acedia and Me*, Norris explored how this once mortal sin of the church fell from that ignoble list, wrapped up into the sin of sloth. When Norris learned the word, learned about its history, she discovered how important it was to have the name of a condition she herself knew well.

Pressed down with a feeling of morbid fatigue, an inertia and listlessness that at times found her binge-reading romance novels but ignoring the writing work she needed to do, Norris alighted on the lost term and researched it as much as I did Bonhoeffer. Careful to distinguish acedia from depression, Norris describes a soul that has succumbed to the temptation of acedia as incapable of "[rousing] yourself to give a damn."[28] An acedic soul has fallen out of love with life itself, unable to care in the face of life's monotony.

For the human heart to keep caring, to keep giving a damn, one cannot avoid the pain of life. At that crossroads between entering into life's troubles or withdrawing from them, acedia offers a deceptive escape: better to slip into the "ease of indifference," the numbing bliss that it promises. It's a shape-shifting condition; the symptoms of acedia begin as an "anxious boredom," develop into "frantic activity" as the sufferer attempts to deny her growing inner pain, and finally mature into "psychospiritual numbness."[29] These very different stages make it tricky to diagnose. Chiefly, it's marked by a restlessness that is so dissatisfied with the present moment or place, and then so desperate for numbing distractions, and finally so overwhelmed by an unending future of this wretched dynamic that a person is unable to work or pray. A soul suffering from acedia constantly looks elsewhere, no matter where it is, to escape the overwhelming tedium of now, until the heart hardens into a stony numbness.

Drawing from Christian monastics who first diagnosed and sought to offer sufferers help for this spiritual condition, Norris learned that one of the most effective acedia-busting practices is praying the Psalms. Those ancient prayers are full of care, replete with life's pain, set in poetic language that wakes up the soul. In the Psalms we hear the voices of others who also contended with life's monotony and frustration and with entrenched communal injustices. Collectively, the Psalms beg for a sign that there is more to life than *this*, ad infinitum; they ask God where God is and whether

God has forsaken us—the very words Jesus uttered on the cross in agony, words he knew from having prayed them all his life. In all their bracing reality, the Psalms offer companionship in suffering and an instructive mirror that shows us who we are and points the way out of ourselves and back into life. The Psalms don't offer an escape from life; they offer a way to *avoid* escaping it—a way back from stone into flesh.

Acedia troubled Bonhoeffer too; he sometimes called it *tristitia*, that inner malaise that weighed on him. A classic case, Bonhoeffer's acedia was an exquisite cocktail of pride, self-righteousness, contempt for others, isolation, and despair. For a long time, only his best friend and confessor, Eberhard Bethge, knew how much Bonhoeffer suffered from this condition. In his cell at the Tegel military prison, where he was held after his arrest for a period of confinement that dragged on for eighteen months, Bonhoeffer wrestled with the meaninglessness of his incarceration.[30] But in the words of the Psalter, in the prayers of Jesus, he found anchor and meaning, company in his solitude, and strength for the days and the nights ahead and the many miseries in each. In all the places from which he longed to find escape from life's travails, prayer opened Bonhoeffer's heart to the word of God, and the word of God gently led him back to his life and responsibility, infused with hope and peace, even in prison.

• • •

When we depart from Berlin, I hope there will be a grassy lawn for the next occupants of our house. I want them to inherit a living, healthy hedge. In the meantime, I have to take care; I must rouse myself to give a damn, do the work necessary to ensure the grass and hedge survive for the next generation of inhabitants. I know I won't always feel like doing these duties, but my faithfulness to these small tasks matters to those who will inherit this yard when they move in.

Of course, it takes hardly any effort not to care, and I am free to take that route. I could simply stop caring: let the grass die, watch the hedge wither, ignore my German neighbor's entreaties, and give no thought to these future residents. I could lie to myself and say that I owe them all *nothing*, that it's not my responsibility to steward. But this would be not only indulgent on my part but also false. We human beings owe one another a lot, all the time, and that includes us maintaining our capacity to give a damn. It's how we stay human for one another. It's how we stay free and how we finally experience joy—a joy that acedia snuffs out.

I wonder sometimes whether the word *acedia* needs to be reclaimed to make sense of our civic and political lives as well. The widespread despair, cynicism, indifference, and hopelessness that plagued monks long ago are, I think, fairly recognizable in neighborhoods and communities today. Distractions surround us, allowing us to slip into the fog of indifference. There, we can anesthetize our disappointments, find scapegoats to blame, and experience (false) release from our responsibility to care. As in every age, we must find a way in this time to recover our cares in the laments of the Psalmist, to let those wise words penetrate our hearts and minds and even revive our civic and political will—not to some lost greatness, but simply to care.

Politics is the hard, often boring work of living a common life. It's the love of neighbor expressed in pothole filling and road paving, trash collecting, and pollution solving, compromise and deliberation, justice and restoration. The Psalms offer us words to recover our sense of civic belonging, rekindle our love for our neighbors and fellow citizens, and maintain them for future generations. They are watchwords, worth recovering.

• • •

Writing at the desk in his bedroom at the Bonhoeffer-Haus near Christmas 1942, Bonhoeffer wondered in his essay "After Ten Years" about the "dearth of civil courage" among his fellow Germans during the Nazi years. Curiously, he saw a lack of civil courage even among those who had joined resistance efforts. Courage and acedia are related: it takes courage to face the truth about ourselves and also to keep alive our capacity to care. Prayer is the water that grows the seeds of courage, that prunes the disease of our hearts and keeps hope alive. In prayer, as the Moravians discovered in their prayer meeting that lasted for an entire century, and as Bonhoeffer knew from praying the Psalms and meditating on Scripture, there is "unsuspected power."

During the Cold War, when the Iron Curtain was drawn to separate the democratic West and the communist East, people who had forgotten how to pray, who didn't know the words, gathered to do so. Starting in 1982 in Leipzig's Nikolaikirche (St. Nicholas Church), people gathered on Monday nights to pray for peace. The prayer meetings grew, and so did the people's courage and hope. So they kept praying, and after praying, they marched on a path in the city that led them right past the headquarters of the State Security (Stasi, in the abbreviated German). Their dreaded Runde Ecke (Round Corner) building was used by the Gestapo during the Nazi era, then handed over to the Soviets at the end of World War II, when it then became the "threatening stronghold" of the Stasi, the East German domestic spy agency. "Conversation ceased" when people passed in front of it during the Stasi's forty-year reign.[31] The people had the courage to march because they had done the hidden work of prayer. They held on to the truth in prayer, and the truth held on to them, protecting them from despair. They prayed for themselves and for future generations of citizens and discovered they were not afraid to march. After seven years, their prayers were answered as the Berlin Wall came tumbling down. Social action and prayer are connected. Like them, we may simply need to recover the words again.

• • •

My son was heavily asleep on my chest, snoring softly, as we sang hymns in the Grosse Saal, the Great Hall, of the Moravian Church in Herrnhut. Called Herrnhut's "living room," it is a cavernous and spare meeting space, full of long white benches and, that night, also full of candles and evergreen boughs, and hymn singers like us. An exquisite 110-point Herrnhuter star glowed and gently turned above our heads, the rising warmth of our songs below causing it to stir. On this Saturday night before the Fourth Sunday in Advent, we sang, heard readings from Scripture, and drank in the bright and subversive joy of the brass band playing from the balcony.

Earlier in the day, we had driven three hours from Berlin in a steady and sullen rain. Dropping our bags at the Jesus Haus, an old turn-of-the-century hospital converted into the meeting place and guest house of a charismatic Moravian community, we headed out to explore before everything closed for the weekend—and for Christmas. Thankfully, the Moravian Star Factory was still open and bustling with business, star makers crafting their wares on display in the main room, delicately gluing star points to their frames. We took in an informative series of panels detailing aspects of the Moravian Church's history and culture, including that century-long prayer meeting and the continued publication of the watchwords.

There, we learned that the star grew out of the Moravian legacy of integrating faith and learning. It was one teacher's inventive way of capturing the mystery and majesty of the star of Bethlehem that led the Wise Men to baby Jesus, and of packing in a geometry lesson in the mix. The teacher taught students how to make these stars, in a Moravian boarding school, out of paper and cardboard, and those students brought the geometric tradition home. A business-man named Pieter Hendrix Verbeek began producing the stars on a larger, more commercial scale with his innovative design using paper on a metal frame.

The business followed the fits and starts of Germany's political life. During the Nazi years, star makers were unable to distribute their product internationally and so took up lampshade making for a time.[32] After the war, the business was nationalized under the Communist East German government and eventually closed in 1968. It relaunched under church management but was still heavily regulated by the state, operating in the "economy of scarcity" that characterized East Germany.[33] It reopened again in 1991, as a free enterprise, a business of the church.

The back of the factory houses a brightly decorated room where children of all ages can make these many-pointed stars for themselves. Long benches line long tables with workstations, and the room is awash in primary colors. With help from watchful attendants, our children picked the colors they wanted for their stars out of the bins available, and my husband and I periodically shepherded the gluing. Finally, three little glowing spiky stars emerged from their work.

I savored these new memories as we soaked in the gentle tones of the Advent hymns in that "living room." When the service concluded, my husband lifted our sleeping son from my arms, and we walked into the cold darkness and down the street to the Jesus Haus.

In nearly every window and above most doorways were glowing Moravian stars, piercing the darkness, sharp and bright, geometric and beautiful. After we tucked everyone into their beds, I noticed a copy of *Die Losungen*, the published watchwords, on the nightstand, and read the words for the day: "Happy are all who take refuge in him" (Psalm 2:12) and "Paul wrote: I know whom I have trusted, and I am sure that he is able to keep safe what he has entrusted to me" (2 Timothy 1:12). I fell asleep marveling at the protection the Moravian refugees found here in Herrnhut, the nurturing that the community offered to Paula Bonhoeffer and the Horn sisters, the strong tower that the Moravian texts became for Bonhoeffer and then countless others because of him. The word that held on to them all continues to shine, piercing the darkness. Bonhoeffer held on to the truth of the word of God, and the truth of the word of God held on to him, even when the darkness finally swallowed him up.

Zionskirche, Berlin

Chapter 5

CROSSING BOUNDARIES

→ *Key: When we venture beyond home with curiosity,*
we are given the chance to understand ourselves, our
world, and our responsibility to that world better. ←

The neighborhood has changed considerably.

A friend invited us to lunch to celebrate her birthday at her favorite restaurant in the city—a raw vegan place in Berlin's Prenzlauer Berg. Gentrified, full of trendy restaurants and shops, but retaining some of its earlier edge, the neighborhood felt so far from our genteel and stuffy one near the Grunewald. Sipping kombucha and admiring the beautifully plated kelp and zucchini noodles with avocado, I had a hard time picturing Prenzlauer Berg as it had been in the past, whether during Bonhoeffer's time or even after the Cold War.

After the Berlin Wall came down in 1989, a famously belligerent squatting culture sprang up in this former East Berlin working-class neighborhood, a social phenomenon that emerged as the broken halves of Germany were brought back together. Reunification is not work for the foolhardy. Repairing tears in the social and political fabric is delicate and difficult work, and new injustices emerge just as others seem to get rectified.

For Prenzlauer Berg, one of the troubles was real estate. Turn-of-the-century buildings once owned by the Communist government-affiliated housing associations changed into private hands. Predictably, rents rose, far outpacing what tenants could pay. Facing eviction, some refused to budge, and a wild, creative, and at times conflicted squatting culture formed in the neighborhood. Over time, gentrification slowly spread, and it brought in its wake restaurants like the one in which we were now singing "Happy Birthday" and munching on slate plates of kelp.

Prohibitive rent hikes were not new to Prenzlauer Berg or other parts of the city. Beginning in the mid-1800s, the ripple effects of Germany's Industrial Revolution, coupled with poor harvests and famine, drove many who lived in more rural areas to cities in search of work. The Potato Revolution of 1847 sparked violence in the streets of Berlin. In what is now Poland, the traditional linen weavers of Silesia revolted as well, unable to compete with the new methods of industrial production, and the Prussian military put them down brutally.[1] Massive internal migration sent desperate and hungry people to Berlin, and tent cities began to form on the city's edge.[2] In an effort to house these massive influxes of people, Berlin began a massive building project, and the tenement buildings put up during this time had a classic design: large apartment structures with inner courtyards, called Hinterhöfe. Alas, these courtyarded housing complexes were "dark, infested, and despised" and very densely populated.[3] The neighborhood in Bonhoeffer's day continued to be rough, crowded, and poor when he rented a small apartment on Oderberger Strasse from a baker in 1932 so he could be closer to a confirmation class he was teaching. Bonhoeffer called the neighborhood "proletarian."[4]

• • •

In very unproletarian ways, we were on vacation in a farming village not far from Freiburg, deep in Germany's Black Forest territory, but my mind was wending its way to Harlem in New York City. Out the window of our Airbnb rental was hilly green pasture, and beyond that the browns, yellows, and reds of autumn trees. The fields were dotted with traditional farmhouses with their steep, sloping half-hipped roofs reaching almost to the ground, wide balconies disclosing magnificent views. Red and white dappled cows grazed on the hill just below our window, lowing periodically. In another pen, a few calves frolicked like preschoolers. When we approached them on a walk, they were both shy and boldly curious in equal measure, taking side looks at us and bumping into one another for courage when we wandered over to the fence to say hello, hands outstretched.

My husband took our three kids out for a morning walk, and from the window I watched them in this idyllic world. A couple of flies buzzed above my head on the screen, trying to find their way back out into the world into which I peered. The bright blue skies of yesterday were now covered with today's clouds, a few low enough to veil and blur the tree-lined edges of these low hills.

Our drive here from Heidelberg on a stretch of the celebrated Schwarzwaldhochstrasse—the Black Forest Highway, the famous B500—offered spectacular valley views and adventurous turns, a welcome change from an earlier stretch of dull highway driving, full of trucks. When the turnoff for the scenic route appeared, we took it and started climbing, our ears popping with the change in altitude. The highway was canopied by tall spruce trees, swaddled by carpets of green moss and browning ferns that gave off a note of cinnamon in the chill air. And before all this sounds too good to be true, know that one of our kids almost immediately began to feel carsick.

The threat of a messy back seat forced us to take many small breaks. We stopped to stretch our legs and peer into the gunmetal waters of the Mummelsee glacial lake, and after another stretch of switchbacking on the way to Triberg, we smirked our way through the incessantly ticking House of 1000 Clocks, a tourist-trap souvenir shop replete with traditional cuckoos. Arriving in Triberg, with all of us now fighting off a creeping feeling of nausea, we stopped yet again to trek up to the town's famous waterfall, the highest in Germany yet tamed by a nearby paved trail.

All along that drive, through various small towns, roadside crucifixes stood on poles—covered with that same steep rooftop so common to houses in this part of Germany, a strange mantle of protection for the crucified Jesus of Nazareth laid bare on a cross. One of these shrines is depicted on the center panel of photographs at the Bonhoeffer-Haus, Jesus on the cross next to a posted threat to Jews, a familiar sight in the Nazi 1930s but latent in culture long before that. Seeing these shrines on the drive, without the anti-Semitic signage, flooded me with an anxiety that I wouldn't have felt prior to volunteering at the Bonhoeffer-Haus. The roadside crucifixes now looked more complicated to me. All the storybook scenery of the Black Forest we took in from the car—the giant spruce trees, the moss, the delightful sensation that Hänsel und Gretel might actually appear—was punctuated by this roadside piety, which now looked strange and forbidding as I held that Bonhoeffer-Haus panel in mind.

For any trip, our family tends to pack more books than clothes, and I did the same in preparation for this one. In addition to a hilariously large pile of books from my own bookcase, I also tucked in Laban Carrick Hill's *Harlem Stomp!* from my children's bookshelf. I planned to do some imaginative journeying on vacation. I wanted to learn more about Harlem and the Harlem Renaissance, and Hill's book was my small window into that world, one just as foreign to me as the landscape out the farmhouse window.

The master poet Nikki Giovanni wrote the foreword to *Harlem Stomp!*, a fact that grabbed my attention. In it, she celebrates the achievements of this remarkable era of human creativity, insight, and reclaimed ambition. The monumental contributions to culture that African Americans made during the Harlem Renaissance grew out of a long, deep suffering of injustice, catastrophic exploitation, and dehumanization. The Harlem Renaissance, Giovanni writes, is evidence of a suffering people's endurance, a creative refusal to believe the lies of the powerful and indifferent, and a great affirmation of the freedom of freed people.

As I paged through the book, immersing myself in the rich illustrations and stories, I was startled by my ignorance. I knew the term "Harlem Renaissance" but only recognized a few of the great names mentioned in the book. Giovanni cautions, rightly, that if the American story now boasts of blues and jazz and the golden treasure chest that is the spirituals (which it does, thank God), "that can only be true if Blacks are an American people."[5] But as an American—as a white American—I did not know this story. Knowing that I did not know it exposed the complications of the American story I am prone to narrate to myself, one as complicated as those roadside shrines.

With help from Hill's book, I looked into another world. There, I learned that the Harlem Renaissance had its own language, traditions, customs, and solutions for day-to-day survival. Jive, dance, rent parties! There, I met Satchmo—that is, Louis Armstrong—who wowed crowds with his musical prowess and unique playing style, and Duke Ellington, who reigned at the Cotton Club just across from the famous Savoy Ballroom. Hill introduced me to Willie "the Lion" Smith and to the famous "cutting contests," musical duels waged by pianists that would go on for hours, in which the musicians would "embroider the melodies" in a realm of "pure improvisation."[6] These were high-altitude flights of human creativity.

I wanted to journey to Harlem because Bonhoeffer had too. Bonhoeffer visited Harlem about halfway through his yearlong residency in New York City, where he arrived for the academic year in 1930 as a Sloane Fellow at Union Theological Seminary. All in all, Bonhoeffer was fairly unimpressed by the American academic theology scene at Union. He thought the students blew a lot of hot air, thinking at such a shallow level that it frustrated him. His experience in New York improved considerably, however, when another Sloane Fellow invited him to visit a church in Harlem. Of the many important influences and places during Bonhoeffer's year in New York, it was in Harlem where he finally found some deep, living theology.

I don't know whether he attended any musical improvisation "battles," but I can imagine Bonhoeffer, the accomplished pianist, completely mesmerized by cutting contests in Harlem just as he had been by Mass in Rome's Sistine Chapel years earlier, when he traveled there with his older brother Klaus. These glowing settings of creative human daring reached a finger out of the dark to feel the divine touch on the other side. I think Bonhoeffer the musician would have been amazed by this realm of genius wholly beyond his culture and vocabulary.

It is doubtful New York would have been as significant or transformative for Bonhoeffer if Albert Franklin Fisher had not invited him to the Abyssinian Baptist Church on West 138th Street.[7] A significant institution then and now, the church was in a highly competitive field of houses of worship. At the time of the Harlem Renaissance, there were more than 160 African American churches in the neighborhood, planted as a result of the huge migratory wave of African Americans, who came north to escape the poverty, indignity, injustice, and violence of the South and try to achieve what the Emancipation Proclamation failed to allow them to do: secure a better life and enjoy a greater measure of freedom.[8] More than just places of worship, the churches were also, in a way, little cities of their own, offering social connection and meaningful help to those who, having fled the Jim Crow South, continued to suffer under the more sophisticated but still unjust prejudices of the American North. Church was a place to recover identity and reclaim dignity after being robbed of both throughout the work week, a place to lay burdens down for a time and to help shoulder others'.

Bonhoeffer's year in the United States revealed the operating power of the "color line" in American life, as W. E. B. Du Bois put it.[9] With the kind of clear-eyed sight that expatriates often develop, Bonhoeffer saw what many white Americans could not (or would not): theirs was a house structured around race, color, and class, and their theology was a load-bearing wall in it.

Dietrich and his older brother Karl-Friedrich exchanged letters during his year in New York in which they talked about race, and Karl-Friedrich admitted to Dietrich that he was so shocked by the race problems in the United States that he had declined a position at Harvard to avoid any personal entanglements in them. He wrote that Germany's "Jewish problem" paled in comparison to America's "black" one.

I found Karl-Friedrich's bald description of American racial injustices from my post-Holocaust position appalling. Both evils—American slavery and the Holocaust—were ruthlessly organized, monetized, and entirely legal according to the laws of their day. But in his starkly worded comparison, I faced a sober indictment. White Americans have not even begun to reckon with our sordid, catastrophic history, our inheritance of guilt and shame, and entrenched injustices. We lag far, far behind Germany's own limping attempts to reckon with its national sins.

My studies in Bonhoeffer's life were prompting me to reevaluate aspects of my own. Without learning about his time in Harlem, I never would have found myself paging through a children's book about the Harlem Renaissance in a Black Forest farmhouse. But there I sat, overwhelmed by how little I knew of this history, even though it belongs more to my national story than Bonhoeffer does. Sitting with that book, I felt thoroughly disabused of my guiltless expatriate identity here in Germany while wholly avoiding my own moral responsibilities, my share in the national guilt and shame, of America's color line.

I'll admit that I judged those roadside shrines in the Black Forest, not least because I didn't see myself as implicated in their complicated guilt. My national story may not have these shrines, but it has lynching trees, statues conferring honor on the dishonorable, coffee counters and water fountains, places where white Americans sneered and shouted and rained violence upon black Americans. These cast a warning, an indictment, of their own.

• • •

When he crossed the wide, watery boundary of the Atlantic, Bonhoeffer was primed to want more than just to passively observe the United States as a tourist. And yet, he found a world quite familiar to the one he had just left in Germany. New York City was in the grip of the Great Depression, suffering from massive unemployment. His year at Union Theological Seminary (1930–1931) was intended to be cross-pollinating, preparatory, and personally and professionally expanding. Here, he could wrestle with his identity and direction and experience the great city of New York. But just like conversation in the seminary classrooms, he found the worship and sermons in (white, wealthy) churches, such as Riverside Presbyterian, flat and self-satisfied. Bonhoeffer was well beyond playing at theology or at church. There were still more boundaries to cross, and his friendship with Fisher, an African American, proved to be incredibly significant—a powerful shift, as it was highly unlikely that Bonhoeffer had ever had a meaningful conversation with a black person in Berlin.[10]

Before coming to New York in the summer of 1930, Bonhoeffer had already had some meaningful boundary crossing experiences. After defending his first dissertation, he worked as an assistant in a German expatriate church in Barcelona, which was his first experience living abroad (1928). The Germans he met in Barcelona seemed quite different than those of Berlin's heady Grunewald. At times he enjoyed the parishioners' hospitality, socializing and taking in entertainments—including bullfights!—but he tested his pastor-theologian wings as well, preparing and delivering sermons and a series of public lectures. Even though he was surrounded by German expatriates, however, he found the scene bereft of the serious intellectual approach to life he was accustomed to in Berlin.[11] Places shape people, and so do shared experiences in those places. The Germans living in Barcelona had not experienced World War I like those in Germany had, and their lives were characterized more by ease and comfort, oriented on profit rather than philosophy.[12]

With its languid afternoons under the Mediterranean sun, Barcelona also shaped Bonhoeffer. Uncharacteristically, he found it difficult to focus, study, and write, often succumbing to sleep as the afternoon sun beat down on his room. When he awoke from these naps, he felt no more inclined to study than when he had drifted off.[13]

He knew he had to write a second dissertation, the so-called habilitation requirement that would allow him to offer lectures in a German university, but he found it difficult to organize himself toward that end. Even for Bonhoeffer, Barcelona proved to be a difficult place to do intellectual work.

That's not to say that Barcelona was only a place of mental atrophy. He wrote sermons and, as noted earlier, a series of fairly serious lectures for a twenty-two-year-old. Notably, however, in his last lecture given in Barcelona, Bonhoeffer toyed aloud with themes more akin with German nationalism—"the Christianity of the Germanic warrior tradition."[14] Despite all he had experienced in the cross-cultural currents of Barcelona, and even despite his liberal, humanist upbringing at home, he had not escaped the dominant tradition of thought in Germany.

Like it did in Germany, the economic suffering in America in 1930 hit vulnerable communities hardest, as crises always do. New York City was no exception. I once asked my grandmother about her memories of living through the Great Depression in the more rural part of upstate New York, and she recalled that for her and her family, that era was not easy, but it was far less traumatic for them than for those whose lives were more dependent on the city's flourishing. She did not suffer the humiliating desperation like the city dwellers did. She and her family and neighbors lived closer to the earth—I often asked her to tell me about helping to slaughter chickens as a girl, a scene I would replay in my mind with fascination and horror. Their rural economy, their web of value and mutual exchange, didn't collapse as severely as the house of cards did downstate.

That suffering was palpable in New York City, and yet in Harlem, Bonhoeffer found a world quite rich in culture that had emerged from even deeper wells of suffering. Harlem caused him to question ideas he once held about America—arguably, ideas that America had (and still has) about itself. Bonhoeffer said that being in Harlem showed him "the real face of America, something that is hidden behind the veil of words in the American constitution that 'all men are created free and equal.'"[15] The reality he saw did not match the words.

Founded in 1808, the Abyssinian Baptist Church was the first African American Baptist church in New York State, established by a small group of worshippers who refused to be forced to sit in segregated seating at another Baptist church in New York City.[16] One hundred years after its founding, the Rev. Dr. Adam Clayton Powell Sr., became its senior pastor, and he set a theological course for the church that was characterized by social activism and community engagement.[17] As the Harlem Renaissance dawned, the church purchased property at its current location and from there was poised to be a key anchor for many people in the Great Migration of African Americans beginning during World War I and in subsequent waves of the "radical rearranging" of America's black citizens.[18]

The church was unlike anything Bonhoeffer had experienced before. Besides its worship services, the church also expressed its life in service to real human needs, offering both spiritual care and practical solutions for its congregants. The tenor of the community reminded him of the intellectual rigor and vitality he was accustomed to in his Grunewald neighborhood back in Berlin; the intensity of these worlds mirrored one another, including the robust intellectualism. Those affiliated with the Harlem Renaissance gave birth to new alphabets, vocabularies, and ways of imagining the world, fostering enormous cultural output, "a literary movement that spoke about black culture, black political agency, and a black Jesus."[19] Unlike the white Christ of European Christianity, so closely tied to colonial endeavors under which nonwhite others were subjected, oppressed, and exploited, the black Jesus of Harlem was a figure who knew suffering and oppression as they did. He was a Jesus from whom white Christians recoiled instinctively.[20]

Because Bonhoeffer, too, was an alien in this landscape, as a German he could see things that white Americans could not see about themselves and their faith commitments. He approached Harlem and the church with rapt curiosity, spending as much of his free time as he could there, reading African American literature, and synthesizing what he was learning experientially with his classes at Union. In this setting Bonhoeffer encountered a theology developed out of suffering and powerlessness, a theology of the cross in which the centerpiece of the cross retained its horror and shame but, paradoxically, offered solidarity and strength to those who clung to it in faith. Many of the congregants of the Abyssinian Baptist Church were middle-class African Americans who, by many standards, had achieved evident success in the world, but they were still black people in a white person's world—more precisely, black Christians in a white Christians' world.[21] This oppressive environment was the crucible in which their theology of the cross had formed.

That theology was sung, preached, lived, and practiced in community. Bonhoeffer collected records of beloved spirituals, and these became albums cherished by Germans in the resistance later on.[22] Bonhoeffer also participated in Sunday school and led two Bible studies. He witnessed how the gospel mattered to the poor, who were served by the church. The teachings of Rev. Dr. Powell long reverberated in Bonhoeffer's imagination, including in the idea he articulated later in his life: the Christological incognito, a way of thinking about Jesus that Jesus himself offered (Matthew 25:31–46). The Christological incognito is Christ obscured by his being "'an outcast among outcasts,' hiding himself in weakness."[23] Clearly, Bonhoeffer gathered far more theological resources in Harlem than spirituals, which were also potent theological tools.[24]

Another friend of Bonhoeffer's at Union, Paul Lehmann, actually grew worried that Bonhoeffer was "spending too much time in Harlem."[25] But what is clear is that Bonhoeffer's deep fascination with, immersion in, and even collection of resources like spirituals in this world served as an important bridge of supplies and reinforcements for resistance and endurance in another world: his own.

• • •

Besides the Bonhoeffer-Haus, one of my favorite places in Berlin to take visitors is the Berlin Wall Memorial and Documentation Center on Bernauer Strasse on the east side of Berlin's Mitte neighborhood, a stone's throw from Prenzlauer Berg. Across the street from the visitor center is a grassy stretch once dominated by the Cold War–era wall and its infamous "death strip." Now, tall, artistic-looking poles of rebar, passable and porous, mark the scar-path of the wall. The center features an excellent museum of the era, those immediate post–World War II years of great power tussles over this ruined and rubbled piece of real estate. The contest was both political and spiritual. The long, cold battle before the wall fell was waged on both of those fronts too.

The most striking feature of the museum is found outside, an overlook onto Bernauer Strasse. One climbs a metal staircase to the lookout, from which a visitor can take in the distinctive towers and spires of the city on a clear day and, below, look into a preserved section of the wall—which, of course, means more than a mere wall. The preserved area lays bare the whole apparatus of control, for the wall answered none of the problems the Soviets hoped it would. They built the wall to stop a mass migration of Germans out of the Soviet-controlled East, another radical rearrangement in which one-sixth of East Germany's population had fled west.[26] From the platform, visitors can also peer down into the death strip, which in some places was up to 160 yards wide, a raked sand pit sandwiched between the wall itself and another interior one. Guard towers punctuated this twenty-seven-mile snaking structure at intervals, equipped with barbed wire, ramparts, trenches, "dogs on cable runs," and trip wires.[27]

As dominating as the structure was before it was torn down in 1989, it began small, with barbed wire rolled out overnight on August 13, 1961. Concrete eventually joined the barbed wire, and then the whole apparatus grew on the ground and up into the air, and by accretions in people's minds and hearts. Someone trying to escape from East Germany didn't just have to scale a single wall. They had to scale two and survive the fish-in-a-barrel design in between them. But before they could even begin to plan such a daring reach, they had to scale walls in their own minds, take flight into hope like a bird, breathe it in, and then chart their course. No wonder so many took to tunneling, which required a subterranean faith of its own.

On one of my parents' visits to see us in Berlin, we visited this wall memorial and museum. We entered the story of Berlin's exile-at-home, listening to video and audio interviews of those who made the escape. We saw how concrete barriers divided families from one another, and how ideologies split soul from spirit. The whole catastrophic structure marked a generation. Privately, friends raised in the "island" of West Berlin say they can tell almost immediately whether someone was raised in the East, a formation that one simply does not shake off or undo. And also privately, in reply, those raised in the East say the same thing about acquaintances and friends from West Berlin.

The upstairs floor of the visitor center focuses on how the Berlin Wall came down, the many attempts to create cracks in it, and the brave souls who disobeyed the oppressive powers. It shows how prayer proved an unstoppable force, beginning with prayer meetings in Leipzig, which sparked the peaceful revolution. The prayers lifted in Leipzig gave the people courage to march around the imagined walls of their city and those in their minds until the wall fell.

In the end, one little word felled it, in what many refer to as a historical accident. Under the pressure of thousands of East German refugees seeking asylum in West German embassies of the Eastern Bloc, the Communist government had been intimating that it would enact changes to its repressive border policies. And when asked at a press conference about when these proposed changes would take effect, the East German spokesperson, Günter Schabowski, looked confused and answered in a harried way that the changes were effective sofort ("immediately"). With that one little word, the journalists in the press conference bolted; the room was vacated in minutes. With that one word, the forbidding spiritual power of the wall was shattered in people's minds, and the crowds gathered to climb on and tear down the wall.[28] But scars remained, and since those days, Germany has also had to grapple with the long, slow work of reunifying a divided people.

From the visitor center, my parents and I walked down Ackerstrasse and navigated various turns until we glimpsed the steeple of the Zionskirche—the Zion Church, the same church my husband stumbled upon during a run in our first weeks in Berlin. This was the parish church where Bonhoeffer took over the large, unruly class of confirmands, a rowdy group of boys whose intractable behavior very likely hastened the previous teacher's early death not long after handing over the reins. On Bonhoeffer's arrival, that pastor led him up a flight of stairs to an upper-story classroom while the boys yelled "Bon! Bon!" in a poor attempt to mock Bonhoeffer's name and threw trash down on them both. The other pastor shouted at them and used physical violence to try to compel order on the group.[29] It was not a good start.

The church building retains clues to its rough and turbulent past, even if the neighborhood around it now features hip restaurants and boutiques. The interior walls are pocked in places, and streaks of light through the windows make the dust in the air sparkle. One of many late nineteenth-century churches, built during a time of purported national piety after German unification, it feels as if it was vacated and never quite reoccupied, more attic than sanctuary. A memorial to Bonhoeffer, a kneeling and deliberately headless figure of a man, his arms outstretched in cruciform love, graces the grassy apron around the church. Bonhoeffer was so moved by the working-class conditions in the parish, on the other side of the city from his parents' wooded suburb, that he decided to rent an apartment on a street nearby, in the Prenzlauer Berg neighborhood, on Oderberger Strasse.[30] He told his landlord to unlock his apartment door to any of these students if he himself was not there to do so, if they needed help.

As we hopped a tram to head home, I couldn't help but think just how far this place was from Bonhoeffer's home in the Grunewald neighborhood. He and these young men shared a common language, but their commonalities stopped there. He was from a privileged, aristocratic world, and he lived with the kind of agency that those in that world grow accustomed to. These students were from an impoverished class, likely crammed in slum-like conditions, their already strapped families scrambling to make ends meet in a Germany that, in 1932, had six million men unemployed.

Bonhoeffer visited each of the boys in their homes, and we know that he was shocked by their living conditions. The quickly built tenement buildings, as I mentioned earlier, were places where the sordid and predatory and impoverished and desperate dwelled together. Artwork depicting life in Prenzlauer Berg and other areas at that time gives us clues as to what that world was like: skeletal sketches of people by artist Käthe Kollwitz (1867–1945), who herself lived in Prenzlauer Berg, or the cartoons and graphic sketches of illustrator Heinrich Zille (1858–1929), who drew scenes of people packed in dark rooms, bedsheets hanging from ceilings to create pockets of privacy, haggard women nursing babies, half-dressed children wandering and fighting, sullen men blankly staring at bottles of alcohol. I'll allow adult imaginations to fill in the gaps of my narrative; those scenes were captured by artists too.

In other words, with its magnificent, large, and fully staffed homes, ample green space, and salon-attending elite classes, Berlin's Grunewald could not have been more different, or further away.

• • •

Bonhoeffer's nomadic adulthood contrasts with the stability of his childhood. He had never ventured outside of Germany before his coming-of-age trip to Rome with his brother Klaus in 1924, a journey that opened windows of theological vision and offered him new perspectives on Christ and the church. His willingness to cross boundaries and allow new places and people to shape him developed into a lifelong pattern. From that first trip to Rome to his wide and eye-opening travels in the United States and other parts of North America in 1930–1931, as well as his expatriate work experiences in Barcelona (1928) and London (1933–1935), Dietrich's travels reaffirmed and strengthened his bonds to Germany. Each place offered him glimpses into other worlds that helped him look back with a clearer eye on his own. His journeys beyond home formed him in a way that eventually led him back.

That pattern is familiar to me in our family's experience in the US Foreign Service. We live as Americans abroad, real and symbolic representatives of our nation in another. Only one member of our family is the paid professional in that capacity, but all of us bear the responsibility of representing our home, so I am never "just me" in relationship to others, and neither are our children. Our job is not to assimilate, though that doesn't mean we don't try to learn, adapt, be polite, and respect the differences of our host country. Without question, we enjoy many privileges and opportunities to see the world that we wouldn't be able to do if not for my husband's work. Yet, moving as often as we do, we have to work to stay curious and open when we sometimes grow tired of being different.

One tricky bit of ethics that I am prone to is believing I am morally exempt as an expatriate. Not that I rob banks or anything like that, but that injustices and troubles that weigh heavily on people in a foreign place aren't my problems. *We're not from here; I didn't make these rules, and I sure won't be able to change them.* Having a mindset of not being "from here" sometimes deceives me into the luxury of not paying attention to my place, much less taking responsibility for that "here" if I do.

Bonhoeffer got involved with the life of the church in Harlem and in the Zionskirche parish even though they weren't his worlds. He likely wouldn't have been as attentive a neighbor to the members of his confirmation class—making home visits, renting an apartment nearby, sharing stories from Harlem with the boys as he did, playing the records he had purchased there, taking them out of the city to his family's summer home in the mountains, and offering dignity by purchasing them cloth for confirmation suits—if he had not also witnessed the church's very practical work in Harlem. He paid attention in New York and learned lessons that mattered to the places he belonged to. He saw what responsibility to others and for others looked like.

When I tell tour groups the story of Bonhoeffer's introduction to his confirmation class at the Zion Church, I cannot help but act it out, putting on a little one-woman show. It's the only part of his life for which I adopt this story-telling technique, and I think the whole scene commands it. I mime-trudge my legs up an imaginary flight of stairs as I narrate, like the elderly and despairing clergyman whom Bonhoeffer was relieving from his agonizing (and clearly inadequate) leadership of the class. With him, Bonhoeffer climbed the stairs too. The clergyman shoved and shouted at the wild young men and finally left Bonhoeffer to fend for himself. Bonhoeffer then stood, silently, for a long time in front of the classroom, as the class whooped and hollered and carried on.[31] Bonhoeffer continued to stand, hands in his pockets.

I stand just like him in the conference room, and then I break out of that posture to act like the crowd of boys, my arms wildly flailing, my mouth and eyes angry and fierce. Quickly, I return to Bonhoeffer's posture, put my hands in my pockets, and reliably, this juxtaposition produces the same result it did in that Zionskirche classroom. My already attentive group of visitors becomes somehow even more watchful, held by the story rather than by my recitation of the facts.

"And when he finally speaks," I say very quietly, breaking the theatrical silence, "he tells them stories from Harlem."[32] Whispered stories, in fact. The shouting, shoving elderly pastor was replaced by a low-talking storyteller, and the hush began in the front of the classroom and then spread throughout the room. Not only did Bonhoeffer tell them stories from Harlem, but he also told them stories from the Bible, "particularly the eschatological passages."[33] The discipline problems that had driven their former instructor up to the brink of death with stress were replaced by "absolute quiet," self-discipline, without any problems of misbehavior. As Bonhoeffer said, "the boys see to that themselves."[34]

• • •

Bonhoeffer's adult life was, as I've said, nomadic, at times confusingly so. He seemed to be constantly coming and going, stopping in at his parents' house since 1935, the Bonhoeffer-Haus, on Marienburger Allee. I know from experience how challenging that itinerant path can be to narrate. Our family comes and goes from places too, and it can be hard for friends to keep track of the timeline and the locations. Similarly, it took me a while to learn the facts and the stories of Bonhoeffer's many trips, like threads in a tapestry.

We received our next assignment, from among a list of places worldwide. I always knew that where I began writing, in Berlin, would not be the place in which I'd first read these words printed in a book. With that new assignment in hand, the emotional stakes we had driven into the ground in Berlin began to loosen and lift. It would always ever be a three-year season.

We'll discover just how much Berlin has planted in our hearts when we are in our next location. We carry each of the places in which we've lived with us, cherishing their inaccessible features, a particular and time-bound taste, sound, or smell. Each place has shaped us, enriched our lives, and simultaneously deepened our love and even longing for our home. Living elsewhere, we cherish even more what is good about America, and what makes Americans who we are. We also agonize over what troubles our nation, its grief, sins, and shame. We are well aware that the America we hold in our minds is often more of a hoped-for idea than a living reality.

Coming to know Berlin through Bonhoeffer's life helped me better see my own. Learning his story and seeing how crossing boundaries in life shaped him have turned my attention to my story, the boundaries I have crossed. Bonhoeffer was able to see his Berlin and its working-class parts better because of his time in Harlem, I think. He was equipped in Harlem to better address the wounds of his Berlin—not only to try to address them, but also to suffer with them, connecting places of suffering and survival with others places of suffering. The boys of the Zionskirche needed Bonhoeffer's Harlem stories; his boundary crossings made critical connections between these distant worlds possible.

Bonhoeffer's story in Berlin narrowed the way I see and think about this city but also sent it sprawling, leaping to other places. His life served as a lens on Berlin, but at the same time it inspired me to seek out books about the Harlem Renaissance, crossing imagined boundaries of history and visiting places that I never imagined for my life's itinerary. Our family sweated out a day of tramping around the island of Fanø in Denmark and slept a fitful night in a tent because Dietrich Bonhoeffer attended an ecumenical conference there in 1934. His life sparked curiosity in our lives, and we all derived so much joy discovering these places in and far beyond Berlin, whether by car, boat, train, or book.

Those of us who treasure and carry diverse places find, like Bonhoeffer, that our hearts can be porous and yet still hold much. We can be open to others and discover that we haven't lost anything of ourselves. Indeed, for Bonhoeffer, his journeys abroad nourished and strengthened his love for his homeland. As he wrote to his dissertation adviser, Professor Reinhold Seeberg, "There can be no doubt that only through active contact with other ways of thought is one led to the formation and comprehension of that which is unique to oneself."[35] This is true not only to the experience of living abroad but also to reading books and visiting places that might not be right around the corner from my life but are foreign *to me*.

• • •

The day was ours to do as we liked, but there were more important claims on it than just what we wanted, important moral encumbrances and civic responsibilities we felt a duty to honor. In this respect it wasn't only *our* day, even if my husband had it off from work and the kids had it off from school. The free time was for freedom, to remember one man and a movement, but freedom is never free. It was the middle of January 2017—Martin Luther King Jr. Day—and to honor him, our family traced his path in Berlin.

One lovely oddity of life at various embassies is that one celebrates both local holidays in the host country and American national holidays. It ensures that American diplomats are somewhat in step with the prevailing customs and practices, free to celebrate with local neighbors in their various festivities, but also appropriately out of step to celebrate our own. After dropping our youngest off at his German preschool, where we knew he'd be much happier playing than tromping around town with us, my husband, our daughters, and I set off into the heart of the city.

We stopped to have brunch at Barcomi's Deli, a New York City–style delicatessen close to both the butter-colored Sophienkirche and the Hackesche Höfe, a warren of courtyards and buildings full of history, Art Deco tiling, and boutique shops and restaurants. This was a neighborhood that once also cradled a vibrant Jewish community. After downing bagels and cream cheese—and on my plate, also plenty of onions, lox, and capers—we made our way to the church, peering into shops as we walked, lingering long over the goodies in the window of the toy shop down the street from the church.

A small plaque just to the left of the ornate iron gates of the Sophienkirche commemorates the historical event for passersby. Although it's permanently affixed all year long, because this day was a holiday, the church had extra posters and signs up with information about Rev. Dr. Martin Luther King Jr.'s visit to the church on September 13, 1964. As we stopped to take in the schedule, out of the corner of our eye we saw our good friend Bill, the embassy's chief spokesperson at the time, walking down the street. We hollered and flagged him down. He had been tackling a few errands on his day off; because his wife was enrolled in a German-language program at the Goethe Institute, and his children were all enrolled at an international school, not an American-affiliated German public school like ours were, the day was business as usual for all of them. So Bill was alone. We begged him to join us and come into the church, noting that the timing could not have been coincidental. As Bill does with most of life's serendipities, he joyfully agreed, a huge grin spreading across his face.

The interior of the church was predictably hushed, with the creaking shifts of old wooden floors and pews as visitors milled quietly or sat. At the front of the sanctuary, up near the raised pulpit on the left, was a small gathering of people. On the floor in front of the altar was a small portable speaker, hooked up to a computer. Banners were hoisted up at the front, and a few volunteers tidied handouts that indicated some MLK activity was happening up there.

As it turned out, the church had already held a special service honoring King that day, and we had missed it. But my husband and Bill, both conversant in German—and, as diplomats, constitutionally wired to relate to others—began speaking with one of the volunteers. They spoke in German for quite some time, so I sat taking in the church scene, studying the resplendent wallpaper along the back wall, and our daughters listened intently since, by that point, they were better able to understand the conversation than I was. Finally, David gave me a summary translation.

For starters, the volunteer was very pleased that two officers from the American embassy were present. Since we had missed the service, he said he would replay an audio recording of Martin Luther King Jr.'s sermon from his 1964 visit for us. Incredibly, this same volunteer said that he had been in attendance that day as a boy when the Rev. Dr. King came to speak. This was his history too.

The Rev. Dr. Martin Luther King Jr. had been in the western sector of Berlin earlier that day in 1964 but crossed the forbidding boundary of the Berlin Wall to deliver a message, and many held on to his words over the twenty-five years from that day until the wall came down. Willy Brandt, West Berlin's mayor during the Cold War, had invited King to come and speak in West Berlin, and he did to a crowd of twenty thousand at the Waldbühne, an amphitheater built as part of the 1936 Olympics complex. US officials confiscated King's passport, possibly to curtail his travel movements, but supposedly due to the tense security situation of the Cold War. Rev. Dr. King was an inspiring but not uncontroversial figure for the State Department, as he had been highly critical of the Vietnam War and of morally unchecked capitalism. Church leaders in East Berlin had also invited him to come and visit them, but without a passport, it wasn't clear how he would be able to cross that formidable boundary. When he got to the border, he offered the East Germans his American Express card as his form of identification. They accepted it as a travel document and let him in—or out, depending on your point of view.

The news spread by word of mouth through East Berlin, in a relational, organic flash: King would be speaking at the Marienkirche! Situated near Alexanderplatz, it's one of the oldest churches in Berlin, dating to the late 1200s. In very little time, a crowd of thousands came to hear King, standing room only, with thousands more outside the church hoping to see or hear or witness something. Then, a new message worked its way to the crowd outside: Rev. Dr. King was heading to the Sophienkirche! All those standing outside the Marienkirche rushed to this second church, the place where we now sat on Martin Luther King Jr. Day in 2017. His second address was standing room only there too.

The volunteer fired up the speaker and clicked a few buttons on the computer, and the crackle of a historic recording piped out. Rev. Dr. King's voice filled the sanctuary again, and his words brought tears to my eyes. This volunteer, now an older gentleman, was eager to revisit that day with us strangers, and I imagined him then as a boy, pressed up against a column in the church, craning to see King ascend the pulpit staircase and stand under its domed canopy. The message he gave in the Sophienkirche was the same one of Christian unity he had delivered earlier in West Berlin, vital truths to those on the other side of the wall, many of whom felt abandoned by the world:

> I am happy to bring you greetings from your Christian brothers
> and sisters of West Berlin. . . . Certainly I bring you greetings
> from your Christian brothers and sisters of the United States.
> In a real sense we are all one in Christ Jesus, for in Christ there
> is no East, no West, no North, no South.[36]

Connecting the East-West division in Germany and the North-South division in the United States, he continued, "For here on either side of the Wall are God's children, and no man-made barrier can obliterate that fact." And then, quoting Scripture, he proclaimed, "Wherever reconciliation is taking place, wherever men are 'breaking down the dividing walls of hostility' (Eph. 2:14) which separate them from their brothers, there Christ continues to perform his ministry."[37]

Tears streamed down my face, hearing that famous and familiar voice, that true son of America, that prophet who brought a message of judgment as a means of confession toward repentance. Here, again, the ministry of the word, infused with theology forged out of the suffering of African Americans, offered hope, light, and vision to a group of East Germans who were now walking in their own dark moment of history. Cut off as they were from loved ones, even cut off from themselves, the words of this preacher from Georgia—a man reviled by many in his own country for threatening the codified systems of entrenched injustice, for calling America to live according to its stated ideals—rang out with the clarity of truth in a city polluted with lies. It was such a privilege to hear those words, sitting just feet from the pulpit in which they were delivered, on the day that honored King's life—one that was cut short at the age of thirty-nine, just like Dietrich Bonhoeffer's. There seemed nothing coincidental about this convergence of moments. Both men crossed boundaries, both acted as bridges between people who knew suffering, and both shared vital words and resources that gave listeners reasons to hope.

After hearing the recording, we thanked the volunteer profusely and stepped with him into a back room to see some other artifacts—among them, records of jazz singers that he cherished. He also gave us a flier for a planned gathering that evening on Pariser Platz, the main square just in front of the Brandenburg Gate and right in front of the US embassy. A group was going to come together to sing spirituals, including "We Shall Overcome," as a way of marking the day and registering the laments of all that has not been overcome.[38] "We have to go," I urged my husband, and later that evening, we arrived to the plaza with small candles and lanterns to hold.

A group of about a hundred formed the gathered choir on the Platz that night, and we lifted our voices together in shared lament and hope. The group was not political, and the gathering was not intended as a demonstration. It had drawn all kinds of people, black and white, German and American, and many others as well. As we joined our voices together in the folksong of the enslaved that became the anthem of the American civil rights movement, right there in the scarred heart of Berlin, all I could think was how little things have changed, how many boundaries still need to be crossed, how far we still need to go, and yet we still have reasons to hope.

Hannah on her bike, at the Jugendverkehrsschule, or "youth traffic school," in the Zehlendorf neighborhood of Berlin

Chapter 6

BONHOEFFER
BY BIKE

→ *Key: We shouldn't just stay in our lane*
when others are suffering in theirs. ←

Like many European cities, Berlin takes bicycling seriously. The
rules governing bike lanes are as formal as the lanes designated
for automobiles, and when we first moved here, we had to learn
to take them seriously too—and quick. Hailing from a car-centric
country, we tended to see cycling as a hobby, only an incidental form
of transportation. We were used to a driving culture in which automobiles dominate the road, a world shaped by the car.

Europe is different. Western European roadways reflect more of
the diversity of human transportation and don't simply cater to the
automobile. Countries here levy heavier taxes on gasoline than the
United States does, parking is at a premium, and, mercifully, it's possible to live without a vehicle in certain urban settings, such as Berlin. It's not always easy, but we know plenty of people who rely solely
on their bicycles and public transportation—including families with
young children, who typically learn to ride bicycles when very young.
For many, the bicycle is their primary vehicle, their form of private
transportation. (And, as Germans will readily advise, if one is properly prepared for cold or nasty weather, it's also an incredibly sensible
way of getting around and a good form of exercise.)

Traffic infrastructure in Berlin reflects the diversity of transport. As the most vulnerable form of transport, pedestrians get a head start at an intersection, signaled by the beloved green and red *Ampelmann*, the iconic symbol of a man signaling to stop or go.[1] Traffic lights for bicyclists also give them a slight head start. As the powerful heavyweights on the road, automobilists are last in line in the right-of-way queue. In this integrated driving culture, everything is calibrated and connected.

That's not to say that the vulnerable rule. Pedestrians and bicyclists still contend with inattentive, impatient, or just plain rude automobilists. Sometimes, tourists or new transplants—including us when we first moved to Berlin—discover the bike lane on a steep learning curve. As tourists walk along, looking up and taking pictures, they often spread across what appears to be a wide sidewalk, totally unaware of traffic laws. The telltale sign of their doom is usually heard, incomprehensibly, and then it is experienced: if a persistent *dring! dring!* on the legally required bike bell fails to clear the path ahead of meandering pedestrians, an angrily yelled "ACHTUNG! ACHTUNG!" often does as the bicyclist attempts to speed through a mass of flabbergasted pedestrians. But the bicyclist is in the right. Disrespecting the bike lane is dangerous.

With a toddler in tow when we first arrived, I immediately learned to give it respect, even with its diminutive, frankly adorable streetlights. I needed to teach our children to do the same. They needed to know, by instinct, to stop and look down the bike lane, just as they would crossing a street. The pathways' forms vary: sometimes, red bricks delineate the lane on a pedestrian sidewalk; other times, there is a painted dotted-line lane on the roadway. Regardless, we learned to pay attention to those cues, developed the habit of looking back for a bike before opening our car doors or turning and not mindlessly wandering into the bike lane.

In our first year in Berlin, we purchased a bicycle installed with a child seat for me to use with our youngest. I did not use it as often as I imagined I would, and my excuses were usually weather related: too cold, too windy, too rainy, too hot. But when I did ride the bike— whether to take our son to preschool or to tool up the road to the nearby grocery store for a few items—I was grateful for those bike lanes and for the culture that respected them.

When our vehicle finally arrived months after we did, my driving habits adapted to that culture. For instance, before making a right turn, I learned to look back hard, way over my right shoulder, to check whether a bicyclist was approaching from behind. I often paid attention to that bike lane long before I made a turn, mentally noting if any bicyclists were nearby.

But when I was on my bike, I was alert for automobile drivers' inattention to me. Traveling on a bike leaves a body more vulnerable than in a car. Without the exoskeleton of a car frame, a bicyclist is still a human body, with all the soft parts exposed. On a bike I felt my physicality, my limits, and the vulnerabilities of my embodiment in a world prone to distraction and mindlessness. Getting around by bike or by foot in a world full of speeding cars offers stark reminders that we are, deep down, fragile creatures.

When my son and I traveled by bike to his preschool, we would bask in the breeze, listen to the leaves rustling as we passed under them, cloud-gaze, and observe things along the roadway not as easily seen from the car—wildflowers in spring, funny stumps of trees, and litter. While he was freer to observe, I had to pay close attention to a whole new landscape of risks. Sometimes he'd shift suddenly

in the seat—"Did you see that, Mommy? Wow!" I would wheel pre-
cariously around piles of wet autumn leaves, marble-like acorns, and
minor potholes in the bike lane, obstacles we could ignore in a car.
On a bike, those small hazards were bigger and more threatening.
We could feel them.

Lest I paint an idyllic picture of Berlin's bike lanes, the same frus-
trations car drivers feel on the road exist in the bike lane. Some bicyclists are speedy; others are slow. Some pass too closely for comfort;
others refuse to get out of the way. The same kind of pressure-cooker
environment that gets automobile drivers huffy and impatient at
rush hour happens in bike lanes too. People can be mindless and
rude on bikes just as easily as they can be in cars. They, too, are just
trying to get to work, run their errands, and get their little ones home
for dinner. But regardless, they are still the more vulnerable travelers, with more skin exposed.

After being on a bike and then back behind the wheel of a car,
I discovered how bicycling had recalibrated my attention to these
more vulnerable travelers. After all, that's how I wanted to be treated
when I was in the bicycle lane, fully aware of the fragility of being
human and of being a body, all bones, muscles, nerves, and skin. In
this respect, walking and bicycling can be profoundly rehumanizing,
our bodies experiencing the world at a slower, breathable pace.

Secluded behind the armored shells of our cars, however, we
don't feel our soft flesh or the hard ground, and we can ignore the
world as it briskly passes by. We forget we're still vulnerable bodies
when gunning that big engine, bulldozing over acorns and plowing
across the quilt-stitches and cobblestones of neighborhoods. This
forgetfulness forms the way we think, and we are prone to believe
our evasions.[2] We are apt to overlook or disregard the vulnerable
around us who travel by foot or bike. They aren't to be pitied; I never

wanted pity on my bike! But as the traveler in the more vulnerable lane, I wanted the respect that protected and honored my humanity. As much as I wanted cars to stay in their lane, I needed them to pay attention to me in mine.

On the roadways of life, even though we travel in separate lanes, we're still connected. What happens in one lane invariably affects the others. Keeping eyes only on one's own lane of travel is foolish. No matter how we travel, we have to keep our eyes open for one another. We have to listen for one another and take it seriously when we hear bells ringing or someone yelling "ACHTUNG!" from another lane.

• • •

"I'm going to read an extended quote delivered by a pastor after Kristallnacht, the so-called Night of the Broken Glass, the country-wide pogrom of November 9 to 10, 1938," I said to the group gathered in the conference room. "One week after that horrifying night of terror, when deeply cultivated anti-Semitism and long-tolerated state-sanctioned persecutions ripened with impunity into emboldened violence across Germany, Confessing Church leader Rev. Helmut Gollwitzer spoke these words in St. Anne's Church in Berlin-Dahlem, the church of the imprisoned Pastor Martin Niemöller." Then I read:

Who should still preach today? Are not all our mouths stopped today? Is it possible today to do anything other than remain silent? What have all the years and centuries of preaching and hearing sermons achieved for us, our people, and our church that we have reached the point at which we stand today, that we now enter as we are entering this church? What do we ask of God, if we now come and sing, pray, read lessons from the

Bible—as if we think God is still here and has not deserted such a patently empty religious hustle and bustle. Our audacity and arrogance must be disgusting to God.[3]

I continued, "That event took place while Bonhoeffer was working with the collective pastorates in eastern Pomerania. He learned that mobs had burned down a synagogue in the town nearby, and, knowing how entrenched anti-Semitism was in Christian theology, he quickly set parameters on how to interpret the moment: this act of terrorism wasn't God's punishment on the Jews. Moreover, he told them, anyone sitting comfortably in a church should know that when synagogues are burned down, the churches will burn next. Bonhoeffer jotted the date in his Bible alongside a verse from Psalm 74: 'They have burned up all the synagogues of God in the land.'"[4]

The group gathered at the Bonhoeffer-Haus that morning was an eclectic mix, some of whom were close friends of mine, some acquaintances, and some new faces. A few children were present too. We represented different faiths as well, including those who identified with no faith. But we all belonged to the American embassy community in Berlin. I felt a duty to tell them who I was and to acknowledge my moral obligations to them.

"Besides being the spouse of a foreign service officer, like some of you are, I am also a Christian, and during this visit together, I will refer to ideas and concepts that are particular to Christian theology and ethics. But learning about Bonhoeffer's life has reminded me just how connected we all are, and how theology is never a private endeavor. What we believe and teach in our faith communities bears upon those who do not belong to them. The way I think, speak, and write about my Christian faith and live it matters to people who do not share my faith. The way we think about, speak of, and act toward one another matters. Even if we do not belong to the same community, our worlds aren't all that disconnected.

"In fact, it is good for us to think aloud about our faith and moral commitments in the presence of those who may disagree with us or hold very different views about the nature of things. Our beliefs are never private, and they may affect others very much. We need to be aware of that effect, how it may bear out on others. During the Nazi era, Christians here and elsewhere failed their Jewish neighbors, and many others belonging to different groups. They were silent when they should have spoken up; they were complicit and, at times, even gleeful participants in persecution. They often used their beliefs to justify violence and genocide, which is abhorrent, but a fact we must acknowledge. They did not see how their lives were connected to one another.

"In this house, this place of memorial and encounter, I urge you to see that we are connected with each other; we belong to one another. What happens in one community often directly affects another. We have to learn to listen for each other, to speak in the presence of one another, and to take seriously when our neighbor tells us they are afraid, or suffering, because of us."

• • •

In his slender 1979 book, *Prayer and Righteous Action in the Life of Dietrich Bonhoeffer*, Eberhard Bethge lamented that even though Hitler had been defeated and Nazism put into history's dustbin, the conditions for his rise and maintenance of power were still at work. As Bonhoeffer spoke of Dummheit—a vivid German word that hardly needs translation into English, but means stupidity or folly—in his 1942 Christmas letter "After Ten Years," Bethge also spoke of stupidity in this book when he argued that it wasn't the uneducated, untrained, or unsophisticated masses that made Hitler possible. Rather, those who claimed to be educated and wielded real power enabled his rule. Folly—great collective stupidity—was in full force among those who claimed to know better. The intellectuals, clergymen, and professionals in a variety of spheres were the fools who thought that they could use Hitler to bring about changes they wanted and contain him, even if they had to hold their noses as they did.

They "stayed in their lane," Bethge said, not troubling themselves with the world beyond their narrow interests, and they limited "their responsibility to the boundaries of their own work," the policies they wanted enacted.[5] Many of these leaders thought of themselves as apolitical, Bethge warned, and thereby allowed Hitler and his ilk to fill the cultural and political vacuum and act with increasing impunity. In the same respect, the church wanted to just sing the refrain "Let the Church be the Church" and claim ignorance about just how useful they were to the Nazis. Over time, the church posed *no real threat* to Nazi power and its sprawling societal corruptions. Grievously so—rather than ask hard and pointed questions of the state, as Bonhoeffer urged, the church either busied itself with its own survival or enthusiastically surrendered itself to greater levels of Aryan captivity. This self-surrender and denial came at enormous cost, Bethge argued: "The longer the resistance was postponed the more costly it became in the end."[6] Bargains with the devil guaranteed there would be hell to pay.

• • •

It was midwinter's eve 2018—the day before the winter solstice, the shortest day of the year. I was scheduled to give a tour on short notice, and, knowing that new locks had been installed at the Bonhoeffer-Haus, I coordinated with Martin ahead of time to make sure I could get into the house before being issued my new key. Standing on the front lawn as we reviewed the procedure for me to unlock the house, I asked him why they needed new locks.

"Well, there have been some break-ins in the neighborhood recently," he said.

"Oh dear, that's awful, Martin. I'm so sorry."

"Well, it's grown darker," he said, and I nodded soberly, as if the darkness were a metaphor of our world becoming dark and strange, old alliances fracturing, even older nationalisms spreading. But then, snapping out of my dramatic reverie, I realized he just meant it was winter; the days were shorter, the hours of darkness longer. Maybe I had drunk too much coffee that morning, but I had become more anxious. The days did feel darker, and not just because it was winter.

When I got back to our house, I set about to do some holiday baking. I wanted to prepare some desserts for teachers' gifts, especially a cranberry cake recipe that calls for fresh cranberries. I had collected, frozen, and hoarded some when they briefly showed up on grocery shelves around Thanksgiving, a commercial hat tip to the Americans in the neighborhood. During the cake's long bake time, I planned to take a bike ride to a few key spots related to Bonhoeffer's life. I wanted to see how they connected, and I thought doing so by bike would help me see it better.

On periodic walks months earlier, I had already attempted to visit some of these places by foot. But I often got very turned around on the streets of that part of the Grunewald neighborhood. Of course, I knew my own neighborhood well, and my neighborhood connects with Bonhoeffer's historic one. Exploring by bike would give me another chance to try to learn these places, a little more swiftly than by foot. So, after closing the oven door, I donned my helmet and set off pedaling down the street with the Grunewald forest on my left, dense with tall pines.

I hung a left onto a narrow cobblestoned street running adjacent to a members-only sports club dating from 1899. Passing it often in my car, I also often wondered whether the Bonhoeffers ever came here. Preparing for his trip to Barcelona after earning his first dissertation, Dietrich wrote the overworked pastor there about suitable dining and tennis attire in society. Was the common practice tails for dinner, or special dress at the athletic clubs? I'd always found that bit of correspondence a little pretentious on Bonhoeffer's part, revealing his aristocratic background. On my many car rides past the sports club, I often saw patrons walking from their spotless black Mercedes-Benzes, Audis, and Land Rovers, clad all in white, tennis rackets resting on their shoulders—a perfect sartorial picture of the Berlin-Grunewald world, largely unchanged between Bonhoeffer's day and now. Pedaling and puffing past in my puffy pink Old Navy coat, there was no question to observers that it was not my world.

Right turn onto Wildpfad, another cobblestone street, down which sits the residence of the ambassador of the Netherlands. Diplomatic residences and offices dot our neighborhood, including the Swedish ambassador's residence, flying characteristic narrow flags on poles out front and featuring a small plaque on the front gate framing the house's place in history. In 1966, the residence was the site of talks between Berlin's mayor, Willy Brandt, and the Soviet ambassador to East Berlin, beginning a season Brandt referred to as "Ostpolitik," a period of détente between the Federal Republic of Germany and the Soviet Union that frustrated the United States. It's a sleek, modern residence, unlike the Dutch residence, which is a commanding grande dame of a house, set at a rakish angle to the road. I made a left turn onto Hagenstrasse, then hung a right onto Richard-Strauss-Strasse, and then a left onto Furtwängler-strasse. Now I was in Bonhoeffer's world, the heart of the Berlin-Grunewald neighborhood.

Lengthy boulevards, diagonal streets, streets with changing names, and periodic circles make the area tricky to navigate. Lacking a solid bird's-eye view of the connections, I had repeatedly made navigational mistakes in the neighborhood. Now, out from behind the wheel of my car, I wanted my body to learn the area.

Up ahead, I saw the spire of the Grunewaldkirche, the parish church of the Bonhoeffer family, which they only occasionally attended. At the age of fourteen, Dietrich and his twin sister Sabine were enrolled in a confirmation class there, and Dietrich received his deceased brother Walter's Bible when he was confirmed there in 1921, using it for the rest of his life.[7] During his years of theological study and writing in Berlin, Dietrich also taught a Sunday school class at this church, and his characteristic skill with children was evident when children from other classes started coming to his.[8] At the Grunewaldkirche, he likely wrestled over whether he should become a pastor, given his heart for people, especially young people, or an academic theologian, given his agile mind and his skillful way with words and ideas. By the end of his life, he fully embraced both of those vocations, living them out in the ways he could wherever he was.

When I got to the sidewalk perimeter, I hopped off my bike and walked up to the front door, passing under a heavy, tangled green vine arching between two stone columns. Just as on my prior walks, I found the door locked, but I made note of the posted Christmas week schedule as well as some upcoming concerts.

My next stop was Bonhoeffer's high school, called the Grunewald-Gymnasium when he was a student and now bearing the name

Walter-Rathenau-Gymnasium. Even the school's name change relates to Bonhoeffer, who reportedly heard the assassins' submachine gunfire that killed Walter Rathenau, the German foreign minister during the turbulent days of the Weimar Republic, who was also Jewish. On June 24, 1922, Rathenau was gunned down not far from his house on the nearby Koenigsallee, as he was heading to work, being driven by a chauffeur. The murderers were identified as members of a far right-wing group, Organisation Consul, committed to fighting "internationalism, social democracy, and Judaism."[9] A memorial to Rathenau now stands there.

Unlike the neighborhood where the Bonhoeffer-Haus stands, the Grunewald neighborhood was the vision of Otto von Bismarck. It was designed for the elites and the well-to-do, and leading figures of science and state (such as Rathenau), "financiers and industrialists,"[10] intellectuals (including the historian Hans Delbrück and Protestant theologian Adolf von Harnack), and "filmmakers and movie stars"[11] resided on these lovely boulevards, as did the Bonhoeffers. When Dietrich returned to Berlin after his first year of university study in Tübingen, he returned to the family's home there. He and Harnack, his professor and neighbor, would commute together from the neighborhood, hopping the train at the Halensee station to the university downtown. It was a ritual that the retired professor reportedly enjoyed as he continued to lecture and hold seminars for special students, Bonhoeffer included.[12]

On my way to the Gymnasium, I made a wrong turn. I made a ridiculous, lost-to-the-world (or, more accurately, a mindlessly-obedient-to-my-Google-Maps-narration) circle, passing the same cars a second time, revealing just how turned around I was. I decided to break out of my unthinking obedience to the GPS and get lost on purpose, which somehow landed me near the school anyway. I glided past the cream-colored stone building slowly, look-ing for a plaque that memorialized its students who were involved in the Widerstand (resistance). A fellow guide at the Bonhoeffer-Haus worked at this school, and seeing that plaque prompted her to learn more about Bonhoeffer. In time she visited the Bonhoeffer-Haus and became a volunteer.

A student sat on the steps outside, scrolling on a smartphone. Beyond him, affixed to the exterior wall of the building, I spotted three large basalt-rock statues between banks of windows. The three male figures have an oddly cruciform look to them, even though they are meant to be embodied virtues. I later learned that the school's plaque for its students killed during the Nazi era bears four names—Dietrich Bonhoeffer, Justus Delbrück, Hans von Dohnanyi, and Ber-nhard Klamroth—and it was placed fifty years after the failed July 20, 1944, assassination and coup attempt.

From there I pedaled to Dietrich's childhood house at Wangen-heimstrasse no. 14, a three-story villa, today an amber-colored dwell-ing along a narrow, cobblestone street,[13] apportioned into apartment housing residences and a few businesses. I stopped to take some pic-tures, which I'd never done on prior visits. The city-issued memorial plaque on the exterior of the property, marking it as the house of Dr. Karl and Dietrich Bonhoeffer, looks just like the one on the Bonhoeffer-Haus. That gave me some license to do so, but I didn't linger long.

I double checked my map on my phone before I headed home, and yet I still managed to head in the wrong direction on Wangenheim-strasse. My Google Maps narrator warned me repeatedly to "make a U-turn, make a U-turn!," but I ignored it. I could see that the road ahead curved sharply to the left, and as I approached that curve, the noise of highway traffic grew. Ah, yes! Berlin's ring road, the A100, passes right through this neighborhood. As I rounded the curve, I saw a pedestrian bridge on my right, spanning that highway, and beyond that, some familiar shops that stand on Kurfürstendamm, that famous boulevard connecting this "millionaire's slum" to the heart of the city. Now I saw how close the Halensee S-Bahn station was to this neighborhood, the very station that Harnack and Bonhoeffer commuted from to the university. Although I had driven along that stretch of road, trying to see why Bonhoeffer went to that station, from the car I couldn't see how it connected. But on bike, I finally saw. Since my getting-lost strategy seemed to be working well, I decided to keep pushing forward to see what other connections might emerge. So I made my way across the bridge.

Pausing in the middle, I watched the cars zooming beneath, like rushing water. I had driven just like these cars hundreds of times under this pedestrian bridge and never noticed it. Reaching the other side, I followed the road as it curved into Auguste-Viktoria-Strasse, marveling at the interconnectedness of these neighborhoods and streets, how close these roads were to my life and yet how unknown they were to me. Exploring by bike helped me to see the arteries and veins of the body of this neighborhood in a way a car drive could not.

After turning onto Paulsborner Strasse, a road that bends past an Italian trattoria, I hung a left onto Hubertusallee. Like one of C. S. Lewis's Pevensie children freshly spat out of Narnia through the wardrobe and back in merry old rainy and embattled England, I was out of Bonhoeffer's pathways and back onto my own. My improvised exploration had helped me better mentally map his places: the neighborhood parish church, its gray stone a centerpiece at a confluence of roads; his high school, a normal-looking place with remarkable alumni; the home where he grew up, well-appointed but hardly unique among all the other well-appointed homes along its narrow street; the train station nearby. They were all so close together, connected by his life. I glanced at the time. The cake would be done baking soon, so, firmly back in my life, I headed home.

The next day, I was back in Bonhoeffer's world, at the Bonhoeffer-Haus for a scheduled tour. I drove that exact stretch of the A100 ring-road highway on my way there, and this time, I didn't simply mindlessly zoom under the pedestrian bridge I had crossed the day before. Instead, I peered up as long as I could to see the connections from a different angle. Spanning the bridge was a banner, something I had missed when crossing it the day before. It read, *Bei Stau, Rettungsgasse!* (In a traffic jam, [make a] rescue lane!)

The Rettungsgasse is one of many impressive aspects of German driving culture. When traffic gets heavy and slows to a crawl on any major highway, German drivers are required by law to create a lane to let ambulances and fire trucks pass through. On a six-lane highway, cars in the left lane hug the median, driving on the left shoulder. Cars in the right and middle lanes tighten up, hugging the right side. These combined efforts create the Rettungsgasse, the rescue lane, and drivers do this whenever traffic forms, whether rescue vehicles are coming or not. Knowing that a Rettungsgasse will form in traffic is not only endearing; it's calming. It's certainly better than drivers fuming behind the wheel and trying to stake out their territory while traffic crawls along.

Seeing that banner got me thinking on my way to the Haus. Stau—bad traffic—is almost always out of our control. Things go wrong, accidents happen, and smoothly flowing traffic snarls and slows to a lurching crawl. A crash early in the day casts an echo long after it's been cleared. And the effects of traffic spill off major arteries onto side streets as drivers try to navigate a way out of the mess.

Stuck in Stau, trudging in traffic, we drivers rediscover just how connected we are. When traffic is flowing smoothly, we don't have to give much thought to others or feel their presence affecting us. But when the Stau of life spreads through our connected world, we find ourselves unavoidably tangled up in the mess, frustrated at being thwarted, at the dynamics beyond our control. The traffic won't untangle unless we are willing to stay patient, even yield, instead of exploding in rage at other drivers.

But while we're stuck in Stau, we can form a Rettungsgasse. My German is schlecht (bad), but my church-related vocabulary gets a regular workout at our bilingual church in Berlin. Retter is a German word I hear a lot in church; we call Jesus our Retter, which means savior, or rescuer. Retter and Rettung are related. We may not be able to rescue ourselves from the Stau of life, but we can learn to make a Rettungsgasse, making space for the good to flow to those who need it rather than only trying to advance our own good.

Bonhoeffer knew that those who claimed to follow Jesus the Retter needed to care about what was happening in the other lanes. The church should not just "stay in its lane" when people in other lanes were in trouble—but, for the most part, it did. But there were some who, when the Nazis pressed hard, kept their wits and formed a Rettungsgasse in the Stau.

• • •

Alison Owings's *Frauen* caught my eye on the shelf of our embassy community's lending library. As soon as I began traveling in her book, eavesdropping on the conversations she recorded in it, I knew it was a world I needed to get lost in and explore. In the mid- to late 1980s, right around the time that the Bonhoeffer-Haus was inaugurated and opened to the public, the American, Owings, then a young writer, conducted a series of interviews with German women who had lived through the Nazi era. She published *Frauen* in 1993 to critical acclaim, offering what some reviewers termed intimate portraits of an enemy. Despite all the extant research on Nazi Germany, Owings felt that too little accounted for the presence, role, and experience of German women—"average" women, whose contributions to civic and political life are so often overlooked in official histories. Armed with a tape recorder, this young freelance journalist reached out to as many women as she could to record their narratives. When she sent out feelers to possible interviewees, she didn't know whether anyone would reply.

But a wide range of women did, reflecting diverse opinions, experiences, and postures. Some were anti-Semites and (still!) Nazi true believers; others lived through the Nazi years by going along to get along; and others took personal risks to push back against Nazi encroachment on life. Some even plotted against them. Surprised by how many women were willing to be interviewed, Owings noted that it "seemed they had been waiting for decades for someone to ask them a question," to peer into their lane of travel and ask them about it.[14] She prepared a few questions, but mostly she just let them talk, listening to what they let emerge. Occasionally she pressed them in an effort to make sense of what they thought and did during those brief and endless twelve years of spiritual and political darkness.[15] Owings stressed that the women's interviews were not intended to represent a segment of the population but only to reveal single human beings navigating that period of time. Her book is a complicated file of testimonies, a chronicle of people's lives and thoughts.

I found that chronicle so compelling, in part, because I fit the category of people she pursued for interviews. I'm exactly the kind of person whom historians and journalists do not pursue for interviews;

my life does not make history. I'm an American Hausfrau whose day-to-day life does not matter to Twitter moments, media headlines, or pundit chatter. It's easy to believe my small actions don't matter to the big historical picture, and I very rarely see my life from a bird's-eye viewpoint, consider the map of my life, or see its continuities and divergences within the larger social or political picture. I don't see myself as an actor in what's happening on the grand stage of history, much less someone who could effect change, produce a bit of friction, or achieve a measure of (big) good. I doubt many of Owings's interviewees did either. But when their children began to learn and make sense of history, many of these women realized that they needed an alibi—an explanation, even proof—for what they did and did not do. I rarely see myself as needing an alibi for history; I just don't think I matter that much to it.

The interviews are as shocking and strange as life in Nazi Germany was; they cannot be boiled down well. And Owings refused, rightly, I think, to draw neat conclusions about any of them. She let each woman be vividly human, allowing them to speak. And in them, we can hear the voices of heroes and those of the pathetic and mealy-mouthed, the unrepentant and incurious, and some of the courageous few who still lived with regret that, despite all they had done, they hadn't done even more.

Like Dr. Kristen Monroe, whose work I discussed in chapter 3, Owings asked in her own way how German women faced tests of character and humanity during the Third Reich. From her vantage point, the answer to that question was "[as] a whole, not well at all." Moreover, she saw that "German women . . . contributed mightily to the atrocious success of the Third Reich," enabling men to commit all kinds of atrocities and joining them in the rapid descent into greater levels of social criminality.[16] Owings wondered too about American women, how they might have fared under these tests, and above all, she wondered about how she would have responded.[17] And then, describing a sensation I have felt many times during our entire tenure in Berlin, she said, "Being in Germany made the test feel closer. Sometimes scenes, or sounds, the look of an old street, made me feel I am *there*, and I sense a terrible might."[18] The test does feel closer in Berlin, a backdrop that charges the imagination, but truthfully, the test is everywhere.

While Owings was hesitant to draw conclusions to her fascinating oral history, her last words in *Frauen*—a "multifaceted warning"—are worth repeating:

> It may be simplistic, but [it] is a warning nonetheless. It is that we are all well advised to take seriously and keep honed and in good repair our peace-minded instructive freedoms—especially public education and a free press. It is that anyone of good will cannot happily go about a private life, but must be alert enough and brave enough to butt in and be assertive the minute that injustice or intolerance, not to mention despotism, is spotted. It is that ignorance, avoidance, and stereotypes of any kind certainly are time-savers, but in the long run break, and reveal plain old human beings, who have a lot more in common as human beings—such as not having chosen where, when, or to whom we were born—than as members of any group. It is that we must cross superficial boundaries and get to know each other as individual human beings. *It is to remember that as individual human beings, we are all connected.*[19]

• • •

The six visits to the traffic school were mandatory. My daughter's teacher passed out a paper that we had to bring with us. Then she had to ride around a little fake town on her bicycle until an instructor said her time was up and be sure to get the paper stamped and signed, bureaucratic proof that she had clocked her time on the training field. Hannah was a fourth grader in Germany, and this was her fate.

All fourth graders in Germany are required to take a bicycle class, with classroom instruction, paper tests, and a final road test as well. Three times in the fall and then three times again in the spring, my daughter and I made our way to a traffic school so she could practice her skills on a diminutive course full of miniature roads, sidewalks, and pedestrian crosswalks. Parents served as "real" pedestrians at times. There were functioning stoplights, stop and yield signs, and even pretend construction sites with temporary cones and barricades rerouting traffic—all the things a bicyclist might face out in the real world.

When we arrived, we got in line together behind the other fourth graders and surrendered her paper at the office. The desk officer issued her a yellow safety vest with a number on it and told her to go stand outside until a loaner bike became available, or at least this was what Hannah reported to me. Without knowing enough German, I couldn't understand what the officer had said to her any more than a dog understands its master. In other words, I could basically follow a pointing finger, maybe chase a thrown ball, pick out the repeated word *Fahrrad* (bike); yelling would mean something to me too. Thankfully Hannah understood, and off she went to join the other fourth-grade bicyclists, helmets on heads.

The most difficult obstacle Hannah faced was one I could not help her with. Yellow-vested traffic minders stood throughout the course, and their job was to watch the children pedaling around, going where they wanted to, for about thirty minutes. The adult minders watched for infractions, and when they saw a child make one, they spoke up, sometimes barking instructions, quizzing the child on a safety rule, or making them physically practice an intersection again. But some of the minders—usually men—seemed to enjoy exercising their power over the kids rather than offering them effective instruction. They would zero in on a kid, catch them doing something petty, and then heap insults on them for being confused.

When Hannah got onto the next available bike, I said to her quietly, "Kiddo, just keep your head down, toughen that skin up, and follow the instructions as best as you can." She had not even left the bike "parking lot" to enter the pretend roadway before an instructor bore down on her, and I had no idea what she had done to invite it, if anything. With him barking at her, I watched her get off and back on the bike, only to be forced to do it again, and again. I could not figure out what minor rule she had already violated.[20] At last, with a final dressing down, he released her to enter the course space, her confidence dragging, which showed up in her tentative pedaling.

It was so hard for me to watch her try to comply, bearing up under the instructor's inordinate attention, suffering the minor but humiliating consequences. It frustrated me more because I couldn't understand what this man was saying to my child, nor effectively argue with him. I felt small and helpless and completely unable to change any of the facts on the ground. I knew that my intervening wouldn't have made her experience easier. But it appalled me more, looking back on it, that the essence of my moral instruction to her was, effectively, "Lie low, kid. That's the way to survive this thing." Even when she followed the instructions of these yellow-vested, sometimes power-tripping traffic minders, she still got an earful of pedantic lecturing. Every time we went, we wanted the half hour to fly by, get our stamp and then get out of there.

When the desk officer slammed that final stamp onto her paper after our sixth visit to the course, I breathed a deep sigh of relief. Hannah had learned to deal better with the instructors, but I couldn't help thinking back to my early inward retreats, my instinctive withdrawal from such minor stresses as fourth-grade traffic school. That stress test revealed a lot to me, and what I saw disturbed me. It was easy to see how the instinct to survive takes over. And in places where civic life dries up and political trust is broken, and the universe summed to zero, it *feels* easier—even wise—to just lie low, keep one's head down, go along to get along. It is a survival strategy, but a diminishing one. I felt helpless at the traffic school, and then I taught that survival strategy to my daughter.

• • •

I hit the curb too hard, and the impact jarred both my body and the bike. My headlight tumbled out of its socket and slammed onto the sidewalk. I squeezed the brakes and scooted out of the bike lane so I didn't jam it up. As I crouched down to take a look at the damage, with my hand on the bars, the bike folded up again, like a newborn foal, and fell to the ground. I got it back up to standing and, this time, stood the bike up more sturdily. No major harm done, it seemed. I saw that a few pieces of plastic had shattered off the frame of the headlight, and I tried to get the bulb back into the socket. After several failed attempts, it finally clicked into place.

I pedaled off again, relieved to see the light glow. It all could have been much worse, I thought, and my mind started focusing forward, more alert now to all the possible obstacles in my path ahead—some odd stick on the street, a kicked-up stone—and wondering what I narrowly missed behind. I was relieved that our son had not been in the bike seat behind me. But my anxious, racing mind continued to ruminate on the bike spokes and all that could get snarled in them, imagining the bike flipping, and worse, my son with me, rotating in the air and then slamming down onto the sidewalk. Once my mind hit that mental curb, it was hard for me to hit the brakes on my anxiety.

Once the inner fear begins to grow, I am tempted to swaddle my life, my family, in mental bubble wrap to stave off the worries. I want to retreat into cocoons of caution, look inward and not outward. I like to think that I'm anticipating dangers and thereby keeping my children safe, but in truth, I'm often just teaching them how to fear and withdraw, how to avoid getting entangled, how to survive and no more.

My bike rides in Berlin remind me that we are all connected in this world. The streets I ride along are connected to others, and what might happen on my street, in my neighborhood, can affect what happens in another place. There's connective tissue linking our lives to others, and these roads are signs of it. Whenever I turn in on myself during a bike ride, when worry bubbles up, it gives me the chance to acknowledge and answer my fears by practicing curiosity, staying inquisitive and creative, and being willing to courageously improvise wherever I am.

Bonhoeffer gave thought to the spokes of wheels too. He saw the connective tissue of civic life in ways that many in his day preferred to avoid. In his searing essay "The Church and the Jewish Question," written in the earliest months of Hitler's tyranny, Bonhoeffer saw that the state posed a threat to the fabric of society, and specifically to its Jewish citizens. A threat to one citizen is always a potential threat to others.[21] Identifying the three tasks of the church in its relationship to the states, his most controversial third point, deviating sharply from Lutheran tradition, was for the church to fall between the spokes of the wheel itself in order to jam it and stop its relentless crushing spin.[22]

Falling between the spokes; jamming the wheel. Bonhoeffer here speaks of the church itself as the jamming agent, shoving itself into a charging wheel. The church needed to be willing to be the thing itself—the branch, the stone, whatever might stop the motion. To let oneself fall into the spokes is an act of nonviolent self-sacrifice, as far from religious zealotry as can be imagined. And it requires paying attention to what's happening to others, a willingness to look beyond one's own lanes, off the routine paths of safety and away from the bottom line of our own personal survival, to be aware of and willing to respond to a vulnerable other. Acknowledging the costs, Bonhoeffer knew we shouldn't stay in our lane if others were suffering in theirs.

Wreath at the German Resistance Memorial, Bendlerblock, Berlin. The plaque reads: "Died Here for Germany, July 20, 1944," listing the names of some of the men involved in the failed plot executed there.

Chapter 7

LIFE AS
ARS MORIENDI

→ *Key: The most masterful lives are those
skilled in the art of dying well.* ←

Benjamin and Brigitte lingered in the room longer than the others in the group, who had already headed down the pine staircase. I remained on the landing outside of Bonhoeffer's bedroom, giving them space to think and feel. Finally they came out, joining me on the landing.

"I'm so glad you could come today," I said, quietly engaging them in small talk, drawing them out of their meditative place. Benjamin turned to me, trying to return my pedantic pleasantries, but his eyes showed how intensely Bonhoeffer's story had moved him.

"Yes," he said, his eyes filling with tears. "What an honor to be in this house." He and Brigitte, his wife, were part of a group from our bilingual church in Berlin, so I knew them from many Sunday services. Benjamin serves as one of our church's interpreters, translating seamlessly between English and German. His ability to communicate between these language worlds is astoundingly fluid.

Quieting my instinct to generate more banter, I replied, simply, "It is."

After a long pause, he continued, "You know . . ." and then paused again, trying to gain composure but finding the task challenging.

"His life was so aristocratic, so comfortable and privileged. I didn't realize quite how high he lived growing up. He really could have lived a much easier life, a more secure life, than he did. It's an amazing thing: his faithfulness to God required him to relinquish his claims to that privilege, to so much. To everything." Here, Benjamin swallowed hard, tears beginning to fall onto his cheeks. "*Everything* was stripped from him. He even let go of his claims to his own life."

I nodded slowly, my eyes closed in earnest agreement, and remained quiet.

"We don't think in those terms much, do we?" he said at last.

I opened my eyes, and said, "No. We don't."

• • •

That same thought came to me during a tour at least a year before that conversation on the landing. I allowed the idea to spool out, warning the visitors—who were strangers to me—that I was thinking on my feet a bit. But the truth of it seemed so plain that I wanted to sound it out.

I had focused their attention on Panel 6, with its photographs of leaders from the Confessing Church and of Finkenwalde, the illegal preachers' seminary that Bonhoeffer headed from 1935 to 1937. The panel had been giving me problems in recent tours, mostly because I needed to give it more study. My mind often went blank when I tried to pair the names and faces of these key Confessing Church leaders in the filmstrip-like image at the top of the panel. Many of them are not well known outside of Germany by nonexperts like me. I knew of Rev. Martin Niemöller, passing his church as I did every day on the way to my son's preschool. I had learned the name of the lone female on the filmstrip, Gertrud Staewen, who was a member of

Niemöller's parish and personally acted to help Jews, securing forged food-ration cards and helping to hide those trying to escape.[1] Before guiding this group, I had studied this particular panel more closely, and so the material was fresh in my mind. My attention was primed for discovery.

I delved into a description of the seminary—one of five started by the Confessing Church—including its bare-bones beginnings and its dependency on the local population for donations of materials and furniture. As I spoke, I was suddenly gut-punched with emotion. I had been swimming around in the facts of the seminary and Bonhoeffer's leadership of this experiment in "new monasticism." But now, as I spoke, I saw it through a different lens.

I had long imagined the Confessing Church as an institutional counterbalance to the Deutsche Christen, the German Christians. And at the beginning of Nazi rule, that picture is somewhat accurate. Membership between these two poles, those who ardently supported the Nazis and those who ardently opposed, was nearly equal, with a large segment of the church found somewhere in the ambivalent middle. In my mind the Confessing Church organization was a solid force with institutional gravitas, bearing the moral mantle of manifest destiny because they were, clearly, in the right. But as the German Christians enjoyed political coordination with the National Socialists, their rule strengthened as the Nazis' did, just as the Confessing Church's resolute stand against these consolidating powers grew weaker.

Never had I imagined the Confessing Church as a scrambling response or an emergency effort, a fragile coming together of factions aiming to mitigate the spiritual hemorrhage caused by the Nazi assault on the church—an assault that the Deutsche Christen welcomed and cheered. Indeed, the Confessing Church was a conglomeration of people holding widely varying positions—many were nationalistic, many anti-Semitic, some quite open to compromise with Nazis, while others in the movement risked their lives to resist them. "The only thing all Confessing Christians had in common was their opposition to the absolute demands of Nazi ideology on their religious faith," as Victoria Barnett put it.[2] Beyond that common point of agreement was a wide field of disagreement about how the church was to relate to the state and to victims of the state. The right and good thing to do was simply not apparent to all, and all kinds of human emotion and weakness clouded and constrained how people made decisions as moral and civic chaos and political fear calcified on society.

The Confessing Church seminary that Bonhoeffer formed was an innovative effort marked by both its brevity and its intensity—terms commonly used to describe something doomed and futile. Indeed, its brief dates, its relatively ad hoc existence, and its far-flung location distant from recognized power centers marked it, by and large, as a failure—at least by the measures I know. It was not a training camp for culture warriors or political agitators; it did not promise or usher in any sweeping transformation of society. Really, it was barely an institution, and it bloomed for a few precious days of history out on what must have seemed like the edge of existence, more wildflower than oak. By all metrics in use today, it was an inconsequential vapor in the hot winds of the era.

The seminary's fleeting and fragile reality gripped me as I described it to the group, and a flood of pity swallowed me as I imagined Bonhoeffer and the seminarians there. They were all young men, at the beginning of their careers and what should have been a flourishing adulthood, but already they were forced to make much larger decisions than I ever did at that age or after. And there was

Bonhoeffer, a young, rising, and accomplished theologian, energetic and humane, with all the pedigree and privilege that, in normal times, would have fast-tracked him into a comfortable academic and pastoral career, earning him plenty of plaudits in life. At Finkenwalde these young men came to study with him, and together they lived in a community on the far reaches of an unquiet sea, trying to build something that would get them to a safe shore, which, for many of them in time, would be the shores of heaven. After the Gestapo closed the seminary just two years after it began, they continued their formative work in collective pastorates, apprenticing with a Confessing Church pastor and receiving instruction midweek. As the Nazis prepared to expand their perverse vision of greatness and inflict it upon more of the world, most of these pastors were forced into military service and died for a cause none of them believed in.

Their presence at a Confessing Church seminary revealed how they interpreted their times, at least with respect to their vocational ministry.[3] Among the students, Eberhard Bethge opposed the Nazification of the church in 1933 and joined the Young Reformation Movement, an early precursor to the Confessing Church.[4] With fourteen other classmates at the famous seminary in Wittenberg, Martin Luther's old seminary, he announced his allegiance to the Confessing Church in October 1934. In coordination with Reich Church authorities in Berlin, the seminary promptly evicted Bethge and these other students. By the time he arrived at the seminary when it was formed in 1935, he had already experienced some of the costs of discipleship.

I had never pitied these men before, nor the seminary, nor Bonhoeffer—never once considered the smaller forms of suffering they tasted. And I wondered what my pity for Bonhoeffer represented, for it seemed strange and worldly. I didn't want to project pathos onto him or think of him merely as a privileged human being who should have been guaranteed a quality of life that most are denied. Peering beneath that pity, though, I discerned a kind of grief, a true wail of lament, over the tragic waste that the Nazi regime made of everyone and everything. Lives that should have been lived, dreams that should have been allowed to breathe and grow. And as a wildflower in that growing field of wreckage, Bonhoeffer's seminary looked so small and ineffective compared to the rapacious juggernaut of the regime and the nauseatingly obedient support it received from the Nazi-affiliated church.

That tour was the first time I ever paired Bonhoeffer's name with failure. It was a new and uncomfortable lens, for it was much easier to think of him as a moral champion, a victor finally receiving posthumous fame. But thinking of him as someone denied a course of life that could have easily been his, repeatedly thwarted in his life's work, working on the edges, feeling the instability and fatigue of it all, caused me to churn with pity and grief. I teared up briefly. In that one moment, I saw how casually I had fashioned him in my mind as a successful hero without considering how much he let go of in life, the many private sufferings and dying-to-self moments he chose, long before the Nazis put him to death in 1945.

I went on in my tour, thinking aloud. "Obviously, Bonhoeffer made his peace with that hard path. The 'normal course of life' was not going to be his. The times offered that normal course to no one. To chart a course of career success in that political and social environment necessitated so much moral corruption, so much ethical atrophy. While it is right to honor him, and I do, it's better to think of him not in terms of heroism and success—even moral success—but to see his life as a masterpiece in the art of dying, a fully lived study in the *ars moriendi*."

Ars moriendi, the art of dying. Roman Catholic friends in Washington, DC, introduced that Latin term to me years ago, and the phrase returned to me as our family visited the Marienkirche (Mary's Church) near Alexanderplatz. This historic church is not far from Berlin's iconic TV tower, the Fernsehturm, which was completed by the East German government in 1969 as part of a massive building campaign to project its Communist greatness by overshadowing the many churches in the neighborhood: the Berliner Dom, the city's national Protestant cathedral; St. Nicholas's (or the Nikolaikirche); and St. Hedwig's Roman Catholic cathedral. The design of the tall TV tower's disco-ball-like sphere under a candy cane-striped antenna, however, reflects a cross of light on sunny days, an unforeseen effect that Berliners refer to as the "Pope's Revenge," poking fun at the shattered hubris of atheistic communism.[5]

Comparatively tiny, but not diminished beneath that hulking tower, the Marienkirche is one of Berlin's oldest churches, sharing that distinction with the nearby Nikolaikirche. Construction on the Marienkirche began in 1270, when Berlin was still a very young city, and the building itself reflects the strata of history, parts of it in granite and the majority in red brick. On the left side of the church's entrance hall is a large fresco—two meters high, twenty-two meters long—behind a thick pane of glass protecting it from the elements and the many visiting tourists. While it is currently under restoration, it's amazing that there's anything there to restore. Painted in the late fifteenth century, sometime between 1470 and 1485, the fresco was covered with layers of whitewash and lost to memory until an architect discovered it in 1860. This *Totentanz*, or Dance of Death, fresco depicts people of all ages and classes—men and women, young and old, wealthy and poor, distinguished and forgotten—holding hands with shroud-draped skeletons who stand between the living, as if they are all line-dancing together. Beneath the images are stanzas of poetry, including the words of the Psalmist, "Learn that you must die, that you may gain a heart of wisdom" (Psalm 90:12).[6]

Meditating on death as a path of wisdom has long been part of the biblical tradition, present in both Judaism and Christianity and formally incorporated into liturgical services such as Ash Wednesday. While signing an ashen cross on a congregant's forehead, a priest utters words from Genesis 3: "Remember that you are dust, and to dust you will return." While the memento mori tradition—whose name is Latin for "remember you will die"—has been a part of religious and secular wisdom traditions, the practice took on a particularly vivid form in medieval Europe as the Black Death, the bubonic plague, ravaged the continent, killing between one-third and one-half of Europe's population.[7]

In the generations after the plague, various artworks captured its horrors but also the hope-filled warning that one could gain wisdom for life by meditating on one's inevitable death. The *Totentanz* fresco in Berlin is one example; many others in the same genre and title exist at churches throughout Europe. Another is a widely circulated set of fifteenth-century manuals of varying lengths that feature woodcut prints of people lying on their deathbeds, tormented by personified temptations and demons, with instructions on the art of dying well. These *ars moriendi* handbooks were widely used throughout Europe and were particularly helpful to laypeople when a priest could not get to a dying person's bedside in time.[8] They offered the hope that a path of life wound even through the valley of death.

• • •

"Bonhoeffer is one of my heroes," a new acquaintance told me brightly when she learned I was volunteering at the Bonhoeffer-Haus. It would have been petty to challenge her. I knew what she meant, having said it myself and meaning it too. It was religious small talk, the back and forth of a light conversation: What kind of music do you like? What's your favorite kind of food? Who are your heroes? Bonhoeffer *is* a hero, without question. But when his story is told in ways that make it thrilling and dramatic—which in parts it was, no doubt—that narrative easily neglects the many smaller deaths and lesser sufferings he experienced.

When I have described Bonhoeffer as my hero, I've meant he is someone I want to affiliate with, or emulate, although if pressed to show how I might imitate him, I would struggle to answer. I want to do the right thing at the hard time, like he did, but much of what I think of as hard about my life is small and pathetic compared to the travails and trials of the Nazi era. I, too, want to make good decisions and disobey powerful pretenders that seek to shape culture to their corrupting will, but by the end of a day, I'm usually tired, and there are dishes to wash, and I'd prefer to not have to make more decisions, much less face down a power. I'm not a hero. Soaking in the details of Bonhoeffer's life, the many discomforts and insecurities he faced long before his death at the Flossenbürg concentration camp after two years of incarceration in various prisons, I cringe at the costs he suffered in life. He seemed to live a life forever accompanied by death, something I try daily to avoid, and he also seemed to live nine lives within a span of thirty-nine short years.

Death invaded his home life early, when he was twelve and the news arrived that his older brother Walter had died from his shrapnel wounds in the Great War (1918). But even before that, as a younger child, Bonhoeffer thought about death and meditated on

Ewigkeit—eternity. Imagining himself on his deathbed, reciting his last words, his fascination and fear of death at bedtime was often so great that he felt faint.[9] He would bite his tongue hard to draw himself out of that black hole in his mind and find solace by picturing angels posted by his bed. As scared as he became, he continued to think about death, almost practicing it.[10]

Death, with its clarifying power, was still on his mind in his magnificent essay "After Ten Years," written at the Bonhoeffer-Haus at Christmas 1942. He gave copies of it as a present to fellow conspirators Hans Oster, Hans von Dohnanyi, and Eberhard Bethge. He hid another copy in the Haus. In the essay, Bonhoeffer reflects on what it means to be human and remain human, and to be a Christian and remain a Christian, in deadly, dehumanizing times.

"Time lost is time in which we have failed to live a full human life . . . [our] losses have been great and immeasurable, but time has not been lost," he begins. The essay ranges widely, addressing the constraints of his fellow conspirators' circumstances and the hope that another kind of nobility will emerge, a new class of noble people who have abandoned vanities and privilege in exchange for quality and freedom. He decries Dummheit—sometimes translated folly or stupidity—as a far deadlier threat than scoundrelism. And then, he writes about death:

> In recent years we have become increasingly familiar with the thought of death. We surprise ourselves by the calmness with which we hear of the death of one of our contemporaries. . . . Fundamentally we feel that we really belong to death already, and that every new day is a miracle. It would probably not be true to say that we welcome death (although we all know that weariness which we ought to avoid like the plague). . . . Nor do

we try to romanticize death, for life is too great and too precious. . . . [We] know too much about the good things that life has to offer, though on the other hand we are only too familiar with life's anxieties and with all the other destructive effects of prolonged personal anxiety. We still love life, but I do not think that death can take us by surprise now. After what we have been through during the war, we hardly dare admit that we should like death to come to us, not accidentally and suddenly through some trivial cause, but in the fullness of life and with everything at stake. It is we ourselves, and not outward circumstances, who make death what it can be, a death freely and voluntarily accepted.[11]

By the time he wrote this essay, Bonhoeffer had accepted that his Christian life, lived faithfully, might lead to "the sacrifice of his Christian reputation," which was perhaps his most difficult lesser death before his final one.[12] His responsibility led him to enter the polluted waters of the world, even into sin, and thus to trust more fully in the grace and righteousness of Christ. The ethics of the times offered no sinless options, and responsibility for Bonhoeffer meant refusing to be a bystander as the country descended deeper into madness. He risked history misinterpreting him, opening himself up to being misunderstood and judged or even derided. This course was the fullest and most responsible expression of his Christian faith.

• • •

One of the things that most shocked me in my early visits to the Haus, before I became a guide, was learning that Germans regarded Bonhoeffer and the other conspirators of the failed July 20, 1944 assassination and coup attempt ambiguously, even as traitors, for a long time afterwards. Most did not celebrate them as heroes, and it took nearly a generation before their actions were reconsidered in a more positive, less uncertain light.[13] Indeed, it took nearly a generation before anyone began to talk about what happened, to sort and sift through the truth of that era. When I heard a volunteer guide say this, it sounded almost nonsensical to me, imagining World War II, as I once had, as a grand morality tale in which the good guys won because it was their moral manifest destiny.

Retold in this century in the film *Valkyrie* (2008), the July 20, 1944, plot led by Colonel Claus von Stauffenberg was the last of many serious attempts to jam the Nazi wheel.[14] As Allied forces pressed in from both west and east against the Nazis late in the war, the Stauffenberg plot also represented the last real attempt from within Germany to communicate powerfully that not all of Germany was as mad as its *Führer*. Stauffenberg was a relative newcomer to the larger Abwehr conspiracy, but he was well aware of Hans von Dohnanyi, Bonhoeffer's brother-in-law, and his significant groundwork in the cause.[15] Bonhoeffer was in prison already when the plot failed, and his links to this larger conspiratorial circle had not yet been uncovered. And until that fateful date, Bonhoeffer had believed his release from prison was possible.[16]

Convinced that Hitler needed to be removed, Stauffenberg volunteered to place a bomb in the middle of a military briefing for Hitler and other senior military officers held at the Nazis' eastern front headquarters, named the Wolf's Lair, far in the east of Germany (now Poland). Stauffenberg excused himself from the room and witnessed the bomb detonate as he left the compound. Believing the mission had been successful, he flew back to Berlin, where he and other Abwehr plotters enacted their coup to take control of the rest of the military and security forces. But within hours, the coup attempt unraveled in a series of miscommunications and stalled momentum. Moreover, they learned that Hitler had survived, and the *Führer* addressed the nation by radio to prove it and mock the conspirators. The briefcase had been moved from where Stauffenberg had first placed it and was sitting against a supporting leg of the massive table at the time it exploded, so the table itself absorbed much of the blast. Stauffenberg and his fellow conspirators were quickly captured, and although one was offered the option to commit suicide, most were immediately put to death by firing squad in the courtyard of the Bendlerblock, the building housing the army's high command.[17]

It was a critical moment of failure. In its aftermath, more than seven thousand were arrested and nearly five thousand put to death, many on very flimsy evidence.[18] As a member of the large conspiratorial network, Bonhoeffer believed his fate was set. Moreover, in September 1944, an extensive cache of files with conspirators' names was found in a farmhouse in the village of Zossen, and Bonhoeffer's name and details of his role were in it. Since his arrest in April 1943, he had been held at Tegel military prison. But the discovery of the Zossen files, laying bare so much of what had been hidden successfully from the Gestapo, precipitated his move to SS headquarters, which signaled a significant turn for the worse for Bonhoeffer.[19] After months in that fearful prison, known for torture, he was transferred to several different locations as the Allied militaries closed in on Berlin, then finally put to death by hanging at the Flossenbürg concentration camp on April 9, 1945—his killing ordered on April 5 by Hitler.[20]

Some immediately referred to Bonhoeffer as a martyr, but few in Germany shared that view. Nor did many Germans see the other conspirators as honorable heroes, instead considering them ambiguous traitors.[21] Many of the conspirators hailed from German nobility and held conservative political views. Their plans to stand up a new government if their plot had succeeded were more informed by a lost world of 1914, before Germany's ill-fated experience with liberal democracy in the Weimar Republic and before World War I. Beyond all their unrealistic political plans, a more depressing reality remained: even if they had succeeded in killing Hitler, the German population was unlikely to have cheered their coup as a liberation from tyranny. More likely, Hitler's death would have made a martyr of the *Führer* since the general public was already so trained to worship him—even if with a fearful awe.[22]

It took considerable time and effort for the conspirators' failures to be celebrated as moral triumphs. Historian Alexandra Richie cautions that many in the West have been raised to think of those conspirators as "the good Germans," the moral heroes in history, vindicated posthumously.[23] But this neglects the fact that, even years after the war, the Führer still registered in the popular imagination as "a figure of hope." In a 1952 opinion poll, a quarter of the West German population saw Hitler in favorable light, and one in ten ranked him just beneath Bismarck among Germany's greatest statesmen.[24]

Like Owings, who traveled to interview German Frauen (women) in the latter part of the decade, Richie traveled to Berlin in the early 1980s and met people who still referred to those conspirators as traitors. In other words, the morality tale was not written from time immemorial. There was a significant struggle over the story itself when the moral rubble started being sifted and sorted, which is itself a story that encompasses prolonged failure to make good sense of such a wretched time.

The work of that story continues—wrestling over events and their meanings, the slow chipping away at stories in light of facts, pursuing the truth, protecting it, and passing it along for future generations. It is the work of historians and theologians,[25] and it is the work carried out at the Bonhoeffer-Haus, by expert guides and passionate visitors. Telling the truth requires seeing people and stories from new angles, listening to a widening chorus of witness, going "beyond" to revisit questions and critically engage the times. One has to be willing to relax certain instincts—the instincts of self-preservation, self-defense, subtle forms of distancing, rationalization, and personal exoneration—in favor of that continued work. Letting go of these well-practiced habits of the heart, at times, means being willing to give an account of moral failure, abdication, and wrongdoing. It is, simply, mortifying, a kind of *ars moriendi* in itself. My German colleagues at the Haus demonstrated to me by example, speaking plainly about hard truths of a past that they inherited. They learned to reckon with a guilt-suffused past in the vigilant present in order to ensure a more hopeful future.

• • •

The unexpected tours were often the most interesting for me. One day I had been sitting for a while, looking out the front window of the Bonhoeffer-Haus, waiting for a scheduled group to arrive. Each passing minute signaled that they weren't going to show; I tried contacting the tour organizer but got no reply. So I sat and read for a while and then finally started gathering my materials together, returning the cups and pitchers of water I had set out for them on the conference table back to the kitchen cupboards. I had just closed the last cupboard door when the doorbell rang. I rushed to the front door, thinking it was the tour group at last, but instead saw a young couple standing at the gate.

I called from the front door to them, "Do you have an appointment with someone?"

They both looked at me curiously and didn't answer, and so I ran out to meet them.

They were Italians traveling through Europe, and they did not have an appointment. Of the two of them, only she could speak some English, but he was the one who was interested in Bonhoeffer. He knew the broad strokes of Bonhoeffer's life. "What a coincidence!" I told her, in rapid-fire English. "Your visit was meant to be. I had been just about to leave, but I still have some time to show you around."

She blinked and asked me to speak more slowly. It was clear that our language differences would be challenging, but she said she would try to translate for her partner. I assured her I would do my best and quickly began recalibrating what would be best to say.

"I do not know who is this," she said haltingly, pointing to the Haus, and then back to her partner. "But he does."

"OK," I said slowly, smiling, and held the gate open to welcome them in.

I had some new points of conversation to include, which I had planned to raise with the group that never showed up. Earlier in the week, I read an advanced copy of Stephen Haynes's *The Battle for Bonhoeffer*, a helpful but searing and complicated account of Bonhoeffer interpretation in the United States. Since he is now such a significant figure in the public domain of popular imagination, Bonhoeffer has been interpreted and reinterpreted, marketed and sold in so many forms, that I despaired as I read Haynes's account that it was possible to say anything about him at all.

One thing I had learned from Haynes was that Yad Vashem, the Holocaust memorial center in Jerusalem, had considered Bonhoeffer for inclusion in its noble register of the Righteous among the

Nations. To merit that designation requires considerable personal sacrifice by a gentile on behalf of Jews during the Holocaust. While Bonhoeffer helped in some operations to get Jews out of Germany, and even though he argued within the Confessing Church that the church should do more to protect Jews from state persecution, the reviewing committee determined that he took no personal risks to save Jewish lives. As laudable as some of his efforts were, the arbiters decided against placing him on the register.

The Italian couple and I walked through the panels—Panel 1, showing points on a map of Berlin in 1935 that were significant to the Bonhoeffer family; Panel 2, with pictures of a young Dietrich and his family; Panel 3, with photos from his school days; Panel 4, with more ominous photos, including one of future Nazi propaganda minister Joseph Goebbels, a panel that tries to capture the growing national crisis in Germany. The story of Bonhoeffer's life was completely new for the young woman—she had never heard of him and was learning as she slowly translated for her boyfriend. He was taking it all in, looking at her and at me, nodding and saying, "Sì, sì!" to signal that he was right with us despite the language barrier. She found it all fascinating too, her admiration for Bonhoeffer clearly building.

As we approached Panel 5, the centerpiece panel with the image of the destroyed Fasanenstrasse Synagogue after Kristallnacht, I brought up this newly learned fact of Bonhoeffer's failure to meet the standards for the Righteous among the Nations. I tried to say what I had learned as simply as I could to facilitate the young woman's translation. But when I told her about the Yad Vashem decision, how Bonhoeffer's resistance work, as important as it was, did not directly save Jewish lives in a way that put him at personal risk, she broke off translating immediately.

"Wait. *What*?! He did not help Jews?!" she said sharply, turning away from the panel to face me with startled eyes.

I realized immediately that I had waded in too far. I tried to backpedal—"No, no, he was a good guy! He was!"—and found myself stumbling more as I did. None of it translated well. To be sure, Bonhoeffer was among the earliest Christian voices to argue that how the church did or did not help Jews (not just non-Aryans, or baptized people of Jewish background) revealed its obedience or disobedience to Jesus. Some parts of the Confessing Church floundered on this subject; many were concerned more with their own survival against the Nazis and much less with the increasing suffering the Nazis inflicted on those beyond the church doors. Bonhoeffer was close to many in the Confessing Church who went to great lengths, assuming real risks, to assist Jewish people. But compared to some whose names do appear on the list—people like Oskar Schindler, whose story was popularly depicted in film, or even Bonhoeffer's own brother-in-law Hans von Dohnanyi, whose story is not as well publicized—in the eyes of Yad Vashem, *Bonhoeffer did not make the mark.*

A pinch of desperation grew within me as I poorly tried to explain what I meant by what I had just said. I wanted this woman, who was learning for the first time about Bonhoeffer's life, fragment by translated fragment, to *like* him, to admire him, just as I did. I wanted him to be an easy hero for her. Inwardly, I kicked myself for trying to be too clever, thoughtlessly incorporating this nuanced point that had so abruptly upended her growing admiration. We continued on with the tour. But as I said goodbye to them at the door and headed home, I returned to interrogate that instinct in me.

Why did I want to *sell* him to her? That wasn't my task as a volunteer. Although each volunteer at the Bonhoeffer-Haus holds Bonhoeffer in great honor and respect, our role is not to tend his cult of personality. Rather, we introduce visitors to his life, to see him in his place and context, and, most importantly, to reflect on his life—its questions, answers, and even some of its failures—with an eye to our own. Ideally, we see where we may need to recalibrate our own course.

Letting go of his own righteousness, Bonhoeffer's decision to move into political resistance came with knowing that he was entering into sin and the possibility that, despite all of his intentions for good, he might be judged differently, his name tied to a legacy of dishonor or disrepute. He had to think beyond those deaths, believing that death did not get the last word. That was all part of embracing responsible action.

• • •

As described earlier, Bonhoeffer returned from his brief second visit to America back to Germany in 1939, and with the help of Hans von Dohnanyi, he began to work as an agent in the Abwehr, or German military intelligence. He continued to travel and engage with his international contacts in the ecumenical movement, his seminary contacts, and other members of the Confessing Church as well. But he was now walking deliberately on a guilt-filled path, a responsible life that drew him more deeply into life's profound brokenness. Bonhoeffer's agent work for the Abwehr required him to lie regularly and practice deceit consciously. He built artifices. His faithful embrace of his responsibilities in no way guaranteed success. But he knew that inaction would have been an even greater failure.

He had been confronted with this truth earlier in life when his twin sister, Sabine, and her husband, Gerhard Leibholz, asked him to officiate at Gerhard's father's funeral. But because the man was not a baptized church member, and was of Jewish background, Bonhoeffer's church superintendent in Berlin counseled him against it. He took that advice and did not officiate at the funeral. It was months before he acknowledged to Sabine and Gerhard what a failure this had been on his part and how tormented he was by regret at the memory. All he could do, he said in a letter, was ask for their forgiveness. This moment of failure showed him a reality he could no longer avoid. He would never be able to navigate a secure, conflict-free course, or even a merely career-minded one, without killing something true in himself.[26] He could not escape the confines of his world. All kinds of deaths were inevitable, and he was responsible for choosing which one he would freely and voluntarily die, which deaths would guide his life.

• • •

The art of dying is a hard sell as a course for a good life, and there is a risk to "paying more attention to dying than to death," as Bonhoeffer put it in a letter to Bethge from prison in March 1944, just before Easter:

> We're more concerned about how we shall face dying than about conquering death. Socrates mastered the art of dying; Christ overcame death as [the last enemy] (1 Cor. 15.26). Being able to face dying doesn't yet mean we can face death. It's possible for a human being to manage dying, but overcoming death means resurrection. It's not through the *ars moriendi*, but through Christ's resurrection that a new and cleansing wind can blow through our present world.[27]

Bonhoeffer paid attention to death with an eye to what came after, which for him meant resurrected life. He believed death opened the door into greater life, and so death itself was not the last word. Death was the last enemy of life, one that Bonhoeffer believed, in Christ, was defeated.

We mostly want to avoid dying and death. We prefer focusing on the glittering images of success as a definition of the good. We want to participate in the next great thing, the big new idea, the surefire social movement that will secure us or help us succeed or bring us to greater life. Bonhoeffer was fully aware of this dynamic, and the price paid for chasing after success:

> When the figure of a successful person becomes especially prominent, the majority fall into *idolizing success*. They become blind to right and wrong, truth and lie, decency and malice. They see only the deed, the success. Ethical and intellectual capacity for judgment grow dull before the sheen of success and the desire somehow to share in it. People even fail to perceive that guilt is scarred over in success, because guilt is no longer recognized as such. Success per se is the good. This attitude is only genuine and excusable when one is intoxicated by events. After sobriety returns it can only be maintained at cost of deep inner hypocrisy, with conscious self-deception. This leads to an inner depravity from which recovery is difficult.[28]

In the thrall of success, we are tempted to blindly, mindlessly follow the one who claims to be successful. But there are always costs of discipleship, whether one is following Jesus—who, as Bonhoeffer put it in the opening lines of one his most beloved books, when he calls a person to follow him, "bids him come and die"—or someone else.

That beloved book of Bonhoeffer—*The Cost of Discipleship*, as it is called in the English-speaking world—is titled *Nachfolge* in German, a word that means "following," or "following after." A little historical detail brings that single word's meaning into sharper relief. At many Nazi rallies, a popular hymn celebrated the Führer and those who identified as his followers: "Führer, command, we'll follow you [wir folgen dir]."[29] Those who followed after Hitler were his disciples, living out his teachings that incurred massive costs. Bonhoeffer deliberately skewered this idolatrous hymn with the title of his book about following Jesus, to ask his reader, Who are you really following, and what does he command of you and demand from you? What deaths will you die—or inflict on others—in your obedience to him?

Bonhoeffer was not tempted to follow Hitler and his movement, but he was tempted to withdraw from the inevitable costs that following Christ would incur. Many facing that temptation spoke of the option to "migrate within," to isolate oneself from the world and its responsibilities. Bonhoeffer saw that withdrawal to an inner world meant neglect of the real one, and in the end, he refused that path by joining the conspiracy, knowing that choice also involved real cost.[30]

. . .

The host and I enjoyed nearly an hour of engaging conversation, although at times I stumbled over my words. He had read a book review I recently published and asked to interview me for his podcast. Never having been on a podcast, I sensed that being interviewed on a podcast was not at all like giving tours in the Bonhoeffer-Haus.

In the final minutes, I felt the fatigue of the long day behind me—in our different time zones, the American host was in the post-lunch slump, but I was nearing my bedtime. My husband sat on a sofa in the living room, listening in, as I conversed with the host by video call at our dining-room table. One of his later questions pushed me into territory I had never talked about on my feet before, and my answer reflected my lack of preparation. Nevertheless, I forged ahead, unbalanced and veering, the recording preserving it for memory. As we said goodbye, I figured he'd notice that I had botched my reply and would sift it all out.

When the podcast episode was finally released, I was excited to listen to it with my husband. After two more distinguished guests discussed Bonhoeffer's life and thought, my interview came on.

I cringed at my many odd verbal tics (my overuse of the word *like* as a filler, for instance) and some oddly phrased sentences that had fallen out of my mouth before I pieced them together well. But then came that question I had felt so shaky answering, and rather than editing it away, the final take made it all sound far worse than I remembered. It had to do with Bonhoeffer and the ethics of assassination. The question was, "What do we do with Bonhoeffer's decision to join a conspiracy that sought, as one of its goals, to assassinate Hitler? Is this a license for a might-makes-right ethics for all so-called 'Bonhoeffer moments?'"

Admittedly, it is one of the thornier ethical questions that emerges from Bonhoeffer's story, and there are many ways to understand his decision and far more ways to misunderstand it and see it as a form of ethical expediency. As Bonhoeffer's story becomes more well known, there are some who invoke his name and life as an ethical ideal, the person becoming a principle, one recast into a doctrine that can be neatly applied to other settings. It's a form of interpretation that is ripe for abuse. The casually deployed phrase "Bonhoeffer moment" has become code in some Christian circles, among certain rhetoricians, as shorthand for "things have become

so bad we're going to have to *do something drastic.*" Regrettably, the
question of assassination quickly emerges, as if the most salient thing
we could wring out of Bonhoeffer's life was that he was willing to do
it or support it, and, therefore, so should we. The host asked me about
"our American political moment," vague and unbounded, and how to
make sense of Bonhoeffer's willingness to assassinate.

Never had a visitor to the Haus asked me a question like this,
which, looking back, is odd. The question seemed to invert all that
could be learned from Bonhoeffer's life, and it framed something like
assassination in itchy, urgent terms, neglecting how long formed and
last-ditch the conspiracy against Hitler was. Early in the Nazi era,
Bonhoeffer engaged with outspoken courage in all kinds of theological battles, urging the Confessing Church to take a stronger stand
on behalf of their persecuted neighbors. He spoke publicly about the
spiritual deformation that a Führer might demand in a radio address
he gave in February 1933, declaring that a leader—which is what
the word Führer meant before Hitler so fully embodied the term—
becomes a misleader when he allows himself to be made an idol by
his followers—or by demanding a kind of worshipping awe that is
only due to God. But his efforts were largely fruitless in effecting the
change he hoped to see. When he returned to Germany to direct
the seminary, he formed practices of community, not battalions of
Christian soldiers. Theirs was not a training camp for armed holy
war, but a bastion of prayer, confession, enduring suffering, ridicule,
and insecurity.

None of those who entered into the conspiracy had a thirst for
blood; none was itching for that fight. Because many of them were in
the military, they also knew, from lived experience, the actual costs
of war. Their motivations to assassinate Hitler and install a new government were varied—some wanted to revive the monarchy, others

a democratic republic. But they all knew they were risking their lives to stop what they knew was a massive evil that had reigned with impunity and terror for over a decade.

Bonhoeffer was valuable to the Abwehr conspiracy for a particular purpose: he had many international contacts because of his work with the ecumenical movement. Hans von Dohnanyi, having drawn Bonhoeffer into the conspiracy, was uniquely positioned as a key leader within it. In 1933 Dohnanyi worked as a personal assistant to the Reich Minister of Justice, and between 1934 and 1938, he carefully documented the many illegal activities and crimes of the Nazis. These pieces of evidence included Hitler's speeches, plans for pogroms against Jews, and Nazi abuse against prisoners of war. When he joined the staff of Admiral Wilhelm Canaris, chief of the Abwehr, in 1939, Dohnanyi was positioned at the heart of the July 20, 1944, conspiracy. The plotters hoped his file of crimes would prove to the German public why they had to stop the madness.

And time to do so was quickly running out. So many firewalls had been breached in the culture. Germany was losing to the Allied forces, a fact Hitler seemed incapable of facing and one that focused the conspirators' resolve to shoulder their responsibilities to one another and the country. Being brought into the conspiracy in 1940, Bonhoeffer's primary role until he was arrested was to communicate with his many international contacts about the plot, chiefly George Bell, Bishop of Chichester, who, as a member of the House of Lords, relayed information to the British government.

But rather than question the interviewer's question, I tried, foolishly, to answer it on its own terms and quickly got tangled up in it. I tried to describe what I thought is often lost in the discussion, that the Nazi era had gone on for so long, had become so deranged and unjust, how the conspirators weren't juiced up for an ideological thrill ride but were already doomed as figures in the Nazi military leadership. They knew how bad things were—not the whole picture, but enough to know something had to be done, as the ship was clearly beginning to sink. And then I said on the recording, "I don't think we're there . . . yet."

My husband and I both blanched hearing that recording. I knew I answered poorly, but my memory had not remembered just how poorly. I managed to sound like I thought there *was* an ethical continuum on which assassination might be contemplated, and that "we" were somewhere along it, moving toward that end, but not . . . *yet*?!

I wish I had said, "If the first thing you suss out of Bonhoeffer's life is 'At what point is it OK to assassinate someone?,' then you are in a far more worrying moral wilderness than you know." But I did not say that, and instead I contributed to the confusion with that menacing little "yet." I did not narrate Bonhoeffer's decision-making well, nor did I call out the immature reasoning that itches for permission to wage violence against a political or theological opponent rather than contend responsibly, prudently, and with ethical honor.

Whatever excitement I had had about being invited onto the podcast was gone. I did not sleep well that night, and my husband and I deliberated whether I should contact the host and ask him to edit that line out of the recording. I asked some friends to listen to it and give me their frank feedback. I wanted them to assuage my fears, but I also wanted them to tell me the truth. They agreed it wasn't the best answer but didn't think it could be heard as advocating for assassination. They recommended I give this question a long think, get some words down on paper, and practice them, which was good advice.

My minor humiliation, with my nausea-inducing nerves and scrupulous sweat, gave me enough of a taste of the fearful risks of speech and action that opens one up to the possibilities of grave misunderstanding. I had stepped into the conversation with enthusiasm, and now all I wanted to do was run from it. Bonhoeffer was such a clear, disciplined thinker, and in that moment, I was painfully not. Stepping as he did into the realm of political action and intentional deception, he also submitted to the possibility of his work being fundamentally misunderstood and judged. He moved toward his responsibilities of living in the world, accepting that none of his actions could be guiltless, for failing to do so incurred another serious moral guilt. My being poorly prepared for a tough but entirely germane question was hardly a small death in life, but it was, to say the least, mortifying.

• • •

> [Bonhoeffer] did not live to see how German Christians felt no guilt over the concentration camps, euthanasia programs, and genocide, and how after the end of the Nazi regime almost all of them would remain in power.[31]

In a 2015 address to a small audience, Dr. Tobias Korenke, a grandnephew of Dietrich Bonhoeffer, wondered aloud whether his family's sacrifices had been worth it. In the last violent outbursts of the collapsing Nazi regime near the end of the war, this one family suffered the loss of four men—two sons, Dietrich and Klaus Bonhoeffer, and two sons-in-law, Hans von Dohnanyi and Dr. Korenke's grandfather, Rüdiger Schleicher.[32] All were put to death during the war's final weeks in the hasty effort to silence those who had been involved in the larger conspiracy against Hitler. Years later, this grandson looked back with adult eyes and wondered about it all.

To be clear, he didn't question their sacrifice, nor did he try to elicit pity from the audience. Rather, he wondered whether anyone could really know what those sacrificed lives meant, what their losses represented, marveling with world-weariness at how the living carried on. He could not imagine the suffering his grandmother carried for the rest of her life. Her fellow citizens had killed her husband, but after the war, life moved on. So many cheered the Nazis, so many more tolerated them, silently acquiescing to the decay, corruption, incendiary use of words, greater levels of physical violence, dehumanizing untruths. So many had stayed silent and inert, obedient in order to survive, and they never had to bear the costs of their inaction.

Yet in this one family, four men were among those who had known and acted, paying for the failed conspiracy with their lives. Their families lived in the ambiguous shadow of their failed cause. There were no ticker-tape parades to thank them. Very few said they had died well, at least at first. Some in the church refused to call Bonhoeffer a martyr because he stepped out of the pure spiritual realm and into the murk of political reality. Dr. Korenke pressed his audience to consider the many costs these men had suffered.

My colleague Gottfried always says in his tours that it took a generation or two before the public began to reckon with what happened. The reckoning continues; the work of remembering is our moral responsibility. We must pay attention to the arguments, consider the costs of inaction and silence, and the risks that others bear when we fail to live responsibly in our times.

When Eberhard Bethge was released from prison, he was astonished to be alive. So many in his family had been brutally put to death, including his own father-in-law—Dr. Korenke's grandfather, Rüdiger Schleicher—who had been taken out of the prison at the SS headquarters and shot along with Klaus Bonhoeffer on a rubble-filled street in Berlin. Reflecting on the risks the postwar period posed, for the costs to be lost from the public mind, Bethge said:

> We were hardy able to imagine that things could simply pick up from the time before 1933, in the church and even more so in politics. That was not possible for us who had a bit of an idea of what had happened to the Jews. . . . We simply could not imagine another Germany just starting up again as if nothing had happened since 1933. It took a while before it was clear to us that just that was probably going to happen after all. . . . You could see and feel it—as if things like concentration camps and the annihilation of the Jews had almost completely escaped them or they had simply closed their minds to it all.[33]

A reckoning was necessary, admissions of guilt were necessary, but on May 8, 1945—the date of Germany's unconditional surrender to the Allied forces—none of those were on the horizon.

Even if their deaths were not honored as sacrifices immediately, these martyrs did not go to the grave in failure. Facing the reality of their deaths, they had seen life on the other side. Klaus Bonhoeffer, Dietrich's brother, answered his grandnephew, Dr. Korenke, best, I think, when he sketched his own vision of the *ars moriendi*—referring, notably, to the lost wisdom of the medieval period—in one of his final letters to family:

> I don't merely want to live, but to do the most I can with my life. Since this must happen through my death, I have made friends with it also. On this ride between death and the Devil, death is a noble companion. The Devil adapts himself to the times and

has even worn the cavalier's sword. This is how the Enlighten-
ment idealized him. The Middle Ages, which spoke of his bad
smell, knew him better.

In any case, it is a much clearer obligation to die than to live
in confused times, which is why those who are destined to die
were always called fortunate.[34]

• • •

As we entered the room, one of the guests was visibly emotional. He
tried to get comfortable standing in the room as I spoke, crossing
and uncrossing his arms, pacing a little, turning around and touch-
ing the bookshelves. He rubbed his face as if trying to wake up, but
it was now clear to me that he was welling up, wiping the tears away,
and struggling to keep composure. This emotional reaction isn't
unusual, especially in a small group. Larger groups of tourists tend
to buffer the room's sensation of sacredness. But with only a few people, already deeply engaged in the story of Bonhoeffer's life from the
overview in the conference room below, the bedroom presses in with
a palpable witness of its own. I feel it too, each time I bring guests up.

This visitor needed to talk and abruptly interrupted my intermit-
tent commentary. He told us that he was realizing some things. He
knew that when he returned to his home in the United States, he had
some difficult work to do. As a pastor, he knew he needed to deliver
a message to his church that his parishioners did not want to hear.
They needed to be confronted about matters of their own discipleship, to hear the word of God and encounter its resolute claim on
their lives. As he spoke, his internal conflict and anguish grew, and
he finally said to the rest of us in the room, with great emotion, "You
don't get it! You aren't facing what I'm facing. I could lose my job!" We

stood for a time in silence. There was nothing to say to this man's discovery except, "Yes, you might." None of us said it, at least not aloud.

As we descended the stairs to gather our things to leave, a couple of the visitors commented on the banister and how lovely it was. Many visitors admire the beauty of the pine banister, and I always agree with them. After visiting Bonhoeffer's room, the banister offers a handhold, a steadying grip, helping us out of our imaginations of his life and back into realities of our own. We aren't Dietrich Bonhoeffer. Even though we all try to imaginatively slip our feet into his shoes, they don't fit us. We have to walk in our shoes, in the circumstances in which we are placed. But Bonhoeffer's life, like many others, can be a helpful model, a sturdy banister, that can help us expand our moral imaginations in our life and times. Smoothed by the many hands that have used it on the way up to his bedroom and the way down to leave the Bonhoeffer-Haus, the banister holds us up as we make our way into the world, the lives we must live, and the deaths we may face—real or metaphorical.

These same visitors told me that on their way to the Bonhoeffer-Haus from the Heerstrasse S-Bahn station nearby, they had happened upon a ceremony for an installation of Stolpersteine (stumbling stones), held just a few blocks from the house. This was incredible news to me. Since it was so hot out, I offered to ferry them in my car to the S-Bahn station and asked whether they would point out those new Stolpersteine to me on our way. They agreed.

Slowly we drove through the neighborhood until they spotted the site. The installation ceremony was done, and a few roses lay on the lawn just off the sidewalk. We parked the car and approached the small brass cobblestones, gleaming in a neat row in the sidewalk, fresh sandy cement around them. These small memorials are found all around Berlin, and throughout Europe, bearing simple facts:

names, dates, fates. Here lived Frau So-and-So, there lived Herr or Dr. So-and-So, born on this date, deported to this place, murdered at this camp, forced to flee on this date. These "stumbling stones," or "tripping stones," are a small form of civic housekeeping, sifting truth from the rubble of lies, a small memorial of the gargantuan cruelty of Nazi rule, but important nonetheless.[35] Without their humble witness, we might otherwise glide through our present without vital knowledge of the past and of the lives torn asunder in the many places all around our modern world. After the morning we had had together, I was glad we pushed on a little further to find these newly laid stones.

My mind was already turning back to the rest of my day, and these visitors were thinking about theirs. I dropped them at the station and pulled away. I needed to get some work done at home, ferry my middle daughter to a doctor's appointment, pick up my son from preschool on the way, and then prepare dinner. The key to the Bonhoeffer-Haus remained on my keychain, and I felt its weight as I went through the ordinary rhythms of the remainder of my day.

Bonhoeffer's desk, in his bedroom in the Bonhoeffer-Haus

Chapter 8

BEFRIENDING BONHOEFFER

→ *Key: We cannot be Bonhoeffer, but we can befriend him,* ←
modeled best by his own friend, Eberhard Bethge.

I n October 1944, Eberhard Bethge was arrested and subjected to Gestapo interrogations. Bethge presumed his interrogators never connected him with his best friend, Dietrich Bonhoeffer, and thus he was spared death. Even though Bonhoeffer was killed right before the end of the war, their friendship did not die with him; having survived as he did, Bethge said their friendship "continued in a transformed way."[1] Unlike his friend, dead at thirty-nine on a Nazi scaffold in the Flossenbürg concentration camp, leaving unfinished fragments of writing behind, Bethge lived to the age of ninety, passing away at his home in March 2000, having gathered up those fragments of that life cut short, fashioning them into a whole for the rest of us.

• • •

"People are so alone these days," a visitor said, with a marked tone of urgency, standing next to the bed, to the small group of us standing in Bonhoeffer's bedroom with him. "It's a huge social need, and it's getting worse. People are so lonely. So many people here in Germany live alone and die alone. Something has to change."

These moments of personal discovery and points of connection between Bonhoeffer's life and the visitors' lives so often happened here. This man's urgent plea squared with recent news articles I had seen about loneliness as a growing problem in Western democracies, a topic that caught my eye too. Not long before this particular tour, I had read that the United Kingdom established a government position to address loneliness and that more European governments, including Germany's, saw social isolation as a significant problem, with older citizens suffering most.[2] The statistics about the number of people living alone, and dying alone, were sobering.

"We're all so disconnected from each other. Well, actually, we're all 'connected' online, and yet we couldn't be farther from each other," the man continued. "We're technologically connected to people thousands of miles away, but we don't talk to our living, breathing neighbors right next door! Honestly, we could do a lot of good by just loving the people near us, whoever they are. Just staying curious about their lives. Letting them know they are seen, loved, and belong. That someone cares about them, today. We have to know how much we matter to each other." We all nodded. His comments as a member of a faith community were infused with a sense of mission, but it was clear, as well, that the problem of social isolation matters for anyone suffering from it.

I was embarrassed to admit at that moment that he was describing my life a little too. When I felt the bite of loneliness here in Berlin, I usually chalked it up to my not being from here or belonging to this place. The American embassy community should be a natural place of belonging for me. Embassies all around the world try to cultivate community, but in Europe, it can be tough because *for crying out loud, you live in Europe*! It's not like it's a hard place to live. Go to museums, drink coffee in a café, go shopping!

But beyond my circumstances, I've always been reluctant to join groups. I often prefer free agency, forming individual relationships with people from a wide range of backgrounds. I love having a diverse set of friends, but if I'm honest, I also prefer to evade the burdens of belonging.

Of course, what I call my personal quirks might not be that personal—they might be explained by phenomena larger than just me. Coming of age in late twentieth-century America, I was raised in a society with an actively fraying relational and civic fabric. Some of that fraying was billed as freedom, escape from the pressures of shame, the demands of tradition, and the encumbrances of relationships. The heavy weights of community life (with all its social pressure) were thrown off, and what remains is a much thinner blanket against the cold of isolation.

By my college days in the late 1990s, more people were bowling alone than joining a league at the alley, as Robert Putnam put it in his groundbreaking book at the turn of the millennium.[3] On a similar theme in one of my college political theory courses, we read Alan Ehrenhalt's *The Lost City*, about the decline of civic belonging in parts of Chicago. Neighborhoods and the friendships forged within them were once cultivated by attentive parents (usually mothers or grandmothers) hollering from kitchen windows at squabbling children playing on the street outside, by neighbors chatting on the front stoop at the end of a day, or by the authority and rhythms of a parish church. All of these social phenomena were already in marked decline as I came into adulthood. And to some of these institutions, many still say, "Good riddance."

Despite promises of renewed connectivity, the internet and the subsequent rise of social media have fundamentally altered civic life. Both nearly infinitely expanded our ability to connect online with friends, old high school classmates, and distant strangers while also keeping us indoors, plugged in, and screen-faced. It's a mixed bag, benefits with real costs. Social media's fevered growth began just as our family entered the foreign service. My fellow diplomatic and expatriate friends and I would often remark just how lucky we were to be living in an age in which it was so easy to stay connected with our loved ones around the world. No more periodic phone calls home; no more need to write letters—or even emails! We could avoid that acute ache of distance, dislocation, and disconnection through the luxurious din of constant digital connection. And indeed, thanks to social media, I can and do feel connected to others all around the world—through regular text, voice, and video contact—with hardly any relational sweat. But the easy bonds of affection online mean I can relate to those I prefer, without cultivating relationships with neighbors where I actually live. If the electricity ever went out, if the digital web ever went dark, I'd feel more of the reality of my actual aloneness.

Twenty years since *Bowling Alone*, lonely bowlers in a globalized world are more tempted now to answer their own sense of dislocation and isolation with much older elixirs, such as nationalism, which is sweeping the globe right now. The digital age produces its own strains of the virus; nationalists today, like those of yesteryear, advocate for identifying with one's own kind, banding together with a tribe of ideologically likeminded individuals, stoking identity consciousness in the expansive digital domain. And whether we identify as fierce nationalists or staunch internationalists, as fascist or antifascist, we signal to our own kind too. Increasingly we have come to believe that we don't have to practice (that is, pretend with) civility and courtesies anymore now that we are habituated to relating behind avatars and pseudonyms, or only with our own kind. None of us expect a neighborhood auntie to come knock our ears for bad behavior out-side with the kids on the block when it all happens inside and online.

• • •

"We really wouldn't know what we know about Dietrich Bonhoeffer if not for his friend, Eberhard Bethge," I said to the gathered group. "We are immensely indebted to him. Yet we so rarely talk about and celebrate Eberhard Bethge. As much as he shied away from it, he, too, deserves our attention."

I pointed to a photo of Bethge with Bonhoeffer on the Confessing Church/Finkenwalde seminary panel. It's an image of the two friends in 1938, taken during the collective pastorates' era in Gross-Schlönwitz, Pomerania (now Słonowice, Poland). The two of them peer down at a paper, trying to make sense of something on it, and the taller one, Bethge, holds the paper in one hand, his other holding his chin, his brow furrowed, in a full-bodied posture of puzzlement. The lighter-haired, balding, shorter Bonhoeffer looks over his friend's shoulder at the paper too. The photo is poetry; it is fitting that Bethge holds the paper, and Bonhoeffer does not. Seven years from the date of that photo, Bonhoeffer would be dead, but Bethge would continue to pore over many more papers and shoulder the story of his friend's life.

The first essay I read in the exhibition catalogue for the Bonhoeffer-Haus, after Martin gave it to me, was one written by Eberhard Bethge, a short recitation on "The Houses at Marienburger Allee 42 and 43." The essay is a clean, crisp account of the story of the houses built by Dr. Karl and Paula Bonhoeffer. Bethge names the many people who lived in them and those who visited from time to time, as he did, and describes some of the interactions between the two houses.

Bethge even gives a postmortem of the Bonhoeffer-Haus as a place of the family, recounting the death dates of Dr. and Mrs. Bonhoeffer, at which point it passed from the Bonhoeffer family and was recommissioned as a manse for a chaplain and his family and then as a meeting place for the students of the Charlottenburg High School. That chaplain was, in fact, the essay's narrator, Eberhard Bethge, and that same Bethge remembers here in this essay, in stoic terms, huddling in the cellar of No. 42 at the end of the war not long after being released from his prison cell. He was accompanied by a fellow former prisoner, a Russian Jew, who had saved Bethge's life when Russian soldiers threatened to shoot them both as they fled.

The report is matter-of-fact and completely unsentimental. Bethge gives us no insight into anyone's feelings, nor any clues about his own inner thoughts. Indeed, he barely acknowledges himself directly, writing about these circumstances related to the house in the third person. He narrates in a self-obscuring manner, not unlike his role in the larger Bonhoeffer story. It is easy to tell Dietrich Bonhoeffer's story and fully overlook the fact that Bethge is one of its major characters, although he never saw himself as anything more than a bit player among other larger leading actors. But so much of what we know about Bonhoeffer, so much of his growing global regard, we know because of this man who never let go of his friendship, even when they were separated by death.

It is fitting that Bethge wrote this contribution on the pair of houses for, in the end, he belonged to these houses as much as Bonhoeffer and his family did. He stayed frequently in the Bonhoeffer-Haus on his visits with Bonhoeffer on journeys back to Berlin, and from his friend's upstairs window, he caught glimpses of the young woman who would become his spouse, Renate Schleicher. She was raised in No. 42, and her uncle Dietrich's lone bedroom window in

No. 43 looks over the other house's back garden, where she and her sisters would play, catching candies that Dietrich would toss down to them during a break in his writing.

Bethge recalled that when the houses were built in 1935, the family spent a happy Christmas there, enjoying the presence of Grandmother Bonhoeffer, who died in the Bonhoeffer-Haus the following month. The houses were surrounded by a pine forest then and were thus even more secluded and quiet than they are today. When the war ended, a new struggle to survive began. The forests were dismantled to fight the cold of winter, the pines cut down and cleared by residents for firewood. It was the same fate suffered by the trees in the Tiergarten, the central park that stretches west from the Brandenburg Gate, which also was stripped bare of its trees for fuel, the natural world reduced to rubble like the built environment around it.

While the story I told in the Bonhoeffer-Haus was largely about Dietrich Bonhoeffer, his family, and the larger work of resistance, I also came to see it as a place of friendship. The Haus silently honors the life and work of Eberhard Bethge, whose presence in Bonhoeffer's life was integral, and whose narration of it is considerable. He was not Bonhoeffer's only friend, but he was his most important one. The Bonhoeffer story the world inherited is, in many respects, the one told by Eberhard Bethge.

Bonhoeffer cultivated friendships with many people that were fruitful and life giving. Those he developed at Union Theological were critical to his theological development, introducing him to ways of thought, approaches to Scripture, and cultural sources that directly nourished his life and work in the hard years that followed. He made friends and trusted contacts during his expatriate residences in Barcelona and London as well. In fact, his minor but not unimportant role as an Abwehr agent was predicated on the fact that he was skilled in the friendly arts. He was neither a master manipulator nor a daring dealmaker, but he knew how to develop relationships, even with people from diverse backgrounds. Those relationships of trust across national and cultural boundaries were central to his value in the larger Stauffenberg conspiracy.

Bonhoeffer's relationship with Bethge came at a critical time, perhaps at just the right time, in the midst of national and church turmoil. The depth of intimacy they enjoyed was forged in the best of ways—incrementally, by prayer and working on a common cause, through letters, and by spending a great deal of time together. If their friendship had not formed or endured as it did, we would not know most of what we know of Bonhoeffer.

The friendship was forged not only along lines of agreement, as they were in their affiliation with the Confessing Church, but also along lines of difference, particularly in their backgrounds and temperaments. Like Bonhoeffer, Bethge was skilled in the arts of friendship,[4] but his roots were humbler than Bonhoeffer's. He was born in a small village in Brandenburg, not far from the border with Saxony-Anhalt, the third child of Elisabeth and Wilhelm Bethge. He was a diligent and accomplished student, endowed with musical abilities. His father, a pastor, died when Eberhard was only fourteen years old, and he announced at his father's funeral that he would follow him into ministry.[5] He and Bonhoeffer both sensed their call to the ministry and the work of theology at an early age. Also at an early age, Bethge made and kept friends well.

By the time he met Dietrich Bonhoeffer at the illegal seminary's first location in Zingst, Bethge had already faced a critical moment of decision about how he would respond to the disturbing changes within the church under Nazi influence, and he had already suffered some consequences for it. Despite being expelled from his seminary after declaring his alignment with the Confessing Church, Bethge and the rest of the candidates were joyful on this new path, freer, and their bold action encouraged others in the nascent Confessing Church too, even though their future was very much in question and now much less secure.

When Bethge and the other seminarians first gathered in Zingst, on the Baltic coast, Bethge was acutely aware that he was not from Berlin. Unlike some of the seminarians with ties to that city's theological scene, he had never heard of Dietrich Bonhoeffer. He felt like a bit of an outsider to the seminary, a country boy among city folk. Many were aware that the young Bonhoeffer, only three years older than Bethge, was a rising star, having provided real leadership in the early days of the Confessing Church, and his position as leader of this seminary at such a young age was proof.[6]

These seminarians knew they were embarking on an altogether new form of theological formation and training, and the times, as their director saw it, demanded it. In shaping this community, Bonhoeffer drew from many Christian traditions and challenged the seminarians with ideas he learned from other friends of his such as the Reformed Frenchman Jean Lasserre. Bonhoeffer met Lasserre at Union Theological Seminary in New York City during their yearlong academic fellowship (1930–1931). Lasserre sought to obey the plain teachings of Jesus in Scripture, including the call to peacemaking, which he understood as a call to pacifism. Bonhoeffer was amazed and instructed by Lasserre and rediscovered the Sermon on the Mount from their discussions. (The two met up later in 1934 at the ecumenical conference on the island of Fanø, Denmark.)[7]

Bonhoeffer's willingness to even entertain pacifism shocked most of the seminarians, who, while members of the Confessing Church, still identified as good Lutherans and, thus, good Germans. Being a good Lutheran and a good German meant inhabiting two worlds at the same time—the spiritual (tended by the institution of the church) and the secular (maintained by the institution of the state)—but these worlds were fully compartmentalized from one another. To those who subscribed to this view, Bonhoeffer's appreciation for pacifism indicated a disturbing leak between these realms, a worrying bleed between two spheres imagined as separate. Pacifism put the claims and authority of Jesus above and, even more worryingly, against the claims and authority of the state.

In other words, Bonhoeffer's pacifism smacked of resistance—that is, *political* resistance—which was unfathomable to them; the word "resistance" was unutterable.[8] Despite their earlier refusal to submit to the Reichskirche and their willingness to suffer the consequences of that refusal, Bethge and these other seminarians were initially worried about discussions of pacifism, in part because it called into question fundamental tenets in their formation as German Protestants and as German citizens. As Bethge put it years later, reflecting on that time, he and the others saw their position in the seminary as one of confession, not of resistance.[9] They belonged to the Confessing Church to witness to spiritual truths within the church, not primarily to oppose the Nazis. Resistance meant working against the state and its God-ordained role. By introducing pacifism as a gospel position, Bonhoeffer helped Bethge and the others critically interrogate their formation as Lutherans. He pressed them to see that the Nazis exploited the Confessing Church's concern for the "pure gospel"—restricting its concerns only to so-called "religious" matters, and not to any "secular" political questions—to terrifying ends. He urged them to see how faith mattered to society and secular political life.

Bonhoeffer's departure from traditional Lutheran teaching on the institutions of the church and the state was significant. The Confessing Church mostly wanted the state to keep to its own affairs and out of the church's, at least in theory. But historically, the church was fully accustomed to serving the interests and ends of the state, always under the guise that the state would respect its ecclesial authority over spiritual matters. Many Christians openly embraced Nazism and claimed Nazi folk religion was Christianity, and they believed that Nazis were fulfilling God's wishes in the world. The Nazis' successes were their proof of this divine favor. For their part, the Nazis exploited the church-state relationship but increasingly demanded more of the church, more naked obeisance, as their power solidified. The Nazis fearlessly claimed God was on their side, and the German Christians enthusiastically agreed.

As the state's harassment and aggression against Jews and others grew more brazen and violent, the Confessing Church still preferred to concern itself with church matters and was reluctant to make a public, united stand on behalf of those not within its fold. More spoke up in defense of baptized church members who, according to the so-called Aryan laws, were considered Jewish or non-Aryan, but their position was still for those within their tribe, not for those found "outside." Early on, Bonhoeffer saw this failure of the church as a theological problem, evidence of the church's complete disorientation about itself. In ways not many did, Bonhoeffer saw that the traditional relationship between the church and state muzzled the church and emboldened the state. In the context of the seminary community, he instituted practices that invited the seminarians to reimagine their lives and responsibilities, practices that called them out of the *German* way of being Christian and into new territory.

Beyond the seminary's classrooms, Bonhoeffer proposed the idea of establishing the House of the Brethren, a community of preachers who would continue in the practices begun with the seminary groups. The council governing the seminary agreed to this other experiment in community, and six stayed on to participate, including Bethge. He served as Bonhoeffer's confessor there, meaning he listened to his regular confessions of sin and became a close confidant and friend. But the Gestapo shut and sealed both the seminary and the House of the Brethren in 1937, after only two short years. *Life Together* is Bonhoeffer's record of and reflection on their experience of communal Christian life.

A natural friendship developed between Bonhoeffer and Bethge. For all their differences in personality—Bonhoeffer was driving, exuberant, cosmopolitan, and intense; Bethge more modest, unassuming, quietly strong, and steady—they matched one another in intellect and theological insight. Bonhoeffer was particularly impressed with the first sermon that Bethge preached on Isaiah 53.[10] They also shared a love of music and enjoyed pairing their musical skills, with Bonhoeffer playing piano and Bethge singing. Their shared knowledge of the language of music gave them insights into so much of their work together and even the dynamics of their friendship. They knew the power of harmony, the possibility of unity in difference, and the importance of a common melodic line.

Naturally, they experienced the normal elbow-knocking of a real relationship. At times, Bonhoeffer demanded a great deal of Bethge; he acknowledged in a letter to Bethge that he knew he "sometimes made life hard for [him]" and asked for his forgiveness.[11] Bonhoeffer was well aware that Bethge patiently endured much in their friendship, such as Bonhoeffer's "tyrannical" ways and "undoubted volatility," without becoming "embittered by it."[12] Indeed, Bonhoeffer could be downright possessive. On one occasion in 1936, he planned a vacation for himself and Bethge. Without checking whether it would be all right with Bonhoeffer, Bethge invited along his cousin Gerhard Vibrans on the trip. Bonhoeffer was completely put out by this—but, unintimidated by Bonhoeffer's clear annoyance of Vibrans's company, Bethge doubled down and invited his brother, Hans, too.[13] In the end, only Vibrans decided to come. As they prepared for the trip, Bonhoeffer tried to limit how much Vibrans would be with them. Bethge confronted Bonhoeffer directly about how tense he was making things, how much his obsessing about the trip was hurting Vibrans's feelings. The three of them reconciled and found a good compromise plan for the trip. But the moment captures how they conflicted in their close friendship at times.

Other shifts and challenges to their friendship emerged, especially as they looked to the future and the possibility of marriage. At the age of thirty-three, Bethge began courting the seventeen-year-old Renate Schleicher, Dietrich's niece, and they became engaged in November 1942. Two months later, Bonhoeffer surprised his family by announcing his engagement to Maria von Wedemeyer, who, at eighteen, was only half as old as Bonhoeffer. She was the granddaughter of a generous aristocratic supporter and patron of the seminary and Bonhoeffer had catechized her in 1937, when she was eleven—but he did not finally confirm her; he flunked her![14] None of the families were initially thrilled with these engagements, likely because of their significant age differences, and they urged both couples to slow things down—for at least a year.[15] With the war at a totalizing tilt, and Germany's military and political situation growing more hopeless, there was "an all-too-common desire for intimacy in those days of mounting personal losses."[16] Bonhoeffer attended Eberhard and Renate's civil marriage ceremony in March

1943 but not their wedding in May 1943.[17] By that point, it was impossible for him.

On April 5, 1943,[18] Bonhoeffer called over to the Dohnanyis', the house of his sister Christel and his brother-in-law Hans, the latter of whom was also his supervisor in the Abwehr-based conspiracy. A strange voice answered the phone, and Bonhoeffer knew instinctively that the hammer was falling, that the Dohnanyis' house was being searched. This was not a surprise—both men knew the Gestapo had been sniffing around the Abwehr, and Hans von Dohnanyi had been warned in late 1942 that he was under surveillance.[19] The Gestapo had focused their attention on a currency irregularity related to an Abwehr mission, Operation 7, in which both Dohnanyi and Bonhoeffer were involved. This irregularity was their opportunity to deal the Abwehr a blow, which the Gestapo were eager to do. Both Dohnanyi and Bonhoeffer had been warned of possible imminent arrests.

Setting the phone down with flooding realization of what was to come, Bonhoeffer went over to No. 42 and asked his sister Ursula to make a meal for him. He returned to his room at No. 43, the Bonhoeffer-Haus, to set out a false diary he had maintained during his Abwehr work, and to hide away other material. Then he went back to No. 42 to sit and eat with Ursula, Rüdiger, Eberhard, and Renate until his father came around four o'clock in the afternoon to tell him there were men up in his room who wanted to talk with him.[20] Bonhoeffer was, finally, placed under arrest, led out of the house with his Bible in hand, and driven away. (Christel and Hans were also arrested; she was released about a month later, but Hans never was.)

Whereas Bonhoeffer hoped his work in the Abwehr would allow him to avoid conscription into military service (a charge the Gestapo leveled at him before they knew of his role in the larger conspiracy), Bethge did not avoid conscription even though he, too, had worked as an agent for the Abwehr, being privy to many of the conversations of the conspiracy. After marrying Renate Schleicher in May 1943, Bethge was sent to military service in Italy, where the family felt he would be much safer than on the front lines.

But the situation in Italy was complicated. From there, Bethge wrote to Bonhoeffer, confiding in him some of his complaints and wondering whether Bonhoeffer might be having a better time in prison. Bethge was likely suffering more than he could or even wanted to say; for one thing, he had to be circumspect about censors, but he also may have been struggling under the moral weight of having witnessed Nazi massacres of Italian civilians and Jews.[21]

Writing from his cell and unaware of these circumstances, Bonhoeffer gently urged Bethge to savor "the polyphony of life," to remember the fullness of his life with his wife and new son, from whom Bethge was separated at the time, and to hold on to the cantus firmus, the strong melody line threaded through the polyphony:

> Where the *cantus firmus* is clear and plain, the counterpoint can be developed to its limits. . . . have a good clear *cantus firmus*; that is the only way to a full and perfect sound, when the counterpoint has a firm support and can't come adrift or get out of tune, while remaining a distinct whole in its own right. Only a polyphony of this kind can give life a wholeness and at the same time assure us that nothing calamitous can happen as long as the *cantus firmus* is kept going.[22]

This strong organizing melody was what Bonhoeffer sought to weave in the seminary community. He wanted all of the Confessing pastors to be able to sing this tune no matter what was being sung around them. With a regular order of Scripture meditation and prayer, he developed their calling to live as ministers of the word no matter where they found themselves. But he did not expect them to reduce the beauty of life to the mere unison singing of the melody line. He wanted them to be able to enjoy and enter into the harmonizing, humanizing lines along that cantus firmus, to which they attuned their lives and around which they organized their living.

By all accounts, Bethge held onto that cantus firmus too. When he was recalled to Berlin from Italy and arrested and interrogated following the failed July 20, 1944, assassination plot, Bethge (like Bonhoeffer) served as a minister to his fellow inmates, praying with and for them, sometimes carrying their last words to their families after they were put to death. The cantus firmus was a theme that Bethge returned to many times in his work on Bonhoeffer's life and thought in later years.[23]

Moreover, when the war ended in defeat for the Nazis and he was released from prison, Bethge's vocation as a "mediator of memories" became clearer and more urgent.[24] The postwar tasks were daunting, including the immediate work of figuring out who was still alive, who was dead, and where they—or their bodies—were. Bethge rode a bike all around Berlin, through the devastated landscape, trying to learn where Bonhoeffer was, for no one knew. After Bonhoeffer had been moved from Tegel to the basement of the SS headquarters in the autumn of 1944, the family's contact with him was severely curtailed. When and where he had been transferred in those last months of the war, and of his life, were still a mystery. Many were in similar circumstances, with trust and social connections so destroyed along with the rest of the city. Widows beseeched Bethge for any information he might have of their imprisoned husbands' final words and hours. Bethge took on the task of piecing together and testifying to what happened.

Through all of this, he maintained his friendship with Bonhoeffer, which was also part of his vocation of memory mediation. As a friend, he was not interested in forming a Bonhoeffer cult; neither in his friendship with him when he was alive nor after his death did Bethge idealize or idolize Bonhoeffer.[25] Those who heard him speak about his friend were amazed at his "selfless witness" and his willingness to talk about Bonhoeffer in "full-blooded" ways.[26] Bethge gathered the unfinished fragments of Bonhoeffer's life and thought, and the sources that formed the foundation of his monumental biography. He was Bonhoeffer's trusted interpreter.

The same could not be said of others. Bonhoeffer's thought was already being put to use—and "creative misuse," notoriously so, in Bethge's opinion—by the North American "death of God" theologians in the 1950s and 1960s.[27] Within twenty years of Bonhoeffer's death, some argued that his ideas were being exploited and he himself was becoming a cult figure.[28] Much later, in an address he gave in honor of Bonhoeffer's seventieth birthday in 1976, Bethge spoke about the importance of "going beyond" Dietrich, as Bonhoeffer himself would have done. He reminded his hearers that *if* Dietrich were still alive, sitting with them on his seventieth birthday celebration, he might rigorously disagree with them on various topics. That was the man Bethge knew; he was devoted to Bonhoeffer but never "slavishly so."[29] He knew his friend as a human being and allowed him his humanity even after death. And that, I think, is one of Eberhard Bethge's greatest gifts to his friend.

• • •

When the gallery organizers gathered us for a meal and a discussion on a lovely terraced apartment on Karl-Marx-Allee, the topic of our dinner discussion was community in place. Each of us lived in Berlin, but none of us was from there. Hailing from different countries, our disciplines were as varied as we were—two photographers (one German but not from Berlin and one Syrian who had fled the civil war), a Russian watercolorist, an Italian portrait artist, a British mixed-media artist, and an American writer and poet (me). The Iraqi calligrapher couldn't come that night, but the organizer told me he was eager to work at words with me. We had all been accepted for residency in the annual collaborative exhibit at the Green Hill Gallery, a venture of Kulturschöpfer, a cultural space in Friedrichshain, one of the hipper neighborhoods in Berlin. Friedrichshain is as far from my home as Prenzlauer Berg was from Bonhoeffer's. It took a long time to get there, and the vibe couldn't have been more different. Whereas my Grunewald-area digs are patrician, tidy, and hoity-toity, Friedrichshain is edgy, aching, stoned, debauched, and bursting with energy and creativity.

"What's been the hardest part of living here, in Berlin, for you?" one of the organizers asked the group as we heaped food onto our plates. None of us knew any of the others well, and getting to know each other was critical to this collective project. So, taking turns, we answered that question honestly and vulnerably. I said, "I don't know about you all, but I'm pretty lonely here. With all the political tension in the United States, I feel more cut off from my own country, more homeless than I ever have. But I blame Berlin for some of my loneliness too. It's been a harder place for to me live than others. I wish I saw more smiles." I could feel everyone watching and wondering where I was heading. I was wondering where I was heading too.

"But if I'm honest, I have to admit that this"—I extended my hands to the others gathered at this table—"is Berlin too, isn't it? Meeting creative people from all around the world in a city so scarred by history. Berlin is so fascinating and so infuriating. Its turbulent past and turmoil encourages and inspires me too. It's complicated. It's all mingled."

To various degrees, others at the table admitted to some loneliness too, and they agreed that, at times, they found German culture grating, painfully direct, and emotionally guarded. People in the city could be so rude. Even the German at the table agreed with this evaluation—"Remember I'm from a village, not Berlin!" We apologized for being so critical of his homeland.

Still, the Syrian shook his head. He had real wounds on this point, and I didn't blame him for feeling wary and distrustful. He said he couldn't simply shake off the stigma of being a refugee, of being a living symbol to many of Germany's "troubles" and fears. Yet he knew the way forward was *here* too. He could not go back; the life he had once known was gone. His home was in ruins, engulfed in civil war, facing global fatigue at its complicated and brutal aspects. He knew he had to put down roots where he was, for however long he was there, and that's why he kept making art. We nodded as he spoke, because that was true for all of us too.

Over the next six weeks, we gathered regularly to plan and create the exhibit. I came as much as I could and didn't give any Bonhoeffer-Haus tours during this stretch of rapid creativity. Rather, after dropping my son off at preschool, I drove out to Friedrichshain, crossing the Spree River heading east. Each time I was fortunate to get a good look at the otherworldly *Molecule Man* sculpture rising one hundred feet out of the river's water, fashioned by American artist Jonathan Borofsky. Three gray aluminum human figures covered in swiss-cheese holes seem to stand on the river, one of the watery boundaries of a once-divided Berlin. Borofsky said he created the piece to show "the molecules of all human beings coming together to create our existence."[30] It is hard to tell whether the humans are wrestling and contending or meeting together and about to embrace.

As I saw it, my task as the lone writer in the art group was to study the other artists as they worked and work out ekphrastic poems—poetry that narrates or reflects on a piece of art, like John Keats's famous "Ode on a Grecian Urn." I watched the portrait artist form people with oil on blank canvases. The watercolorist created fleshy florals on thick homemade paper. Full of texture and candy-like color, the little inedible dessert-like sculptures the materials artist fashioned were at once abstract and surprisingly compelling. With exacting precision, the calligrapher made words dance on a page in patterns only made by schools of fish or flocks of birds, his brushstrokes like an orchestra conductor's gestures. The two photographers captured images that revealed what we couldn't see without their eyes or their lenses. We each posed for them, and they each used different techniques to make these photographs. The diversity of skills was astounding. I took this all in, writing poems for each artist, themes about their vocations rising up like cream.

We worked together in the same studio space, knocking elbows and bumping canvases, stepping over half-completed projects on the floor, laughing and commiserating, cleaning up after one another, and talking together through new ideas and risky endeavors. A few times, we yelled and got grouchy. Yet creative insight was forming not just in us but *between* us, and we saw how the others were influencing our own work. Because we did not all share a common language, we also relied heavily on those who were able to translate for others. That a coherent project emerged from this eclectic mix of backgrounds, languages, nationalities, disciplines, and individual perspectives was a singular grace. In a world flirting again with nationalism, hunkering down into corners of sameness and practicing contempt for the different Other, our exhibition looked like a fool's errand to some, but to us and others, a miracle. As the organizers knew, that miracle is why they keep offering this annual residency.

At the opening night vernissage, friends and passersby from the street took in the exhibit. We participants did too. The curators had organized our work on the gallery's walls into a story, a polyphonic arc that we artists were not able to see from our close-in perspective. There my poems hung, next to the materials installations, next to the photographs, next to the calligraphy, next to the watercolor, next to the oil paintings. Juxtaposed, each piece gave the others a harmony, a richer meaning than if they had been hanging alone, and yet they each held their own melodic line. Walking through the final exhibit, we marveled at what we accomplished together. We saw how our loneliness had been answered too. But had we not come together to risk creative cooperation, as flesh-and-blood people, we never would have seen that miracle. With our egos checked at the door and hearts opened to possibilities unavailable in a zero-sum universe, we created something new together. We ventured beyond ourselves in ways unachievable if we had only clung to our own kind. This joint project knit us together in the process, a grace in our lonely Berlin with other lonely Berliner transplants. For a time, we could not call ourselves lonely with any accuracy.

• • •

While Bonhoeffer returned to New York in June 1939 for that well-intentioned but ultimately misguided attempt to avoid military service, Bethge remained in his leadership role in the Confessing Church. He wrote a letter to Bonhoeffer's parents, thanking them for their continued hospitality: "I would like to take Dietrich's departure as the occasion to give special thanks to you for offering me so often the privileges of a guest in your family. . . . Above all, I will not forget the experiences of the past half year." He later wrote, "I can only say that in your home I have been able to reach decisive and committed viewpoints and clarity in this matter, for which I am and will remain particularly grateful."[31] The house held memories of those difficult days in ways that few places did. It still does.

As one of Bonhoeffer's "singular friends," Bethge cherished his memories from that house and that upstairs bedroom. The two were incredibly close, sharing a bank account, giving gifts together with funds drawn from that account, and sleeping in the same attic room.[32] (Bethge reported that they "were both late sleepers!"[33]) They were together so much in that room.

When Bonhoeffer returned to Germany from New York after those short, tortured weeks away, he also returned to the house. It became "the true center of his life," and I wonder whether the words Bethge wrote to the elder Bonhoeffers returned to him as he wrote again of that "true center" in his biography of his friend later on.[34] As a way to protect and preserve that center, Bethge envisioned the Bonhoeffer-Haus as the place that it is today. The world owes him much for introducing us to his friend; for preserving, interpreting, and advancing his memory in story; and for preserving and inspiring the existence of the Bonhoeffer-Haus in place.

In 1983, Bethge initiated the project to make the house a place of memorial of Bonhoeffer's life and legacy and for others to encounter his life too.[35] It would not be a cult temple in which Bonhoeffer would be revered but a place in which he and the many others who lived and visited there could be remembered and honored. Bethge knew that memories need more than words to be sustained and passed along—they also need places.[36] And in those places, others can see better too, to make their own decisions or to gain a new view on things or to find clarity.

The Bonhoeffer-Haus reminds me that relationships are central to the business of our common good, our common lives. A home is one of the small and seemingly insignificant places where trust is built hour by hour, day by day, while attending to household tasks. It's a place where families tackle the business of a day but also debate, write down thoughts, peer from windows, recite poetry, and sing. A house is a place to welcome visitors, even strangers, to offer them a meal, courtesy, and respect. A house is a place to remember—to look at old photos, tell and hear old stories, and think ahead to the future—for keeping memories well-tended is part of what keeps us human, as Bethge once said:

> Commemoration renders life human; forgetfulness makes it inhuman. We know of course about the grace of forgetting. But even when remembrance carries grief and shame, it fills the future with perspectives. And the denial of the past furthers the affairs of death, precisely because it focuses exclusively on the present. The degree of accountability regarding yesterday is the measure of a stable tomorrow.[37]

And a house is a place where friendships can be discovered, sustained, and even rekindled. Our friendships need places too.

• • •

In all our digital connectivity, one thing I think we may have forgotten is the fact that we humans are not, and can never really be, digital creatures. We cannot undo our embodied nature, our being emplaced, and we also cannot undo our fundamental sociality: our need for each other and for relationships. We need friendships. In addition to food and water to keep us alive, we also need relationships. We enter this world deeply dependent on those around us to care for us, love us, feed us, clean our bodies, and see and talk to us. We need that care when we depart this world too. In the space between those early tender years and our later frail ones, we also need love and connection.

Even though we hyperconnected sophisticates may recoil at the idea, we still learn best, and remember best, with our bodies and alongside others. People matter to places. When people make pilgrimages to places, those pilgrims often quickly discover that the journey to a place is as important as the place itself. Relating to, at times dealing with, one's fellow pilgrims reveals even more of what the pilgrimage might mean. How we live while on pilgrimage reveals how we live in life: whether we care for a straggler or leave them behind, how we deal with someone who annoys us or talks too much or who espouses ideas that offend us. As we discover our instincts for taking offense and withdrawing, we are given opportunities to forgive and offer friendship.

Places offer us another layer of embodied learning. We hear, smell, touch, and sometimes even taste a place, our senses enlivening what our minds can only partly comprehend. We smell spices, breathe in new air, taste new things, and discover that we are not so different from one another at all. We are all human, beautifully and infuriatingly so.

When one enters the Bonhoeffer-Haus, it is as if one has crossed a threshold into another time, a gripping moment in history. And yet, this feeling of that perilous time also recedes when one discovers it is simply a house. It has a smell, the floorboards creak, and there are views out the window into the garden next door.

I've never met Eberhard Bethge, nor have I met Dietrich Bonhoeffer. I have wondered at times, as I've sought to imagine them in the Bonhoeffer-Haus, what it would be like to be Bonhoeffer's friend. We so often try to imagine ourselves as Dietrich, but imagining ourselves as Eberhard might be a better practice. As Bonhoeffer's friend we are less the star in a hero's tale and more like a person entrusted to interpret his ideas in this world, allowing him his humanity and thinking beyond him as well, as Bethge did. For, ultimately, I think Bonhoeffer would have us not focus on him but embrace the responsibilities of our own lives, like relating to our neighbors, lonely as they and we may be, but always, always human.

• • •

Another visitor, on the doorstep of Bonhoeffer's bedroom, told me she had once heard Eberhard Bethge give a lecture at Princeton Seminary. "It was many years ago," she stressed, brushing gray hair from her forehead. I urged her to tell me what she remembered, and she simply replied, "He was a great man who carried a sadness with him."

To describe himself, Bethge once said, using the Hebrew term for the Holocaust, "My biography carries the burden of the Shoa,"—and with it, too, the responsibility of friendship.[38]

Königin-Luise-Strasse 15, Berlin-Dahlem; the former Institute of Anatomy of Freie Universität Berlin (Photo: Emunah A. Rankin)

Epilogue

A TALE OF
TWO HOUSES

Not long after kissing my husband and our older two children at the door before they hustle to the public bus stop for work and school, I drive our youngest to his bilingual preschool. From our house, we head south on a stretch of road called Clayallee, named after General Lucius Clay, the military governor of US-occupied Germany after World War II who orchestrated the Berlin Airlift during the 327-day Soviet blockade (1948–1949).[1] Further north, the road is called Hohenzollerndamm, after the long-reigning imperial house of Prussia, which ruled in Germany until the end of World War I in 1918, when it was replaced by the short-lived democratic Weimar Republic. The names of this one north-south artery on the west side of Berlin capture much of Germany's long and tumultuous history.

Next, we turn west on Königin-Luise-Strasse, or Queen Louise Street, named after the beloved Prussian queen who, before she died at the age of thirty-four, personally persuaded Napoleon to agree to better terms following a defeat to France.[2] This street leads through the heart of Dahlem, a comfortable neighborhood on the west side of the city. At the intersection of Pacelliallee and Königin-Luise-Strasse stands the modest spire of St. Anne's, the parish church of Martin Niemöller, that important place of meeting for the Confessing Church. As a functioning parish, it is also a living monument to its long and significant history. A church has sat at this location since the medieval era, and like so many other churches dating from that period, the current building stands in the freely rakish angle predating modern urban planning, with its building materials revealing layers, like visible memories. In the spring, purple blooms of lilac bushes ring the building, the whiff of their luxuriant scent in the air, a brief display of victorious color. For most of the year, these bushes are common and uninteresting, reduced to a brown tangle of branches in the winter, or to ordinary green bushes in the summer.

The main street of this community stretches beyond St. Anne's and features an ice cream shop, a burger joint, a lovely bookstore and stationery store, an Apotheke (pharmacy) with a Germanic blackletter typeface sign, and a specialty tea shop. There is an abundance of college-age students around, for Dahlem is home to the Freie Universität, the Free University. Students, scholars, and scientists established the Free University of Berlin in their 1948 exodus from the Universität Unter den Linden, under Soviet control. With financial and moral support from the American Allied forces, they established the new university as a refuge for study and research far from the political pressures and persecutions of the Communists, and other American institutions invested in its development. From the little island of West Berlin, physically isolated during the Cold War years, the university sought formal partnerships with other academic institutions around the world, a calculated investment in relationship.[3]

President John F. Kennedy visited the Freie Universität in 1963, just after he gave his well-known "Ich bin ein Berliner" speech outside the Rathaus, the city hall, in the Schöneberg neighborhood, to a huge crowd of West Berliners (estimates vary widely, between 120,000 and 450,000).[4] Immediately after, he traveled to Dahlem and addressed a crowd of 20,000 at the Free University. Popular culture ensures that most know that one quintessential line from the earlier speech, with its uniquely Kennedy-accented German. (And no, he didn't say, "I am a jelly doughnut"—although Berliners are indeed jelly doughnuts, they are also denizens of the city.) But no single iconic phrase from the Dahlem speech stands out, certainly not in public memory. But of the two speeches he gave that day, says Josef Klein, an expert in political linguistics, the one he gave in Dahlem is the more important one.[5] Klein believes the first, iconic speech, with its soaring emotion and powerful rhetoric, was meant for a general audience, offering them spine-strengthening encouragement.

But in the second speech of the day, Kennedy made more careful arguments, Klein believes, aimed at Germany's civic and political leaders and centered on the liberal democratic values of truth, justice, and freedom.[6] Kennedy reaffirmed the United States' commitment to West Berlin against the Soviet Union, no matter what, in a solidarity of freedom. He also urged his listeners to consider what truth requires—dealing in facts and reality, not relying on slogans to think (or as Klemperer put it, letting the words do your thinking for you) or indulging in nostalgia. Finally, Kennedy expressed his hope and belief that the conflict between Western democracies and the Communist East, and other autocratic nations of the world, would be resolved not through military strength but through renewed commitments to the values and practices of freedom, soft powers that attract and persuade, working together for the sake of the world. He closed, "There is work to be done, obligations to be met, obligations to truth, to justice, and to liberty."

Further down the Queen's Street stands a markedly curious building in the midst of the idyll of Dahlem. Clearly once a stately structure, No. 15 Königin-Luise-Strasse sits now as an abandoned and thoroughly vandalized building. It's large, surrounded by untended and overgrown grounds that help obscure the blighted structure when leafed out.

Passing this building each day with my son on our way to his preschool, I watched it decay further during our three years in Berlin. In our final year, I drew my son's attention to it as well. Periodically he asked me why the building "looks so hurt," which was a good question. Together, we made a game of spotting and counting the number of Polizei (police) vehicles parked outside of it. Many days, we counted more than one, with officers patrolling, checking locks on the fence. It was a morbid game. Indeed, the whole structure is a metaphor in civic morbidity.

It will come as no surprise to anyone reading this far that I developed a strong fascination with this building and spent a significant amount of time researching it, though I did not explore its physical grounds for myself. (Nor do I condone anyone doing so!) Watching the ever-increasing security measures over these three years—the various stages of fencing, barbed wire and razor wire, posted notices, and that regular police presence—I knew that to cross these barriers, much less enter the devastated structure, would constitute trespassing at best and be dangerous at worst. But I discovered that not all who trespass the grounds vandalize them. Indeed, my research introduced me to the curious corners of the internet where people write about and photograph abandoned places. My research depended on these risk-takers.[7]

This husk of a building was once part of the Free University, its Institute of Anatomy, opened for instruction in 1949, closed in 2003 when the institute merged with another university, and abandoned in 2005.[8] From the fragments I gathered, it was purchased to be redeveloped as a commercial site. But a series of disagreements and lawsuits between the owners and the local government left it orphaned and uncared for, utterly exposed to those who don't care for it, who mean to exploit it for their own ends, or who just get a thrill from trespassing and vandalizing.

Because it was once a place to study anatomy, the building has lecture halls and the kind of infrastructure necessary for handling cadavers while instructing students. There are large slabs where specimens were laid out and dissected, morgue-sized refrigerators, and oddly shaped sinks that cast a creepiness over the place. To an amateur like me, (obviously) prone to wild flights of imagination, it looks like a place of torture.

But it's an abandoned place of learning, and the only torture happening in it now is inflicted by trespassers against the building itself. It is not enough to say the place has been ransacked, though it has. It is covered in graffiti inside and out. Not a single window in the stately structure remains intact, and in three years of passing by it, I have watched even the last shards of window glass busted out, leaving only empty window frames.

But these descriptions hardly capture the kind of existential war at work within the building. One day not long ago I saw the Hakenkreuz (swastika) etched on a jutting shard on an upstairs window; someone took the time and risk to scratch it on that peninsula of broken glass. In just a couple of days, the window shard was gone. Perhaps it fell out, a natural mercy, or perhaps it was removed by the Polizei, since it is an unlawful symbol in Germany today. The building seems to be at war with itself, and the warring parties are largely invisible. Those who have trespassed with cameras capture the devastation as a journalist might in reports from front lines. One intrepid explorer said that a creepy man emerged from the shadows, telling him to pipe down. The building is a magnet for all kinds of ominous activity.

My fascination with this building stands as an asymmetrical counterpoint to the Bonhoeffer-Haus, a tale of two houses. The ruins of this one structure, neglected by its owner, held in the limbo of unresolved conflicts, threaten the peace and order of the whole lovely neighborhood. Despite all the security spent on it, the private war in and over the property threatens other places with its chaos and violence. The private dispute has become increasingly public and increasingly unavoidable. Neglect and entrenched refusals to cooperate and compromise have allowed a sore to fester. The building is an agonizing symbol of the failure of responsible people to address difficult questions and find reasonable, proximate resolutions. This structure issues a warning, one that will grow with further decay.

But to be accurate, it is *not* decay. On the grounds of old family farms in the American northeast where I was raised, barns built and tended by families once connected to the earth now melt down to the ground. These softening, shrugging structures don't always bear the ravaged marks of psychosocial hostility like this old anatomy institute does. Rotting in forgotten wildernesses, they are like autumn leaves decomposing on a forest floor. It's sad; don't get me wrong. But that kind of decay is natural and normal, in the way that human limits are normal, or change is inevitable. The shackled and shot-through institute looks more like the result of human failure, exploitation, more the results of human sin—omitted and committed, to use the church language—not just human limitation.

Driving past it most days, I try to get a good look to monitor its conditions, the way one cranes to see a devastating car wreck, wondering how anyone is going to walk out of the catastrophe. The wounded hulk of the place remains, day after day. No one is coming to the rescue, and no one is making a Rettungsgasse for this once beautiful structure of learning—at least not yet. We disconnected bystanders drive by. When I've brought the subject up at dinners with friends, they remark, "Oh, yes! I've seen that place! What's its deal?" And I tell them what I've learned, and we are left to just say, "Huh," because it is not ours to care for. We don't belong to it. None of us hold the keys.

• • •

Eberhard Bethge compared two places as well, two houses, one of horror and one of hope. In his address at the inauguration of the Bonhoeffer-Haus on June 1, 1987, he spoke of two memorials that were "fatefully inter-related despite their asymmetry."[9] These two memorials were set aside and preserved in the same year, 1987, on the 750th anniversary of Berlin's founding. They focus on two worlds, but they share an inescapable bond.

The first is the Reichssicherheitshauptamt on what was once called Prinz-Albrecht-Strasse—the Reich Central Security Office, or SS headquarters—which housed a number of nefarious outfits of the Nazi security establishment, including the Gestapo, the SS, and the RSD (a branch of SS Security).[10] In its place now stands the Topography of Terror museum, and Bethge called it "the headquarters of terror" in his Bonhoeffer-Haus address. Political prisoners were brought here for interrogation and not usually held there long. It was known as a place of "intensified interrogation," a euphemism for torture. Dietrich Bonhoeffer was among its prisoners for months.

Bethge linked this place of horrors to the Bonhoeffer-Haus that day, for they were, in his mind and in memory, still locked in an "unequal struggle," an uneven contest of remembrance. These two places represent so much of "how things were" then, Bethge said; the buildings house the memories of warning and sober truths. One place stood once to "assure the security of the Third Reich," projecting its awful power. Its corridors and hallways were staffed with people convinced of their might and right, inflicting great law-lessness and disorder while claiming to be doing the work of law and order.

But there were other kinds of centers, other places, then too. Those gathered at the Bonhoeffer-Haus for its inauguration in 1987 commemorated these "weak centers for the destabilization of the Third Reich." Armed only with bonds of trust, these places, Bethge said, seemed fragile in their small scale and their lack of hard weaponry. They never intended to be centers of resistance, but in a multitude of "undesired and unrehearsed" ways, they were forced to be. Having become such centers, these small places now also must be honored and remembered for their moral authority. Memory must not only tend the looming and large places of power. As Bethge put it on that opening day:

> Marienburger Allee 43 was certainly in no way a headquarters, but it was a center, continually devoted to a culture from which it never allowed itself to be alienated and which it was bent on preserving under all circumstances for the benefit of others. A refuge and resource for energy to hold out and to motivate ever anew.[11]

Though small compared to the large footprint of the Reich Security Headquarters, the Bonhoeffer-Haus's memories could not be left just to melt into forgetfulness, lost through neglect. The memory merited tending, the place deserved visits, and the lessons of this "weak" center needed to be taught to the next generation. Those gathered for its consecration to that purpose—all those who had worked to make the Bonhoeffer-Haus what it is, with all its thoughtful elements—were involved in a moral act of defiance against forgetfulness, the deadly ether of nostalgia, and the mere sloganeering of heroes. They were there to tell the truth, the whole truth, and to preserve a taste of reality. They committed to memory what was required of all the small places when the large places failed.

This memory work remains critical; it is required to maintain freedom. We are not responsible for the history we inherit, but we are responsible for its memory and what we teach the next generation. Like it or not, we are responsible for our places.

• • •

I am caught between the two worlds in which I live. My Berlin days have seen some American heartache. Far from my native land, yet living as a representative in one of its diplomatic outposts, I see from a distance that my country is struggling to fulfill its task of keeping house. We are failing to model what civic housekeeping requires, and we are suffering because of it. Our children will suffer more if we keep this up.

In its plainest meaning, civic housekeeping is what is required to live life together, the habits and practices that keep our communities and nation. At times it involves work that no one much enjoys doing but is necessary for common life. We all love a good meal, but someone has to wash, dry, and put away the dishes. We may love a beautiful garden, but we have to do the work to keep it alive. I can't stand to do laundry, so my husband often takes up that task. But whether I do it or he does, doing the laundry is one way we show love for our most immediate neighbors—our family. And civic and political housekeeping is what loving our neighbors looks like.

Civic housekeeping is an old term due for another look, just like *acedia*. It was coined by Jane Addams over a hundred years ago, when, on a trip to London as a young woman, she was shocked by the sight of poor people digging through rich people's discarded produce. She returned to the United States and set about taking up responsibility in places where the vulnerable—newly arrived immigrants, mostly— were set upon by all kinds of exploiters and societal predators. She opened Hull-House in Chicago for lectures and gatherings, battling civic and political corruption with this house open to the excluded. But she didn't stop there. She also became the garbage collector for Chicago's nineteenth ward, taking on the city's corrupt aldermen. All of it was civic housekeeping.

We cannot be Dietrich Bonhoeffer, but we can be responsible for our houses—the large and small ones alike. While we may never step into the pages of history the way Bonhoeffer did, we can each step toward caring for our civic Haus. Our tasks may be very different in the houses we keep, but when we each take up civic housekeeping in our small part of the world, the ripples from our weak centers reverberate even to the large ones. Small acts in the aggregate can shake the clay feet of the powers that do not care about common life or human flourishing. Some of these powers are, in fact, our own stubborn indifference to one another, our refusal to give a damn about our fellow human beings.

As a small act of moral practice, I sought to remember what the Bonhoeffer-Haus has meant to me and to use the keys there to open up the rooms of my own life, my house. In the Bonhoeffer-Haus I saw again the power of civic stories, the narratives of neighborhoods, the bigger stories of which our small lives are a part. We need to pay attention to those stories. Some need revision and correction; some require confession and penitence. Where the stories have been lost, misused, or abused, we need to recover the facts, love them into a narrative, and hand them along in humble truth. That is what happens during every tour for every visitor and every tour group that comes to hear the stories of the Bonhoeffer-Haus and find their own lives expanded.

In the Bonhoeffer-Haus, I saw that Bonhoeffer was who he was because he belonged to people and places. It matters that we know who we belong to, practice including those we may have been taught to exclude, and offer correction to those entrenched stories.

In the Bonhoeffer-Haus, I saw how Bonhoeffer held on to the truth and how the truth held on to him through very dark days. As a Christian, I share his belief that the truth is the word of God, in all the meanings of that theologically rich term. You may not share that belief, but there are things you point to as true and inviolable. Hold on to those truths, practice them, and trust that the truth will hold on to you. There's a lot of wisdom in the world, found in some of the world's great literature. Poetry, like the Psalms in the Bible, is a robustly practical way of fighting despair. The Psalms hold deep human truths, and these are available to all, no belief-strings attached.

In the Bonhoeffer-Haus, I saw how Bonhoeffer understood himself, his world, and his responsibilities to that world when he ventured beyond it. Not all of us may travel far from home or live beyond our native lands, but we all need to venture beyond ourselves and our routine paths. Encountering difference is a fast way to discover what you cherish about where you come from and to see that human beings, fundamentally, share more in common than what divides us.

In the Bonhoeffer-Haus, and in other places of Bonhoeffer's life, I saw how risky it is not to pay attention to the other lanes in life and how everything connects. I found the metaphor of the Rettungsgasse—the rescue alley—an especially powerful image to hold on to in the Stau (the traffic) of life, or in places of impunity, exploitation, or predation.

In the Bonhoeffer-Haus, I saw how Bonhoeffer's life was a masterpiece in the art of dying, and that his surrender of privilege allowed another kind of nobility to emerge, one of quality, crossing cultures, and living one's life in service to others. Meditating on death has remarkable clarifying power, and Bonhoeffer walked more responsibly in life's hard paths knowing that death was not the final word.

In the Bonhoeffer-Haus I saw the importance of friendship and how thinking about how I could be a friend to Bonhoeffer was a better mental game than imagining being Bonhoeffer himself. He and Eberhard Bethge practiced the art of friendship and offered each other real companionship, and even after death, Bethge continued being Bonhoeffer's friend. How I interpret Bonhoeffer matters to my friendship of him.

Before we leave Berlin, I will surrender my key to the Bonhoeffer-Haus, but I will not surrender these keys, ones that I will carry to the houses of my life, my community, and my nation. You carry keys as well, and ideally, they are to places you care for and love, to places for which you may carry responsibility, whether you like it or not. You may never visit the Bonhoeffer-Haus; I never expected to when we moved here! But now that I have, and since I carried its key for a time, I hope my memories shared here will help you look in your hand, on your keychain, and see how the keys to Bonhoeffer's house might help you better care for your own. Our civic house begs for attention, and those of us who belong to the small centers of a house can make a difference. The small efforts and the weak centers still matter, and those who will live in them depend upon us to care.

Endnotes

Chapter 1: Visiting the Haus, Holding a Key

1. An excellent new biography of the Rev. Martin Niemöller demonstrates the many complications of the relationship between church and state in Germany prior to the rise of National Socialism and how Niemöller navigated those cultural entanglements. See Matthew D. Hockenos, *Then They Came for Me: Martin Niemöller, the Pastor Who Defied the Nazis* (New York: Basic Books, 2018).

2. Because Niemöller spoke various forms of this poem extemporaneously, many versions of it are extant in print and online. I have used the version that is displayed on a wall in the US Holocaust Memorial Museum (USHMM). For more information about this poem from the USHMM, please see https://encyclopedia.ushmm.org/content/en/article/martin-niemoeller-first-they-came-for-the-socialists.

3. The image also appears in the Yad Vashem Holocaust Museum in Jerusalem.

4. Bonhoeffer's original books and papers are archived in the Staatsbibliothek in Berlin, Germany.

5. For more information about the Gleis 17 memorial, see its listing on the Information Portal to European Sites of Remembrance (Gedenkstättenportal zu Orten der Erinnerung in Europa), https://tinyurl.com/y36updyb.

6. See the T4 Denkmal website, https://www.t4-denkmal.de/eng, and Henry Friedlander, *The Origins of Nazi Genocide: From Euthanasia to the Final Solution* (Chapel Hill: University of North Carolina Press, 1997). It is important to note here that Dr. Karl Bonhoeffer's role in the treatment of psychiatric patients, particularly forced sterilizations, has come under increased scrutiny and protest. The psychiatric clinic at the Charité has a memorial site and online information about the center's medical crimes and complicity in National Socialist policies. See the Charité's English page about the memorial, https://tinyurl.com

/y3aqsj7s. Dr. Max de Crinis, who took over the chair after Dr. Bonhoeffer's retirement, was a key figure in the T4 program.

7. Michael Sontheimer, "Why Germans Can Never Escape Hitler's Shadow." *Der Spiegel*, March 10, 2005, https://tinyurl.com/y6kn7djy.
8. Frank Zeller, "Germany's Post-War Justice Ministry Was Infested with Nazis Protecting Former Comrades, Study Reveals," *Telegraph*, October 10, 2016, https://tinyurl.com/y4zpv9w2.
9. See Laura Fabrycky, "Let's Quit the Tug-of-War over Dietrich Bonhoeffer's Legacy," *Christianity Today*, September 20, 2018, https://tinyurl.com/ydfhr9h9.

Chapter 2: Learning the Story

1. For an excellent summary of this essay and some of its challenges, see Victoria Barnett, "Dietrich Bonhoeffer: 'The Church and the Jewish Question,'" United States Holocaust Memorial Museum, https://tinyurl.com/y3h8rnxb.
2. Eichmann was in hiding in Argentina when the Israeli Mossad abducted him and brought him to stand trial in Jerusalem. He was hanged in June 1962 for his crimes against the Jewish people. For more, see "Adolf Eichmann," Holocaust Encyclopedia, United States Holocaust Museum Memorial, https://tinyurl.com/y4e9kcca.
3. Victor Klemperer, *The Language of the Third Reich: LTI—Lingua Tertii Imperii: A Philologist's Notebook*, 3rd ed., trans. Martin Brady (New York: Continuum, 2006), 9–14.
4. Klemperer, *Language*, 14.
5. Erik Larson, *In the Garden of Beasts: Love, Terror, and an American Family in Hitler's Berlin* (New York: Broadway Books, 2011), 134.
6. Larson, *Garden of Beasts*, 134.
7. Hitler's psychological assessment by the predecessor agency to the Central Intelligence Agency, the Office of Strategic Services, is available online. See Henry A. Murray, "Analysis of the Personality of Adolf Hitler: With Predictions of His Future Behavior and Suggestions for Dealing with Him Now and after Germany's Surrender," 1943, Donovan Nuremberg Trials Collection, Cornell University Law Library, https://tinyurl.com/y2w8u5ln.
8. Eberhard Bethge, *Friendship and Resistance: Essays on Dietrich Bonhoeffer* (Grand Rapids: Eerdmans, 1995), 35.

Chapter 3: Sources of Identity

1. Bethge, *Dietrich Bonhoeffer: A Biography*, rev. ed. (Minneapolis: Fortress Press, 2000), 14.
2. Bethge, *Dietrich Bonhoeffer*, 17.
3. Bethge, *Dietrich Bonhoeffer*, 29.

4. Bethge, *Dietrich Bonhoeffer*, 14.
5. Wind, Renate, *Dietrich Bonhoeffer: A Spoke in the Wheel* (Grand Rapids: Eerdmans, 1992), 3–4, 23–24; Kindle LOC 72 of 1717, and 242 of 1717.
6. Bethge, *Dietrich Bonhoeffer*, 15, quoting from *I Knew Dietrich Bonhoeffer: Reminiscences by His Friends*, ed. Wolf-Dieter Zimmermann and Ronald Gregor Smith, trans. Käthe Gregor Smith (New York: Harper and Row, 1966), 22–23.
7. *Catalogue of the Exhibition*, ed. Board of the Bonhoeffer House (Berlin, 1996), 29.
8. Ferdinand Schlingensiepen, *Dietrich Bonhoeffer 1906–1945: Martyr, Thinker, Man of Resistance*, trans. Isabel Best (New York: T&T Clark International, 2010), 2.
9. "It is said of [Dietrich] Bonhoeffer's parents that on their golden wedding anniversary they counted up all the days they had been apart during 50 years of marriage, and it didn't even amount to one month" (Schlingensiepen, *Dietrich Bonhoeffer*, 3).
10. Schlingensiepen, *Dietrich Bonhoeffer*, 3.
11. Bonhoeffer, Emmi Delbrück, "From "The House on the Wangenheimstrasse," *Catalogue of the Exhibition*, ed. Board of the Bonhoeffer House, 23.
12. Bonhoeffer, E., "House on the Wangenheimstrasse," 22.
13. Bethge, *Dietrich Bonhoeffer*, 18.
14. Bethge, *Dietrich Bonhoeffer*, 47–48.
15. Translated from *Widerstand und Ergebung*, 403–4, as cited in Dietrich Bonhoeffer, *A Testament to Freedom: The Essential Writings of Dietrich Bonhoeffer*, ed. Geffrey B. Kelly and F. Burton Nelson (San Francisco: HarperSanFrancisco, 1990), 542–43.
16. Mary Bosanquet, *The Life and Death of Dietrich Bonhoeffer* (New York: Harper & Row, 1968), 17. By Hitler's count, the Holy Roman Empire was the first *Reich*, the German empire was the second, and Hitler's twelve short, disastrous years constitutes the *Drittes Reich* (Third Reich).
17. Steve Ozment, *A Mighty Fortress: A New History of the German People* (New York: HarperCollins, 2005), 14.
18. Bosanquet, *Life and Death*, 17.
19. Rörig (1882–1952) was a professor of history who specialized in German cities and the Hanseatic League. After teaching in various university towns in Germany, he finally settled at Berlin's Humboldt University. See Roland Pauler, "Rörig, Fritz," *New German Biography* 21 (2003), 736–37, https://tinyurl.com/y4q4mkhs.
20. Fritz Rörig, *The Medieval Town* (Berkeley: University of California Press, 1967), 28.
21. Royalty and nobility also offered these zones of sovereign protection, as when Duke Frederick the Wise, the Elector of Saxony, gave his protection to Martin Luther. In 1520, the Pope declared Luther a heretic. As

sworn defender of the faith, the emperor Charles V summoned Luther to Worms to defend himself before an imperial assembly (diet). The assembly issued the Edict of Worms (1521), declaring Luther an outlaw who could be captured or killed without legal consequences. Flaunting the emperor's decree, the Duke of Saxony staged Luther's "abduction" to bring him under his protection but could only guarantee his safety if he stayed within his realm. Bruce L. Shelley, *Church History in Plain Language* (Dallas: Word, 1982), 260.

22. Rörig, *Medieval Town*, 27.
23. Rörig, *Medieval Town*, 138.
24. Rörig, *Medieval Town*, 138.
25. Rörig, *Medieval Town*, 142.
26. For instance, the man who planted the bomb under Hitler's conference table was Colonel Claus Philipp Maria Schenk Graf von Stauffenberg. His name signifies Prussian nobility, for *Graf* is the title of count, and *Schenk* means "cupbearer." Today, the headquarters of the German Defense Ministry resides on a street named in Stauffenberg's honor.
27. Dietrich Bonhoeffer, *Letters and Papers from Prison: The Enlarged Edition*, ed. Eberhard Bethge (New York: Collier Books, 1971), 13.
28. Bosanquet, *Life and Death*, 18.
29. "It was taboo to talk about one's ancestors or put on airs about them" (Schlingensiepen, *Dietrich Bonhoeffer*, 1). Nazis required people to demonstrate "pure Aryan descent by means of an *Ahnenpaß*, or certificate of ancestry" (Marsh, *Strange Glory*, 295), and Bonhoeffer attempted to get one when he was waiting for his final clearance from the Abwehr, or German military intelligence, as a double agent. Charles Marsh, *Strange Glory: A Life of Dietrich Bonhoeffer* (New York: Knopf, 2014).
30. Schlingensiepen, *Dietrich Bonhoeffer*, 2.
31. "Nothing could be more mistaken than to assume that in the German, French and English towns of the eleventh or twelfth centuries there was any kind of economic or social equality" (Rörig, *Medieval Town*, 21).
32. Schlingensiepen, *Dietrich Bonhoeffer*, 8.
33. Bethge, *Dietrich Bonhoeffer*, 12.
34. Marsh, *Strange Glory*, 167.
35. Alexandra Richie, *Faust's Metropolis: A History of Berlin* (New York: Carroll & Graf, 1998), 425.
36. Marsh, *Strange Glory*, 167.
37. Wind, LOC 878 of 1717.
38. Wind, LOC 887 of 1717.
39. Bethge, *Dietrich Bonhoeffer*, 506, quoting from Bonhoeffer, *Testament to Freedom*, 270 (see DBW 14: 924).
40. I am indebted to Dr. Bryan T. McGraw at Wheaton College (IL) for introducing me to her fascinating work.

41. Kristen Monroe, *Ethics in an Age of Terror and Genocide: Identity and Moral Choice* (Princeton, NJ: Princeton University Press, 2011), 190, 200.

42. Kate Connolly, "Sex Parties, Bloody Duels, and Blackmail: Life at Court of Last Emperor," *Guardian*, September 2, 2010, https://tinyurl.com/y4r3whoe.

43. Bonhoeffer, *Letters and Papers*, 13, 14, 15.

Chapter 4: The Watchwords

1. Bethge, *Dietrich Bonhoeffer*, 634–50.

2. Marsh, *Strange Glory*, 276–77.

3. Marsh, *Strange Glory*, 281.

4. Bethge, *Dietrich Bonhoeffer*, 653: "they say that it was like an answer to a prayer when my coming was announced."

5. Schlingensiepen, *Dietrich Bonhoeffer*, 230: "Today's *Losung* speaks dreadfully of God's incorruptible judgement" (DB-ER 653–54).

6. Schlingensiepen, *Dietrich Bonhoeffer*, 230.

7. Schlingensiepen, *Dietrich Bonhoeffer*, 230, from DB-ER 658, 661.

8. Karen Marsh, *Vintage Saints and Sinners: 25 Christians Who Transformed My Faith* (Downers Grove, IL: InterVarsity Press, 2017), 113.

9. Kai Dose, "A Note on John Wesley's Visit to Herrnhut in 1738," *Wesley and Methodist Studies* 7, no. 1 (2015): 117.

10. John Wesley, "John Wesley the Methodist: Chapter VII—The New Birth," Wesley Center Online, accessed January 9, 2019, https://tinyurl.com/y3fz2r5j.

11. Bethge, *Dietrich Bonhoeffer*, 35.

12. Schlingensiepen, *Dietrich Bonhoeffer*, 10n6.

13. While Bonhoeffer thought the Moravian texts were a good place to begin, he prized even more highly reading Scripture as a whole: "There can be no doubt that the daily Bible passages published by the Moravian Brethren, for example, are a real blessing to all who have ever used them. This was discovered by many to their grateful astonishment particularly during the church struggle. But there can be equally little doubt that brief verses cannot and should not take the place of reading the Scripture as a whole. . . . Holy Scripture is more than a watchword." Dietrich Bonhoeffer, *Life Together* (New York: Harper & Row, 1954), 50.

14. *New monasticism* is a term Bonhoeffer used in a letter to his brother Karl-Friedrich on January 14, 1935: "The restoration of the church will surely come only from a new type of monasticism which has nothing in common with the old only an uncompromising attitude of life lived in accordance with the Sermon on the Mount in the following of Christ. I believe it is now time to call people to this" (Bonhoeffer, *Testament to Freedom*, 424).

15. Bonhoeffer, *Testament to Freedom*, 424.

16. Bonhoeffer, *Life Together*, 50.
17. Harnack was born and raised in Wisconsin but married a German, and the two were living and working in Germany when Hitler came to power. A lecturer in English literature and a translator, respectively, Mildred and her husband both actively spied against the Nazis. She was beheaded and her body studied at Humboldt University for the effects of stress on menstruation. For an excellent overview of her life, see Shareen Blair Brysac, *Resisting Hitler: Mildred Harnack and the Red Orchestra* (New York: Oxford University Press, 2000). See also Emily Bazelon, "What Happened to the Remains of Nazi Resistor Mildred Harnack? Now We Know," Slate, November 7, 2013, https://tinyurl.com/y3575qsf.
18. Bethge, *Dietrich Bonhoeffer*, 420.
19. Bethge, *Dietrich Bonhoeffer*, 462.
20. Bosanquet, *Life and Death*, 159.
21. Bosanquet, *Life and Death*, 157.
22. Bosanquet, *Life and Death*, 157–59.
23. Dietrich Bonhoeffer, *The Prayerbook of the Bible* (Minneapolis: Augsburg Fortress, 1970).
24. Geffrey Kelly and F. Burton Nelson, *The Cost of Moral Leadership: The Spirituality of Dietrich Bonhoeffer* (Grand Rapids: Eerdmans, 2002), 231; Eric Metaxas, *Bonhoeffer: Pastor, Martyr, Prophet, Spy* (Nashville: Thomas Nelson, 2010), 367–69.
25. "Above all, the Psalms enabled [Bonhoeffer] to cope with his own shutting moods amid all the vicissitudes of his ministry, including his imprisonment." (Kelly and Nelson, *Cost*, 232)
26. Kelly and Nelson, *Cost of Moral Leadership*, 227.
27. Bonhoeffer, *Prayerbook of the Bible*, 26.
28. Kathleen Norris, *Acedia and Me* (New York: Riverhead Books, 2008), 3.
29. Ian Irvine, "*Acedia, Tristitia,* and Sloth: Early Christian Forerunners to Chronic Ennui," *Humanitas* 12, no. 1 (Spring 1999): 89.
30. Kelly and Nelson, *Cost of Moral Leadership*, 233.
31. "Runde Ecke History," Citizens Committee of Leipzig, "Runde Ecke" Memorial Museum and Stasi Bunker Museum, https://tinyurl.com/y3cw8htk.
32. Dorothee Theile, *Morning Star, O Cheering Sight . . .: The Moravian Star and Its History*, 3rd ed., trans. Jacob Watson, Deborah Hübler, Peter Vogt, and Jill Vogt (Herrnhut, Germany: Comenius-Buchhandlung GmbH, n.d.), 37–67.
33. Theile, *Morning Star*, 63.

Chapter 5: Crossing Boundaries

1. Richie, *Faust's Metropolis*, 159.
2. Richie, *Faust's Metropolis*, 160.
3. Richie, *Faust's Metropolis*, 162.

4. Bonhoeffer House, *Catalogue of the Exhibition*, 117–18. The word *proletarian*, McCormick Theology Seminary professor Dr. Reggie Williams notes, is one Bonhoeffer also used with respect to New York's Harlem neighborhood. See Reggie Williams, *Bonhoeffer's Black Jesus* (Waco, Texas: Baylor University Press, 2014), 113.
5. Laban Carrick Hill, *Harlem Stomp! A Cultural History of the Harlem Renaissance* (New York: Little, Brown Books for Young Readers, 2009), 3.
6. Hill, *Harlem Stomp!*, 95.
7. I follow Dr. Reggie Williams's lead in calling Mr. Fisher by the name Albert. Williams's account stands apart from nearly all other biographical depictions of Fisher, which call him Frank. Williams spoke with Fisher's family members, and none of them recall him being called Frank or Franklin (Williams, *Bonhoeffer's Black Jesus*, xii).
8. Hill, *Harlem Stomp!*, 81.
9. Williams, *Bonhoeffer's Black Jesus*, 37.
10. Charles Marsh writes that Bonhoeffer's passing references to "Arabs, Bedouins, and Negroes" during his travels in Libya with his brother Klaus were made more as an observer of a scene than a participant in it (Marsh, *Strange Glory*, 115).
11. "He never refused invitations to social gatherings but gracefully bore with the banalities of the conversation and accompanied on the piano the orgies of sentimental singing, to the delight of all but himself" (Bosanquet, *Life and Death*, 67).
12. Marsh, *Strange Glory*, 68–69.
13. Marsh, *Strange Glory*, 79.
14. Williams, *Bonhoeffer's Black Jesus*, 14; Marsh, *Strange Glory*, 85.
15. Marsh, *Strange Glory*, 116. Drawing on Williams's research, Marsh highlights that Bonhoeffer's use of the word *veil* is an allusion to Du Bois's *The Souls of Black Folks*, which Bonhoeffer had read for a course with Reinhold Niebuhr (compare with Marsh, 106, 116).
16. "History," Abyssinian Baptist Church, https://tinyurl.com/y39zyscz.
17. "History," Abyssinian Baptist Church.
18. Williams, *Bonhoeffer's Black Jesus*, 82.
19. Williams, *Bonhoeffer's Black Jesus*, 54.
20. Williams gives an extended summary of W. E. B. Du Bois's *Darkwater* essay "Jesus Christ in Texas," in which the Christ figure's race is unclear to his hosts at a dinner party: "he could be Jewish, a mulatto, or a Negro, they cannot tell," but the reality remains that "in a white-centered world, Jesus becomes a frightening disruption" (Williams, *Bonhoeffer's Black Jesus*, 60), a stranger they are neither attracted to nor follow but repelled by and shun.
21. Williams, *Bonhoeffer's Black Jesus*, 88–89.
22. Charles Marsh writes, "singing the Negro spirituals and listening to recordings of them would become a vital part of the dissident circles that gathered around Bonhoeffer" (119).

23. Marsh, *Strange Glory*, 118.
24. Marsh, *Strange Glory*, 116.
25. Marsh, *Strange Glory*, 118.
26. "Construction of the Wall in August 1961," Berlin Wall Memorial, https://tinyurl.com/yypkfwdf.
27. Maria Nooke, "From the Building of the Berlin Wall to the Fall of the Berlin Wall: A Short History of the Division," in *Where in the World Is the Berlin Wall?*, ed. Anna Kaminsky (Berlin: Bundesstiftung zur Aufarbeitung der SED-Diktatur, 2014), 12, 21.
28. Evoking a line from Martin Luther's "A Mighty Fortress" hymn, "one little word shall fell him," the *Economist*'s obituary headline for Schabowski was titled "One Little Word." *Economist*, November 7, 2015.
29. Bethge, *Dietrich Bonhoeffer*, 226–29.
30. While I have relied heavily on the work of others, this one piece of information—that the church is in Mitte and Bonhoeffer's apartment is in Prenzlauer Berg—flies against all the scholarship and is possibly my one correction to the dominant Bonhoeffer record. But even this is not my own correction. It is Gottfried Brezger's, my colleague at the Bonhoeffer-Haus.

    "No, no, it is not Prenzlauer Berg! It is Mitte!" Gottfried corrected me on a tour late in my time at the Bonhoeffer-Haus. After two years of developing my own *Berliner Schnauze* (lip, but literally "snout") and thus having enough cultural capacity to know I should engage him directly in reply, I said back forcefully, "No, Gottfried! It is called Wedding in many biographies, which is wrong, but I have studied the maps and it's close enough to Prenzlauer Berg. Perhaps it's far-west Prenzlauer Berg? Eberhard Bethge says so!"

    And Gottfried retorted, "No, it is Mitte," and then, smiling, he said firmly, "Eberhard Bethge got it *wrong*, and now everyone does." So, for the record, the Zion Church is in the the Mitte neighborhood, and Dietrich's rented apartment on Oderberger Strasse stands in Prenzlauer Berg. (And thanks to Gottfried for his deep, generous knowledge.)
31. Eberhard Bethge writes that "the minister tried to force the throng back into the classroom by shouting and using physical force" (Bethge, *Dietrich Bonhoeffer*, 226). Then he briefly introduced the new instructor and slipped away, "leaving Bonhoeffer standing silently against the wall with his hands in his pockets. Minutes passed" (Bethge, *Dietrich Bonhoeffer*, 226).
32. Bethge, *Dietrich Bonhoeffer*, 226.
33. Bethge, *Dietrich Bonhoeffer*, 226.
34. Bethge, *Dietrich Bonhoeffer*, 226.
35. DBW, Vol. 10, 119.
36. Paul Kengor, "Martin Luther and the Berlin Wall," *Washington Post*, October 30, 2014, https://tinyurl.com/y53sbheb.
37. Kengor, "Martin Luther."

38. For more on the story of this song, see—and hear—Noah Adam, "The Inspiring Force of 'We Shall Overcome'," National Public Radio, August 28, 2013, https://tinyurl.com/y6cy3a7a.

Chapter 6: Bonhoeffer by Bike

1. For more on the *Ampelmann*, an East German design for pedestrian signals that was so beloved that it continued for public use past Germany's reunification, see "The History of Pedestrian Crossing Lights" on the *Ampelmann* website https://tinyurl.com/y3tapb29. (This iconic and now well capitalized symbol boasts its own brand-centric line of merchandise—oh, the ironies!)
2. On evasion and "easive thinking," I was particularly helped—not a surprise, for her thought always helps mine—by Jean Bethke Elshtain in her essay "Politics without Cliché," *Social Research* 60, no. 3 (Fall 1993): 433–44. In it, she draws on ideas developed by the Czech dissident playwright and then post-Communist president, the late Václav Havel.
3. Bonhoeffer House, *Catalogue of the Exhibition*, 39.
4. Bethge, *Friendship and Resistance*, 6.
5. Bethge, *Prayer and Righteous Action*, 34.
6. Bethge, *Prayer and Righteous Action*, 39.
7. Metaxas, *Bonhoeffer*, 38–39.
8. Metaxas, *Bonhoeffer*, 64.
9. Rabitz, Cornelia, "Chronicle of Right-Wing Terrorism in Germany," *Deutsche Welle*, November 23, 2011, https://p.dw.com/p/13Ert.
10. Marsh, *Strange Glory*, 6.
11. Marsh, *Strange Glory*, 6.
12. Schlingensiepen, *Dietrich Bonhoeffer*, 27.
13. Marsh, *Strange Glory*, 6.
14. Alison Owings, *Frauen: German Women Recall the Third Reich* (New Brunswick, NJ: Rutgers University Press, 1993), xvi.
15. "Brief and endless" is a phrase from Goethe: "Choose well, your choice is brief and yet endless." In my study I remembered reading it but have completely lost the reference. My apologies to whoever from my bibliography introduced me to it.
16. Owings, *Frauen*, xxv.
17. Owings, *Frauen*, 475.
18. Owings, *Frauen*, 475, emphasis original.
19. Owings, *Frauen*, 476, emphasis mine.
20. Her infraction was failing to mount the bike from the righthand side *prior* to kicking up the kickstand. She had kicked up the kickstand and then mounted the bike from the left.
21. Putting it more expansively in his famous letter from jail, Rev. Dr. Martin Luther King Jr. wrote, "Moreover, I am cognizant of the interrelatedness of all communities and states. I cannot sit idly by in Atlanta and not be

concerned about what happens in Birmingham. Injustice anywhere is a threat to justice everywhere. We are caught in an inescapable network of mutuality, tied in a single garment of destiny. Whatever affects one directly, affects all indirectly." Martin Luther King Jr., "Letter from a Birmingham Jail," April 16, 1963.

22. Bosanquet, *Life and Death*, 120.

Chapter 7: Life as *Ars Moriendi*

1. Staewen is buried in the cemetery that surrounds St. Anne's Church in Dahlem.

2. Victoria Barnett, *For the Soul of the People: Protestant Protest against Hitler* (New York: Oxford University Press, 1992), 5–6.

3. John de Gruchy, *Daring, Trusting Spirit: Bonhoeffer's Friend, Eberhard Bethge* (Minneapolis: Fortress Press, 2005), 12. "By identifying with the Confessing Church and especially the decision at Dahlem, he and his companions had made a choice that now determined their future."

4. Bethge, *Friendship and Resistance*, 2. The Young Reformation Movement formed in response to the German Christian Formation Movement and petered out in the infamous "brownshirt" synod. Not long after, Martin Niemöller formed the Pastors' Emergency League, which then joined forces with the members of the Young Reformation Movement to form the Confessing Church.

5. "Berlin TV Tower," Berlin.de: The Official Website of Berlin, https://tinyurl.com/y4nkee59. The popular story about the reflection cross being the Pope's revenge was specifically to punish the German Democratic Republic's government for removing crucifixes from churches.

6. The Marienkirche website has an English-language page with some information about the fresco. See "English Information," Marienkirche, https://tinyurl.com/y5eefr77.

   An exhaustive history and image-rich study of the Berlin fresco is available on the webpage "The Dance of Death in Berlin," where the writer compares Berlin's *Totentanz* fresco with other more well-known ones, including those in Lübeck and Tallinn, and it's possible to explore it there with panel-by-panel imagery of the massive fresco. "The Dance of Death in Berlin," Døden fra Lübeck, https://tinyurl.com/yyjb3sk7.

7. Ole J. Benedictow, "The Black Death: The Greatest Catastrophe Ever," *History Today* 55, no. 3 (March 2005), https://tinyurl.com/y3fym47d.

8. Austra Reinis, *Reforming the Art of Dying: The* Ars Moriendi *in the German Reformation (1519–1528)*, (London: Routledge, 2007), 3–4. This larger study points to the effects of the Reformation on the prevailing Roman Catholic teaching on death and dying and how the Lutheran tradition focused more on the assurance of salvation at the time of death.

9. Marsh, *Strange Glory*, 3–4.

10. Marsh, *Strange Glory*, 3–4.
11. Bonhoeffer, *Letters and Papers*, 16.
12. Bethge, *Dietrich Bonhoeffer*, 678.
13. See Bethge, *Dietrich Bonhoeffer*, 931. Bethge distinguishes between the honor given to men such as Bonhoeffer, whom the British called martyrs, and the honor that the church in Germany gave to Protestant pastor Paul Schneider as a martyr but refused Bonhoeffer.

    Recognized as the first Protestant pastor who died in Nazi custody, Schneider was a German pastor and Confessing Church member who spoke out against the Nazis and refused their orders. Imprisoned at Buchenwald, routinely beaten and punished for his continued outspokenness, he was put to death by lethal injection. A short profile of Schneider is available at *Gedenkstätte Deutscher Widerstand*, https://tinyurl.com/yyc4h4pq.
14. For an excellent documentary film about the plot, including interviews with some of the conspirators' family members, see Pierre Isbouts, dir., *Operation Valkyrie: The Stauffenberg Plot to Kill* (2008; New York: Koch Entertainment, 2008, DVD).
15. Bethge, *Dietrich Bonhoeffer*, 803.
16. Bethge, *Dietrich Bonhoeffer*, 811, 827.
17. The *Bendlerblock* still stands in Berlin, on a street since renamed for Colonel Stauffenberg, and has an excellent free memorial and museum dedicated to all those who resisted National Socialism from various sectors of civic life. One passes through this courtyard to reach it, the memorial to Stauffenberg and the other conspirators within it.
18. "The July 20, 1944, Plot to Assassinate Adolf Hitler," Holocaust Encyclopedia, United States Holocaust Memorial Museum, https://tinyurl.com/y6aamg6j.
19. Bethge, *Dietrich Bonhoeffer*, 799
20. Bethge, *Dietrich Bonhoeffer*, 899.
21. Richie, *Faust's Metropolis*, 544.
22. Richie, *Faust's Metropolis*, 544.
23. Richie, *Faust's Metropolis*, 545.
24. Richie, *Faust's Metropolis*, 545.
25. See, for example, Victoria Barnett, "Review Essay: Interpreting Bonhoeffer, Post-Bethge," *Contemporary Church History Quarterly* 20, no. 3 (September 2014), https://tinyurl.com/lplrle5.
26. Wind, Renate, LOC 830–36 of 1717.
27. Dietrich Bonhoeffer, *Letters and Papers from Prison*, Dietrich Bonhoeffer Reader's Edition (Minneapolis: Fortress Press, 2015), 322.
28. Dietrich Bonhoeffer, *Ethics*, Dietrich Bonhoeffer-Reader's Edition (Minneapolis: Fortress Press, 2015), 36.
29. Schlingensiepen, *Dietrich Bonhoeffer*, 206. See also Brian Murdoch, *Fighting Songs and Warring Words* (New York: Routledge, 1990), 128–29.

30. Schlingensiepen, *Dietrich Bonhoeffer*, 249–50.
31. Renate Wind, LOC 627 of 1717.
32. Dr. Tobias Korenke is deputy chairman of the board of the Erinnerungs- und Begegnungsstätte Bonhoeffer-Haus eV—the Bonhoeffer House.
33. Bethge, *Friendship and Resistance*, 7–8.
34. Bethge, 929; quoting from Dietrich and Klaus Bonhoeffer, *Auf den Wege zur Freiheit: Gedichte und Briefe aus der Haft* (1946).
35. Eliza Apperly, "The Holocaust Memorial of 70,000 Stones," BBC, March 29, 2019, https://tinyurl.com/y56dczp2.

Chapter 8: Befriending Bonhoeffer

1. Bethge, *Friendship and Resistance*, 87.
2. Rick Noack, "Isolation is Rising in Europe. Can Loneliness Ministers Help Change That?" *Washington Post*, February 2, 2018https://tinyurl.com/ybagv6hs. See also Guido Kleinhubbert and Antja Windmann, "Alone by the Millions: Isolation Crisis Threatens German Seniors," trans. Paul Cohen, *Der Spiegel*, January 10, 2013, https://tinyurl.com/atokkpj.
3. See Robert Putnam, *Bowling Alone: The Collapse and Revival of American Community* (New York: Simon & Schuster, 2000).
4. De Gruchy, *Daring, Trusting Spirit*, 212.
5. De Gruchy, *Daring, Trusting Spirit*, 2.
6. De Gruchy, *Daring, Trusting Spirit*, 16.
7. Bonhoeffer House, *Catalogue of the Exhibition*, 68. I also want to remember our family's short overnight visit to the island, where we slept in a tent at a campground and ate danishes at picnic tables the next morning—all thanks to Bonhoeffer's peripatetic life!
8. De Gruchy, *Daring, Trusting Spirit*, 19.
9. Bethge, *Friendship and Resistance*, 18–19.
10. De Gruchy, *Daring, Trusting Spirit*, 17.
11. Bonhoeffer, *Letters and Papers*, 129.
12. De Gruchy, *Daring, Trusting Spirit*, 62; quotation from Letter to Bethge, February 1, 1941.
13. Marsh, *Strange Glory*, 253. Humorously, beginning a passive-aggressive campaign against Bethge's invitations to others, Bonhoeffer asked Bethge to think of the poor car, crushed by the weight of so many (four!) people in it: "'About the car,' he said, 'the axle will be scraping along as it is with three people. It will be worse with four. . . . And then over the mountains!'" (253).
14. Marsh, *Strange Glory*, 336.
15. The Schleichers insisted that Eberhard and Renate take a one-year break, and "with no knowledge of Eberhard and Renate's situation," Maria's mother did the same for Dietrich and Maria, "as must have been a

common remedy to protect girls not yet finished with their schooling" (Marsh, *Strange Glory*, 334).

16. Marsh, *Strange Glory*, 335.

17. De Gruchy, *Daring, Trusting Spirit*, 67.

18. Whether this phone call took place on April 4 or April 5 is, clearly, in dispute among the biographers. Bethge himself is credited with giving two fairly different accounts of those days. The timeline is less my concern— I'm not a Bonhoeffer biographer—but it's worth noting that these days' events are fuzzy. Some say Bonhoeffer was at the Schleichers' residence when the Gestapo arrived and his father came to get him. Others depict Bonhoeffer sitting in his room, waiting for them to come. The important element in the various accounts, to my mind, is that Bonhoeffer was prepared for this eventuality and had laid his groundwork of deception. He was not caught off guard by the agents' arrival; he was expecting it and ready for it.

19. Bethge, *Dietrich Bonhoeffer*, 781.

20. Schlingensiepen, *Dietrich Bonhoeffer*, 316.

21. De Gruchy, *Daring, Trusting Spirit*, 74–77.

22. Bonhoeffer, *Letters and Papers*, 303.

23. Bonhoeffer, *Letters and Papers*, 83.

24. Bonhoeffer, *Letters and Papers*, 91.

25. Bonhoeffer, *Letters and Papers*, 133.

26. Bonhoeffer, *Letters and Papers*, 135.

27. The publication of John Robinson's *Honest to God* (1963) expressed this theological movement's ideas in a way that captured public imagination. For a helpful overview of the movement and key figures in the British and American scene from that era, see William Hamilton, "The Death of God Theology," *Christian Scholar* 48, no. 1 (Spring 1965): 27–48.

28. In 1965, American theologian Harvey Cox argued that it was time for the academy to "move 'beyond Bonhoeffer'" and that theologians should "let Bonhoeffer rest in peace and not use him to justify our own positions or turn him into a cult figure" (de Gruchy, *Daring, Trusting Spirit*, 141).

29. De Gruchy, *Daring, Trusting Spirit*, 144.

30. Borofsky, Jonathan, "Molecule Man, 30 meters tall, aluminum, permanent installation, Spree River, Berlin 1997," https://tinyurl.com/yxluo7ep.

31. De Gruchy, *Daring, Trusting Spirit*, 41.

32. Marsh, *Strange Glory*, 237.

33. Bethge, *Friendship and Resistance*, 73.

34. Bethge, *Dietrich Bonhoeffer*, 685.

35. De Gruchy, *Daring, Trusting Spirit*, 180.

36. De Gruchy, *Daring, Trusting Spirit*, 181.

37. Bethge, *Friendship and Resistance*, 105.

38. Bethge, *Friendship and Resistance*, 105.

Epilogue: A Tale of Two Houses

1. "Lucius Clay Dies; Led Berlin Airlift," *New York Times*, April 17, 1978, A1.
2. For more on the "fiercely anti-Napoleonic" Queen Louise's prudent interactions with Napoleon, see Andrew Roberts, *Napoleon: A Life* (New York: Penguin, 2014), 393.
3. "Foundation and History," Freie Universität, https://tinyurl.com/yym 6rfb7.
4. Jesse Greenspan, "JFK Tells West Berliners That He Is One of Them, 50 Years Ago," History, June 26, 2013, https://tinyurl.com/y3kcf67q.
5. "Rhetoric of Encouragement: Kennedy's Speech at Freie Universität, an Interview with Political Linguist Josef Klein," Freie Universität Berlin, https://tinyurl.com/y42cevce.
6. Audio file of Kennedy's speech, Freie Universität Berlin, June 26, 1963, https://tinyurl.com/y6l6bf2s.
7. See especially Ciarán Fahey, *Abandoned Berlin* (Berlin: Bebra Verlag, 2015). Fahey's synonymous website has the most up-to-date information on his prior research. His is by far the most elegant and strives for journalistic accuracy, with snappy commentary and writing. There are plenty of other websites devoted to this genre of adventuring, with varying degrees of quality and all kinds of strange pictures.
8. "Anatomy Institute," *Wandering Wolf Child* (blog), https://tinyurl.com /y3mtge5w.
9. Bethge, *Friendship and Resistance*, 73.
10. The street name was changed to Niederkirchnerstrasse after World War II.
11. Bethge, *Friendship and Resistance*, 74.

Bibliography

"Abandoned Anatomy Institute, Berlin." *Wandering Wolf Child* (blog). https://tinyurl.com/y3mtge5w.

Abyssinian Baptist Church. "History." https://tinyurl.com/y39zyscz.

Apperly, Eliza. "The Holocaust Memorial of 70,000 Stones." BBC, March 29, 2019. https://tinyurl.com/y56dczp2.

Barnett, Victoria. "Dietrich Bonhoeffer: 'The Church and the Jewish Question.'" United States Holocaust Memorial Museum. https://tinyurl.com/y3h8rnxb.

——. *For the Soul of the People: Protestant Protest against Hitler.* New York: Oxford University Press, 1992.

——. "Review Essay: Interpreting Bonhoeffer, Post-Bethge." *Contemporary Church History Quarterly* 20, no. 3 (September 2014): https://tinyurl.com/lplrle5.

Bazelon, Emily. "What Happened to the Remains of Nazi Resistor Mildred Harnack? Now We Know." Slate, November 7, 2013. https://tinyurl.com/y3575qsf.

Benedictow, Ole J. "The Black Death: The Greatest Catastrophe Ever." *History Today* 55, no. 3 (March 2005). https://tinyurl.com/y3fym47d.

"Berlin TV Tower." Berlin.de: The Official Website of Berlin. https://tinyurl.com/y4nkee59.

Berlin Wall Memorial. "Construction of the Wall in August 1961." https://tinyurl.com/yypkfwdf.

Bethge, Eberhard. *Dietrich Bonhoeffer: A Biography*. Rev. ed. Minneapolis: Fortress Press, 2000.

———. *Friendship and Resistance: Essays on Dietrich Bonhoeffer*. Grand Rapids: Eerdmans, 1995.

———. *Prayer and Righteous Action in the Life of Dietrich Bonhoeffer*. Belfast: Christian Journals, 1979.

Board of the Bonhoeffer House, ed. *Catalogue of the Exhibition*. Berlin; 1996.

Bonhoeffer, Dietrich. *Letters and Papers from Prison: The Enlarged Edition*. New York: Macmillan, 1971.

———. *Life Together*. New York: Harper & Row, 1954.

———. *The Prayerbook of the Bible*. Minneapolis: Augsburg Fortress, 1970.

———. *A Testament to Freedom: The Essential Writings of Dietrich Bonhoeffer*. Edited by Geffrey B. Kelly and F. Burton Nelson. San Francisco: HarperSanFrancisco, 1990.

Bonhoeffer, Emmi Delbrück. "From: The House on the Wangenheimstrasse." In *Catalogue of the Exhibition*, edited by the Board of the Bonhoeffer House. Berlin: 1996.

Borofsky, Jonathan. "Molecule Man, 30 meters tall, aluminum, permanent installation, Spree River, Berlin 1997." Borofsky.com. https://tinyurl.com/yxluo7ep.

Bosanquet, Mary. *The Life and Death of Dietrich Bonhoeffer*. New York: Harper & Row, 1968.

Brysac, Shareen Blair. *Resisting Hitler: Mildred Harnack and the Red Orchestra*. New York: Oxford University Press, 2000.

Citizens Committee of Leipzig. "Runde Ecke History." "Runde Ecke" Memorial Museum and Stasi Bunker Museum. https://tinyurl .com/y3cw8htk.

Connolly, Kate. "Sex Parties, Bloody Duels, and Blackmail: Life at Court of Last Emperor." *Guardian*, September 2, 2010. https://tinyurl.com/y4r3whoe.

de Gruchy, John W. *Daring, Trusting Spirit: Bonhoeffer's Friend, Eberhard Bethge*. Minneapolis: Fortress Press, 2005.

Dose, Kai. "A Note on John Wesley's Visit to Herrnhut in 1738." *Wesley and Methodist Studies* 7, no. 1 (2015): 117–20.

Elshtain, Jean Bethke. "Politics Without Cliché." *Social Research* 60, no. 3 (Fall 1993): 433–44.

"English Information." Marienkirche. https://tinyurl.com/y5eefr77.

Fabrycky, Laura. "Let's Quit the Tug-of-War over Dietrich Bonhoeffer's Legacy." *Christianity Today*, September 20, 2018. https://tinyurl.com/ydfhr9h9.

Fahey, Ciarán. *Abandoned Berlin*. Berlin: Bebra Verlag, 2015.

Freie Universität. "Foundation and History." https://tinyurl.com/yym6rfb7.

Friedlander, Henry. *The Origins of Nazi Genocide: From Euthanasia to the Final Solution*. Chapel Hill: University of North Carolina Press, 1997.

Greenspan, Jesse. "JFK Tells West Berliners That He Is One of Them, 50 Years Ago." History, June 26, 2013. https://tinyurl.com/y3kcf67q.

Hamilton, William. "The Death of God Theology." *Christian Scholar* 48, no. 1 (Spring 1965): 27–48.

Hill, Laban Carrick. *Harlem Stomp! A Cultural History of the Harlem Renaissance*. New York: Little, Brown Books for Young Readers, 2009.

Hockenos, Matthew D. *Then They Came for Me: Martin Niemöller, the Pastor Who Defied the Nazis*. New York: Basic, 2018.

Isbouts, Jean-Pierre, dir. *Operation Valkyrie: The Stauffenberg Plot to Kill*. 2008; New York, Koch Entertainment, 2008, DVD.

Irvine, Ian. "*Acedia, Tristitia*, and Sloth: Early Christian Forerunners to Chronic Ennui." *Humanitas* 12, no. 1 (Spring 1999).

Kelly, Geffrey, and F. Burton Nelson. *The Cost of Moral Leadership: The Spirituality of Dietrich Bonhoeffer*. Grand Rapids: Eerdmans, 2002.

Kengor, Paul. "Martin Luther and the Berlin Wall." *Washington Post*, October 30, 2014. https://tinyurl.com/y53sbheb.

Kleinhubbert, Guido, and Antja Windmann. "Alone by the Millions: Isolation Crisis Threatens German Seniors." Translated by Paul Cohen. *Der Spiegel*, January 10, 2013. https://tinyurl.com /atokkpj.

Klemperer, Victor. *The Language of the Third Reich: LTI—Lingua Tertii Imperii: A Philologist's Notebook*. 3rd ed. Translated by Martin Brady. London: Continuum, 2006.

Larson, Erik. *In the Garden of Beasts: Love, Terror, and an American Family in Hitler's Berlin*. New York: Broadway Books, 2011.

Marsh, Charles. *Strange Glory: A Life of Dietrich Bonhoeffer*. New York: Knopf, 2014.

Marsh, Karen. *Vintage Saints and Sinners: 25 Christians Who Transformed My Faith*. Downers Grove, IL: InterVarsity, 2017.

Metaxas, Eric. *Bonhoeffer: Pastor, Martyr, Prophet, Spy*. Nashville: Thomas Nelson, 2010.

Monroe, Kristen. *Ethics in an Age of Terror and Genocide: Identity and Moral Choice*. Princeton: Princeton University Press, 2012.

———. *The Heart of Altruism: Perceptions of a Common Humanity*. Princeton: Princeton University Press, 1996.

Mouw, Richard. *Adventures in Evangelical Civility: A Lifelong Quest for Common Ground*. Grand Rapid: Brazos, 2016.

Murdoch, Brian. *Fighting Songs and Warring Words*. New York: Routledge, 1990.

Murray, Henry A. "Analysis of the Personality of Adolf Hitler: With Predictions of His Future Behavior and Suggestions for Dealing with Him Now and after Germany's Surrender," 1943. Donovan Nuremberg Trials Collection. Cornell University Law Library. https://tinyurl.com/y2w8u5ln.

Noack, Rick. "Isolation Is Rising in Europe. Can Loneliness Ministers Help Change That?" *Washington Post*, February 2, 2018. https://tinyurl.com/ybagv6hs.

Nooke, Maria. "From the Building of the Berlin Wall to the Fall of the Berlin Wall: A Short History of the Division." In *Where in the World Is the Berlin Wall?* Edited by Anna Kaminsky, 10–26. Berlin: Bundesstiftung zur Aufarbeitung der SED-Diktatur, 2014.

Norris, Kathleen, *Acedia and Me*. New York: Riverhead, 2008.

"One Little Word." *Economist*, 7 November 2015.

Owings, Alison. *Frauen: German Women Recall the Third Reich*. New Brunswick, NJ: Rutgers University Press, 1993.

Ozment, Steven. *A Mighty Fortress: A New History of the German People*. New York: HarperCollins, 2005.

Pauler, Roland. "Rörig, Fritz." *New German Biography* 21 (2003): 736–37. https://tinyurl.com/y4q4mkhs.

Paulick, Jane. "Remembering Martin Luther King's Visit to Berlin." *Deutsche Welle*, November 11, 2014. https://tinyurl.com/y66qd77o.

Putnam, Robert. *Bowling Alone: The Collapse and Revival of American Community*. New York: Simon & Schuster, 2000.

Rabitz, Cornelia. "Chronicle of Right-Wing Terrorism in Germany." *Deutsche Welle*, November 23, 2011. https://p.dw.com/p/13Ert.

Reinis, Austra. *Reforming the Art of Dying: The* Ars Moriendi *in the German Reformation (1519–1528)*. London: Routledge, 2007.

"Rhetoric of Encouragement: Kennedy's Speech at Freie Universität, an Interview with Political Linguist Josef Klein." Freie Universität Berlin. https://tinyurl.com/y42cevce.

Richie, Alexandra. *Faust's Metropolis: A History of Berlin*. New York: Carroll & Graf, 1998.

Rörig, Fritz. *The Medieval Town*. Berkeley: University of California Press, 1967.

Schlingensiepen, Ferdinand. *Dietrich Bonhoeffer 1906–1945: Martyr, Thinker, Man of Resistance*. Translated by Isabel Best. New York: T&T Clark International, 2010.

Shelley, Bruce L. *Church History in Plain Language*. Dallas: Word, 1982.

Sontheimer, Michael. "Why Germans Can Never Escape Hitler's Shadow." *Der Spiegel*, March 10, 2005. https://tinyurl.com/y6k n7djy.

T4 Denkmal. https://www.t4-denkmal.de/eng.

Theile, Dorothee. *Morning Star, O Cheering Sight . . .: The Moravian Star and Its History*, 3rd ed. Translated by Jacob Watson, Deborah Hübler, Peter Vogt, and Jill Vogt. Herrnhut, Germany: Comenius-Buchhandlung GmbH, n.d.

United States Holocaust Memorial Museum. "Adolf Eichmann." Holocaust Encyclopedia. https://tinyurl.com/y4e9kcca.

———. "The July 20, 1944, Plot to Assassinate Adolf Hitler." Holocaust Encyclopedia. https://tinyurl.com/y6aamg6j.

Wesley, John. "John Wesley the Methodist: Chapter VII—The New Birth." Wesley Center Online. https://tinyurl.com/y3fz2r5j.

Williams, Reggie. *Bonhoeffer's Black Jesus: Harlem Renaissance Theology and an Ethic of Resistance*. Waco, TX: Baylor University Press, 2014.

Wind, Renate. *Dietrich Bonhoeffer: A Spoke in the Wheel*. Grand Rapids: Eerdmans, 1992.

Zeller, Frank. "Germany's Post-War Justice Ministry Was Infested with Nazis Protecting Former Comrades, Study Reveals." *Telegraph*, October 10, 2016. https://tinyurl.com/y4zpv9w2.

Index